Simone de Beauvoir

MANCHESTER
UNIVERSITY PRESS

TEXTS · IN · CULTURE

This series offers a set of specially commissioned, cross-disciplinary essays on a text of seminal importance to Western culture. Each text has had an impact on the way we think, write and live beyond the confines of its original discipline, and it is only through an understanding of its multiple meanings that we can fully appreciate its importance.

TEXTS · IN · CULTURE

Simone de Beauvoir's
THE
SECOND SEX

New interdisciplinary essays

RUTH EVANS

editor

Manchester University Press
Manchester and New York

distributed exclusively in the USA by St. Martin's Press

Copyright © Manchester University Press 1998

While copyright in the volume as a whole is vested in Manchester University Press, copyright in individual chapters belongs to their respective authors, and no chapter may be reproduced wholly or in part without the express permission in writing of both author and publishers.

Published by Manchester University Press
Oxford Road, Manchester M13 9NR, UK
and Room 400, 175 Fifth Avenue, New York, NY 10010, USA

Distributed exclusively in the USA by
St. Martin's Press, Inc.,
175 Fifth Avenue, New York, NY 10010, USA

Distributed exclusively in Canada by
UBC Press, University of British Columbia, 6344 Memorial Road,
Vancouver, BC, Canada v67 1z2

British Library Cataloguing-in-Publication Data
A catalogue record is available from the British Library

Library of Congress Cataloging-in-Publication Data
Simone de Beauvoir's The second sex: new interdisciplinary essays /
    Ruth Evans, editor.
        p. c.m. — (Texts in culture)
        ISBN 0-7190-4302-6 (cl). — ISBN 0-7190-4303-4 (pb)
        1. Beauvoir, Simone de, 1908—Deuxième sexe. 2. Beauvoir,
    Simone de, 1908—Criticism and interpretation. 3. Beauvoir, Simone de,
    1908—Influence. 4. Women. 5. Women and literature. 6. Feminism.
    7. Feminist criticism. I. Series.
    HQ1208.S53   1998
    305.42—dc21   97-21594

ISBN 0-7190-4302-6 *hardback*
ISBN 0-7190-4303-4 *paperback*

First published 1998

02 01 00 99 98   10 9 8 7 6 5 4 3 2 1

Typeset in Apollo by Koinonia, Manchester
Printed in Great Britain by Bell & Bain Ltd, Glasgow

Contents

for Lucy Mills and Thomas Mills

Series introduction

Texts are produced in particular cultures and in particular historical circumstances. In turn, they shape and are shaped by those cultures as they are read and re-read in changing circumstances by different groups with different commitments, engagements and interests. Such readings are themselves then re-absorbed into the ideological frameworks within which the cultures develop. The seminal works drawn on by cultures thus have multiple existences within them, exerting their influence in distinct and perhaps contradictory ways. As these texts have been 'claimed' by particular academic disciplines, however, their larger cultural significance has often been obscured.

Recent work in cultural history and textual theory has stimulated critical awareness of the complex relations between texts and cultures, highlighting the limits of current academic formations and opening the possibility of new approaches to interdisciplinarity. At the same time, however, the difficulties of interdisciplinary work have become increasingly apparent at all levels of research and teaching. On the one hand the abandonment of disciplinary specialisms may lead to amorphousness rather than challenging interdisciplinarity: on the other, interdisciplinary approaches may in the end simply create new specialisms or sub-specialisms, with their own well guarded boundaries. In these circumstances, yesterday's ground-breaking interdisciplinary study may become today's autonomous (and so potentially circumscribed) discipline, as has happened, it might be argued, in the case of some forms of History of Ideas.

The volumes in this series highlight the advantages of interdisciplinary work while at the same time encouraging a critical reflexiveness about its limits and possibilities; they seek to stimulate consideration both of the distinctiveness and integrity of individual disciplines, and of the transgressive potential of interdisciplinarity. Each volume offers a collection of new essays on a text of seminal intellectual and cultural importance, displaying the insights to be gained from the juxtaposition of disciplinary perspectives and from the negotiation of disciplinary boundaries. Our editorial stance is avowedly 'cultural', and in this sense the volumes represent a challenge to the conception of authorship which locates the significance of the text in the individual act of creation; but we assume that no issues (including those of disciplinarity and authorship) are foreclosed, and that individual volumes, drawing contributions from a broad range of disciplinary standpoints, will raise questions about the texts they examine more by the perceived disparities of approach that they encompass than by any interpretative consensus that they demonstrate.

All essays are specially commissioned for the series and are designed to be approachable to non-specialist as well as specialist readers: substantial editorial introductions provide a framework for the debates conducted in each volume, and highlight the issues involved.

Stephen Copley, University of York
Jeff Wallace, University of Glamorgan
General Editors

Acknowledgements

I owe thanks to Stephen Copley, Diane Elam, Claire Gorrara and Jeff Wallace for reading parts of the manuscript and for offering invaluable advice. I am grateful to the series editors, Stephen Copley and Jeff Wallace, for general help on a range of issues. I am also indebted to my former editor at Manchester University Press, Anita Roy, and to my current editor, Matthew Frost, for their patience and good advice. I would also like thank Stephanie Sloan at MUP. I owe thanks to Martin Coyle, David Bryant, Peter Garrett and Russell West. I would particularly like to thank Dr Nora Sellei of the Department of English Literature at L. Kossuth University, Debrecen, Hungary, for inviting me to give a paper on *The Second Sex* and for generously supplying me with information about the reception of Simone de Beauvoir in Hungary. My children deserve especial thanks: this book is dedicated to them.

Abbreviations

All references to *The Second Sex* are to Simone de Beauvoir, *The Second Sex*, trans. and ed. H. M. Parshley (Harmondsworth: Penguin, 1972). All references to *Le Deuxième Sexe* are to Simone de Beauvoir, *Le Deuxième Sexe*, 2 vols., Collection Idées (Paris: Gallimard, 1977).

DS   *Le Deuxième Sexe* [DS1 = volume 1; DS2 = volume 2]

EA   *The Ethics of Ambiguity*

MLF   Mouvement de Libération des Femmes

NQF   *Nouvelles Questions Féministes*

QF   *Questions Féministes*

SS   *The Second Sex*

Chronology

Cultural history bearing on the writing and reception history of *The Second Sex*

1399   Christine de Pisan, *L'Épître au dieu d'amour* [*Epistle to the God of Love*]: defends women in France against dominant clerical misogyny, as part of larger debate, the 'querelle des femmes', surrounding the reception of the controversial thirteenth century poem *Le Roman de la Rose* [*Romance of the Rose*]

1673   Poulain de la Barre, *De l'égalité des deux sexes* [*On the Equality of Both Sexes*]

1787   Marquis de Condorcet, *Lettres d'un bourgeois de Newhaven à un citoyen de Virginie* [*Letters from a Bourgeois of Newhaven to a Citizen of Virginia*]: demands political rights for women

1789   French Revolution: proclamation of the *Droits de l'homme et du citoyen* [*Rights of Man and of the Citizen*]

1790   Marquis de Condorcet, *Déclaration des droits et l'admission des femmes au droit de cité* [*On the Admission of Women to Citizens' Rights*]

1791   Olympe de Gouges, *Déclaration des droits de la femme et de la citoyenne* [*Rights of Woman and of the Female Citizen*]

1792   Mary Wollstonecraft, *Vindication of the Rights of Woman*

1807   Georg Hegel, *Phenomenology of Spirit*

1843   Flora Tristan, *Union ouvrière*: on the double oppression of working women

1848   Karl Marx, *Communist Manifesto*

1897   Marguerite Durand creates *La Fronde*, first feminist daily newspaper, produced uniquely by women

1908   January 9: Simone de Beauvoir born in Paris

1916   Hélène Brion, *La Voie féministe: femme, ôse être!* [*The Feminist Way: Woman, Dare to Be!*]

1918   Voting rights for women over thirty in Great Britain

1928   Women over twenty-one get the vote in Great Britain

1929   Beauvoir graduates from the Sorbonne: she is only the ninth woman in France to become an *agrégée* of philosophy

       Virginia Woolf, *A Room of One's Own*

1931–43 Beauvoir teaching in *lycées* in Marseille, Rouen, and finally Paris

1933   Sigmund Freud, 'Femininity'

1940   France defeated by Germany; women play large part in the *Résistance*

1943   Beauvoir publishes first novel, *L'Invitée* [*She Came to Stay*]

         Jean-Paul Sartre, *L'Être et le néant* [*Being and Nothingness*]

1945   Beauvoir helps to launch the journal *Les Temps modernes* to which she is a regular contributor

1945   April: vote is given to women in France

         May 8: VE Day ends war in Europe

         Jean-Paul Sartre, *Les Chemins de la liberté* [*Roads to Freedom*]

1946   October: Beauvoir begins writing *Le Deuxième Sexe*

         French Constitution recognises equality of women in most spheres

1947   Beauvoir, *Pour une morale de l'ambiguité* [*The Ethics of Ambiguity*]

1948–9   Three chapters of *Le Deuxième Sexe* published in *Les Temps modernes*

1949   Simone de Beauvoir, *Le Deuxième Sexe*

1952   H. M. Parshley's translation, *The Second Sex*, published by Alfred A. Knopf (USA)

1953   H. M. Parshley's translation, *The Second Sex*, published by Jonathan Cape (UK)

1954   End of French control of Indochina

1954–62 Algerian war of independence

1958   Beauvoir, *Mémoires d'une jeune fille rangée* [*Memoirs of a Dutiful Daughter*]

         Geneviève Gennari, *Simone de Beauvoir* [first scholarly study of *Le Deuxième Sexe*]

1963   Betty Friedan, *The Feminine Mystique*, dedicated to Simone de Beauvoir

1967   Neuwirth Law authorises sale of contraceptives in France

1968   Students riot in Paris; workers strike; one of many diverse and influential women's groups, 'Psychanalyse et Politique' ['Psych et Po'], established: rejects socialist 'phallic' feminism in favour of sexual difference

         Prague invaded by Soviet and Warsaw-Pact troops

         Mary Ellmann, *Thinking about Women*

1969   Monique Wittig, *Les Guérillères*

1970   Kate Millett, *Sexual Politics*

         Germaine Greer, *The Female Eunuch*

         MLF [Mouvement de Libération des Femmes], initials coined by press to style radical women's groups in France, generally adopted by public to name French women's liberation movement

1971   *Manifesto of the 343*: public declaration in *Le Nouvel Observateur* by a number of women that they had had illegal abortions, signed *inter alia* by Beauvoir

Beauvoir joins the MLF: Gisèle Halimi and Simone de Beauvoir co-found the women's pressure group, *Choisir*

1972   H. M. Parshley's translation, *The Second Sex*, published in Penguin Books

Jacques Lacan, *Le Séminaire livre xx: Encore* [on female sexuality]

Equal Rights Amendment approved by US Congress

1973   Elaine Marks, *Simone de Beauvoir: Encounters with Death* [first English-language study of Beauvoir]

Gisèle Halimi, *La Cause des femmes*

US Supreme Court rules that individual states may not prohibit abortions during the first six months of pregnancy

Giscard d'Estaing establishes Secretariat of State for the Status of Women

1974   Another women's group, the 'Ligue du droit des femmes', established, with Simone de Beauvoir as president

Luce Irigaray, *Speculum de l'autre femme* [*Speculum of the Other Woman*]

Julia Kristeva, *Des Chinoises* [*About Chinese Women*]

Annie Leclerc, *Parole de femme*

1975   Hélène Cixous, 'Le Rire de la Méduse' ['The laugh of the Medusa']

Repeal of French law forbidding abortions ['Veil law']

1977   Beauvoir accepts directorship of journal *Nouvelles féministes* (later *Questions féministes* and then *Nouvelles questions féministes*)

Luce Irigaray, *Ce Sexe qui n'en est pas un* [*This Sex which Is not One*]

1978   US Equal Rights Amendment just fails to be ratified for adoption

1979   Julia Kristeva, 'Le Temps des femmes' ['Women's time']

1980   Elisabeth Badinter, *L'Amour en plus: histoire de l'amour maternal, 17e–20e siècle* [*The Myth of Motherhood: An Historical View of the Maternal Instinct*]

Sarah Kofman, *L'Énigme de la femme, la femme dans les textes de Freud* [*The Enigma of Woman, Woman in Freud's Writings*]

1981   Newly-elected socialist President Mitterand establishes a Ministry of Women's Rights; Yvette Roudy appointed minister

1986   April 14: Beauvoir dies

1989   Michèle Le Doeuff, *L'Étude et le rouet* [*Hipparchia's Choice*]

1990   Toril Moi gives annual Bucknell Lectures in Literary Theory; published as *Feminist Theory and Simone de Beauvoir*

1991   Susan Faludi, *Backlash: The Undeclared War against American Women*

1992   US Senator Pat Buchanan declares 'The real enemy we have to defeat right now is radical feminism.'

1994   Toril Moi, *Simone de Beauvoir: The Making of an Intellectual Woman*

1996   6–8 September: 'Simone de Beauvoir: Ten Years On': conference held in Dublin to mark 10th anniversary of Beauvoir's death

1

Introduction: *The Second Sex* and the postmodern

RUTH EVANS

A return to Beauvoir?

The essays collected in this volume revisit a complex work of theoretical philosophy, written in French in 1949 and first available in English translation in 1953. Though often assessed retrospectively as a momentous book, *The Second Sex*'s impact on English speakers was not immediate, and it is not now accorded, either in France, Britain or America, an assured place within philosophical, feminist or literary history. Ironically, its status as a 'cult book' for the year 1966[1] – a category Will Self (writing in the Observer *Life* magazine) defines as 'a text that influences mainstream culture only after its slow diffusion through the traditionally thin ranks of the avant-garde'[2] – was only recognised in 1996. And despite Le Doeuff's assertion that Beauvoir's thoughts 'galvanized women's movements pretty well everywhere and helped them get going'[3] it has never been an inaugural text for modern feminism.[4] Largely unacknowledged by the French, by philosophers and by the women's movement alike, *The Second Sex* erupts into the present in a manner that dislocates it from its 'proper' place in the scheme of things, confounding attempts to present the truth of its history or its place in history. As all the contributions here demonstrate, to revisit *The Second Sex* today produces the uncanny effect of belatedness that Freud called *Nachträglichkeit* (deferred action),[5] as new events and new knowledge endow the text with 'untimely' meanings. If the post-

modern is not simply 'the contemporary' but is, as Diane Elam
has argued, 'a way of thinking about history and representation',[6] then *The Second Sex* thinks through the question of postmodernity from its own geographical and temporal dislocations,
returning to haunt both the present and the future.

This volume is about that haunting. In admittedly far from
unified ways, each essay in this collection inscribes the uncanny
time of Beauvoir's text as a space of otherness that opens itself up
within the modernist project of feminist liberation. Atack's deconstructive reading finds an other to *The Second Sex*'s 'language of
linear rationality' in its 'multilayered ironic textuality' (p. 55)
and use of double structures of narration. Rodgers problematises
the nationalist histories of feminism that have excluded *The
Second Sex*, and by putting it 'beside' as well as 'within' feminism
she also problematises the traditional account of feminism's
genealogy. Where previous readers have found the author of *The
Second Sex* a 'realist', Sage finds a *romancier*, 'a writer who
systematically destabilised the relations between past and
present, work and world, on which realism depends' (p. 97).
Mackenzie, writing philosophy, finds Beauvoir's understanding
of the category of the Other uncannily similar to that found 'in
those feminisms strongly influenced by Derridean deconstruction'
(p. 139); in other words, she locates where Beauvoir's Woman-as-
other (this 'other' is confusingly capitalised in Parshley's English
translation) crosses over to assume the place of the Other as
language. Horton finds a productive tension between Sartrean
'freedom' and the 'situated' subject that renders Beauvoir's
understanding of subjectivity other to the modernist Enlightenment tradition of analytic philosophy. Finally, Ward Jouve's
fictional agonistics finds in women's troubled relations with each
other an alternative to the utopia of equality supposedly represented in *The Second Sex*.

To some readers, however, it will seem both perverse and
anachronistic to claim *The Second Sex* as postmodern. Anachronistic, because the book does not fit the chronology of 'now': not
only was it written in 1949 but its existentialist conceptual appa-
ratus is 'outdated', and it is not (nor has it ever been) the *dernier
cri* of feminist theory.[7] Perverse, because the word is that postmodernism appears to threaten the political coherence of the

women's movement by precipitating a crisis in its theoretical foundations: identity, history, the body, and emancipation.[8] These charges must be answered. Given the popular conflation of the postmodern with 'the look of the contemporary', there is an understandable danger that readers will suspect this introduction of simply tarting up a text that is *passé* in order to fix the consumer's gaze. But the essays in this volume do not claim for *The Second Sex* a new 'relevance'. More radically, they invite the reader to relive the twentieth-century past by recognising in the text the uncanny recurrence of preoccupations that supposedly arose after it was written: in short, they address the book's untimeliness.

Nor does this collection seek to engage with debates about the relationship between feminism and postmodernism: it does not want to rescue feminism from postmodernism, nor conversely to argue, as does Diana Coole, that feminism's 'own inner logic already reconstructs it as postmodern'.[9] While I agree with Coole that feminism and postmodernism are implicated in one another, to elide both categories is to lose their respective capacities to question each other's periodicity, and thus to challenge traditional historical narratives of both feminism and modernity. Nor does this collection use postmodernism in order to correct past errors in feminist readings of *The Second Sex*, or to suggest that Beauvoir's text was prescient. Those critical moves would leave this introduction – and *The Second Sex* – still within a modernist chronological frame. Repeatedly, though not consistently, the essays in this collection suggest that the text's critique of how 'woman' is represented in history and how she might be represented in the future is not only positioned within a dislocated narrative framework but is received by readers today in a way that disturbs and challenges the conventional periodicity of women's time.

This ironic revisiting of the modern within the postmodern, in order continually to open up new spaces for thinking modernity, is a point made by Jean-François Lyotard. For Lyotard, the postmodern is not simply that which comes after the modern: it 'is undoubtedly a part of the modern'. However, a 'work can become modern only if it is first postmodern. Postmodernism thus understood is not modernism at its end but in the nascent state, and this state is constant.'[10] The postmodern does not simply follow the modern in a chronological unfolding but is rather a constant revisiting of the conditions that made modernism possible. According to Lyotard, the paradoxical time of the postmodern is the tense of the future anterior: the artist and writer work without rules 'in order to formulate the rules of what *will have been done*.'[11] Postmodern texts 'always come too late for their author, or, what amounts to the same thing, their being put into work, their realization (*mise en oeuvre*) always begin too soon. *Post modern* would have to be understood according to the paradox of the future (*post*) anterior (*modo*).'[12] The work of art may be assigned to a particular moment in the linear chronology of literary history, but it does not necessarily inhabit that temporality.[13] It exists both too early and too late.

As Beauvoir interprets it, the tense of existentialism is also the tense of the postmodern. The book's most memorable statement – 'One is not born a woman, rather one becomes one' ('On ne naît pas femme: on le devient', DS1,285; SS295; Atack's translation, p. 43) – writes the future for women in a version of the paradoxical tense of the future anterior. In Atack's gloss, 'Our essence is created by what we do, it is the consequence of what we do. We will, therefore, be *what we will have done*' (p. 53; emphasis mine). In 1979 Beauvoir claimed: 'I think that *The Second Sex* will seem an old, dated book, after a while. But nonetheless ... a book which will have made its contribution.'[14] While the first half of this statement bows to a conventional view of history as the displacing of the old by the new, the second half signals an unfinishedness to interpretation in the aporia of a future that has already taken place. As Sage observes, recent readings of Beauvoir's representations of the body and female sexuality are now making sense of what looked to 'a whole generation of feminists ... like nonsense' (p. 116). In this light, *The Second Sex* contributes less to a modernist project of liberation than to a rethinking of the conditions under which feminism takes effect. Therefore, I want to move on now to a consideration of the place of *The Second Sex* within feminist historiography.

The Second Sex: making history?

Important new readings by Toril Moi, Judith Butler, Jane Heath, Michèle Le Doeuff, Margaret Simons, Nicole Ward Jouve and Lorna Sage have brought Beauvoir's undeniably feminist work back before a feminist critical gaze. Yet Beauvoir has been subject to considerable feminist woman-bashing. *The Second Sex* has stood accused of miming phallogocentric thinking, while elsewhere it has been largely ignored by feminist critics.[15] As Rodgers's essay in this volume observes, Beauvoir's feminism has always been perceived by Anglo-American feminists as 'humanist, existentialist and egalitarian' (p. 59), in other words, not feminism's cutting edge. In part, *The Second Sex*'s exclusion from feminism is discursively produced by the powerful allegory that has underwritten feminist historiography, namely the agon between (naïve humanist) Anglo-American feminism and (sophisticated) French feminist theory.[16] Although the notion of French thought as unitary is an Anglo-American fantasy,[17] it nevertheless remains the case that no major French academics work on Beauvoir.[18]

In these debates – and regrettably also in this volume – it seems as if Beauvoir's readers exist only on the shores that bound the Atlantic: France, Britain and America. But *The Second Sex* is read outside this golden triangle. In Hungary, for example, Beauvoir's and Sartre's work began to be read in translation after 1956, with critics emphasising Beauvoir's repudiation of her bourgeois background and her conscious identification with anti-fascism and oppressed groups. *The Second Sex* appeared in Hungarian in 1969. Unsurprisingly, it was never influential, certainly not in the sense that it had an impact on a movement. Socialism was deemed to have brought about equality for all, and there is no deep-rooted feminist tradition in Hungary. Remarkably, none of the Hungarian editions of *The Second* Sex has a preface, inviting still-unresolved questions about official perception of the work's ideological impact and the lack of desire to control readers' responses. After all, the book's demystification of domesticity is severely at odds with the belief in Hungarian society that a woman's place is in the home. One Hungarian academic, Nora Sellei, has pointed out that in the prefaces to translations of Beauvoir's other works her texts are never evaluated in aesthetic terms.[19] Reading *The Second Sex* with attention to its textuality might indeed prove to be productive for Hungarian feminists, but there is no way of predicting how it will be read within the changed cultural and social formation of post-1990 Hungary, or what kinds of political implications renewed attention to the work might have for nascent Hungarian feminism.

A postmodern feminist historiography is not a narrative of winners and losers.[20] In Rodgers's cultural history, *The Second Sex* does not emerge triumphantly as winner to replace its earlier 'loser' status amongst leading 'French feminists' and amongst those feminists in Britain and the US who have taken Cixous, Irigaray and Kristeva as synecdoches for French feminism *tout court*. Instead, Rodgers demonstrates how *The Second Sex* has been subject to a kind of cultural *Nachträglichkeit*, as French feminists rewrite their own narratives of feminism to include Beauvoir. This 'deferred' time of *The Second Sex* points not to a narrative of progressive emancipation but to the politics of history-making, further problematising what Rodgers describes as 'the difficulty of the task, so crucial to feminism, of creating a genealogy of women' (p. 88).[21]

The 'difficulty of the task' is also figured by the dynamic of what Susan Gubar describes as 'feminist misogyny': 'the uncanny mirror-dancing that repeatedly links feminist polemicists to their rivals and antagonists.'[22] Thus Antoinette Fouque accuses Beauvoir of imposing a 'matricidal and motherless feminism' (Rodgers, p. 68), while Chantal Chawaf accuses her of bringing 'more grist to misogyny's mill' by not breaking with 'the forces that suffocate and drag women down to a primary and repulsive maternity' (Rodgers, p. 69). Cixous rejects Beauvoir, but equally Beauvoir rejects Cixous: 'There is something false in this search for a purely feminine writing style' (Rodgers, p. 70). Gubar observes that 'As a genre, feminist expository prose inevitably embeds itself in the misogynist tradition it seeks to address and redress.'[23] In pointing to the eerie appropriateness with which recent feminist criticism has aligned itself with traditional misogyny in attacking 'incorrect' forms of feminism, Gubar seeks to delimit feminist thinking from within the metaphysical assurances in which it is held (truth/falsehood, feminism/misogyny, internalisation/demystification). Not only does this challenge the assumption that there is a right or wrong way to do feminism, but her analysis also suggests that when feminists repudiate Beauvoir this can no longer be satisfactorily explained as 'bad faith': the internalisation of patriarchal thinking. Instead, this self-divided reception of *The Second Sex* reveals the extent to which a unitary feminist identity is disrupted.

The figure of the mother looms large in critiques of Beauvoir and in the construction of a genealogy of women. As Rodgers says, post-1968 feminists rejected the 'possessive, castrating image of the mother, and were as a consequence prone to denigrate the work of previous women' (p. 88).[24] The rejection of Beauvoir as mother complicates feminism's Oedipal drama, for it also – ironically – implies a rejection of the Beauvoir who distanced herself from the mother glorified by Cixous and Kristeva.[25] This rejection also results from feminism's later taking up of psychoanalytic criticism, in which the figure of the mother is also a figure for feminism's movement first to the preOedipal, and then to the Lacanian Other of language and the unconscious.[26] In rejecting Beauvoir as the 'mother' of feminism, feminists may thus be rejecting what they take to be Beauvoir's refusal of the (m)Other, of a (sophisticated) poststructuralist and postmodern feminist politics. Yet 'the mother' in psychoanalytic feminist criticism is a deeply conflicted figure, projected as capable of healing feminism's rifts but also bringing into feminism an otherness that divides it against itself. As Gallop says, 'If "the figure of the mother" blesses the marriage of psychoanalysis and feminism, the mother as other presides over their divorce.'[27] The intrusion of this otherness into *The Second Sex*'s otherwise non-psychoanalytic feminism is attested by several essays in this volume that open up the work's status as a deconstructive 'writing' (Atack, Sage, Mackenzie, Ward Jouve). Sage, for example, argues that Beauvoir 'orphaned' herself by lopping off the past, making herself motherless but in so doing releasing herself into being a writer (p. 110). To understand more about *The Second Sex*'s troubled relationship to feminist historiography, it is necessary to turn to Beauvoir's representation of history.

The problematic of history in *The Second Sex*

In her Introduction Beauvoir states that women 'have no past, no history ... of their own' (SS19). Yet she does not set out to write that history for them. Instead she charts modes of female alienation. Her analysis concentrates on demonstrating how the various versions of 'female difference' are male fictions: 'the whole of feminine history has been man-made' (SS159). Beauvoir explicitly rejects any assertions of the value of the 'female domain':[28] it precisely does not have 'value', which is an existentialist ideal that historically only men have possessed.[29] She is wonderfully ironic about the masculine ideal of femininity embodied, for example, in Proudhon's 'ardent litanies to the "true woman"', commenting that 'In spite of this devotion, he was unable to make his own wife happy: the letters of Mme Proudhon are one long lament' (SS143). The existential frame, rather than being a limitation on Beauvoir's feminist project, becomes a way of questioning the adequacy of realist chronological history for a feminist politics by casting doubt on the subject of that history. 'History' for Beauvoir must begin not by rescuing women from obscurity or celebrating their heroic roles but with the politics of representation. It must admit, in Elam's words, 'that there is a politics to our definition of the political.'[30]

    Where traditional feminist history has sought, in Friedman's formulation, 'to discover the "truth" of women's history that could shatter the "myths" and "lies" about women in the standard histories' – a goal that 'operates out of a positivist epistemology that assumes that the truth of history is objectively knowable'[31] – *The Second Sex* resists both telling the 'truth' about women and the assurance of a conscious position of knowledge. One way in which it does this is by 'ironically install[ing] suspicions about discourse at its very beginning' (Atack, p. 55). In the French edition, the text is framed with two epigraphs (omitted in Parshley's translation), the first by Pythagoras and the second by a little-known (male) French feminist of the seventeenth century, Poulain de la Barre:

> Il y a un principe bon qui a créé l'ordre, la lumière et l'homme et un principe mauvais qui a créé le chaos, les ténèbres et la femme. [There is a good principle which created order, light and man and a bad principle which has created chaos, darkness and woman.]

> Tout ce qui a été écrit par les hommes sur les femmes doit être suspect, car ils sont à la fois juge et partie. [Everything which has been written by men about women must be suspect since they are simultaneously judge and litigant.][32]

According to Pythagoras, the case against women is decided by pre-existing narratives that consign her *a priori* to an ethically inferior place. But Poulain de la Barre's recognition of vested interests disorganises the 'right' of the good principle to speak the truth about the other. As Atack notes: 'the double structure of hierarchical binary opposition [in Pythagoras] is met with another double structure which sets a frame (of argument, *interest*, and duplicity) by which the former may be read' (p. 55). Men are not neutral observers of 'women's case', but women will not be neutral observers either: 'Man is at once judge and party to the case; *but so is woman*' (SS27: emphasis mine). Only an angel or hermaphrodite, Beauvoir teases, would be able to step outside sexual difference.

Beauvoir's Introduction thus begins by recognising gender in terms of Lyotard's differend (*différand*): 'a case of conflict [as distinguished from a litigation] between (at least) two parties, that cannot be equitably resolved for lack of a rule of judgment applicable to both arguments. One side's legitimacy does not imply the other's lack of legitimacy. However, applying a single rule of judgment to both in order to settle their differend as though it were merely a litigation would wrong (at least) one of them (and both of them if neither side admits this rule).'[33] In *The Second Sex* the *querelle* – intellectual dispute – between men and women cannot be resolved according to a single rule of judgment. Men presume to invoke a 'universal' law by which to judge the dispute, but that law is partisan. In the words of Poulain de la Barre, 'Being men, those who have made and compiled the laws have favoured their own sex, and jurists have elevated these laws into principles' (SS22).

Women cannot answer or refute men's claims about them (which wrong them) because they are caught in a double bind, supposed to abide by the rules which would allow women to claim damages but in fact suffering a wrong which cannot be 'judged' since the rules only respect the interests of one of the parties: men.[34] But this does not mean elevating women's interests,

as Beauvoir makes clear: 'We should consider the arguments of
the feminists with no less suspicion, however, for very often
their controversial aim deprives them of all real value. ... People
have tirelessly sought to prove that woman is superior, inferior,
or equal to man. ... If we are to gain understanding, we must get
out of these ruts; we must discard the vague notions of superiority, inferiority, equality which have hitherto corrupted every
discussion of the subject and start afresh' (SS26–7). Of course
Beauvoir's style here is problematically magisterial (installing
authority where she most means to call it in question) but she is
also clear that there is no way of deciding once and for all the
question of sexual difference, of what 'women' are (there are no
angels or hermaphrodites, no way of getting outside gender).
Beauvoir's position is uncannily close to Lyotard's: 'I don't know
whether sexual difference is ontological difference. How would
a person *know*?'[35] Not only is it impossible to know what the
ontological difference is, but there is no way – because of the
differend – of being able to find out. The differend is a figure for
the difficult politics of representation, for what makes representation difficult in the first place: the attempt to put into words
something that cannot be because of the incommensurability of
knowledges that precludes an objective perspective.[36]

It is true that Beauvoir seems to argue for women's ethical
rightness to judge the case. But she is very clear about 'relativity
of interest' (SS28): women may be more qualified to speak for
women but she explicitly distances her project from the language
of rights and identity politics: 'books by women on women are
in general animated in our day less by a wish to demand our
rights than by an effort towards clarity and understanding'
(SS28). Moreover, as Atack argues, *The Second Sex*'s narrative
strategies confuse the identity of the narrating voice, frustrating
'attempts to fix an identified gender position within discourse'
(p. 53) and hence to install an ontological foundation for the
'truth' of women's case.

Yet central to *The Second Sex* is the question of woman as a
subject in history. Contesting the view proposed by Hegel that
only man could ever be a historical agent,[37] Beauvoir claims for
women the right to engage in a 'project' that will confer meaning
on their existence: 'What [women] demand today is to be

recognized as existents by the same right as men and not to subordinate existence to life, the human being to its animality' (SS97). But while she sweeps away the grand narratives of psychoanalysis and Marxism, rejecting 'both the sexual monism of Freud and the economic monism of Engels' (SS91), Beauvoir problematically makes existentialism her theoretical foundation: 'Underlying all individual drama, as it underlies the economic history of mankind, there is an existentialist foundation that alone enables us to understand in its unity that particular form of being which we call a human life' (SS91). It is therefore useful to remind ourselves that though deeply influenced, as Mackenzie demonstrates, by Hegel's insight that consciousness arises in intersubjective recognition,[38] Beauvoir does not set out to write a 'system',[39] and that existentialism is a structure of *alienation* – 'the existent succeeds in finding himself [*sic*] only in estrangement, in alienation' (SS88) – into which, as Atack reminds us (p. 41), Beauvoir intrudes the otherness of psychoanalysis by choosing Lacan's mirror stage as an analogy for that structure (SS297).

Despite Le Doeuff's claim that *The Second Sex* is 'a prolongation of the reading of Hegel' (Rodgers, p. 65), and despite the fact that Beauvoir talks about 'progress' (SS148) and the 'evolution of woman's condition' (SS152), Beauvoir is absolutely clear that this evolution has not been 'a continuous process' (SS128) and that nothing can be known in advance about women's condition. Beauvoir's position on women's autonomous agency may not be logically consistent (as Mackenzie points out), but *The Second Sex* is at no point committed to grand narratives of the end of history. In Atack's words: 'We are not determined by our natures or by pre-existing religious or social scripts. There is no final and glorious end to history or politics.' (p. 40)

Instead of filling in the blanks in women's history, *The Second Sex* chooses to pose questions about the narrating of past events.[40] The text juxtaposes psychological and anthropological case studies, historical narratives, literary examples and personal anecdotes. As Atack comments, this technique allows Beauvoir to dramatise 'arguments about gender relations and female identity through history' within a frame of the *querelle*, and that this allows her to represent the *querelle* as existing 'in the here and now, in the eternal present of the debate over interpretation' (pp. 51–2). What Atack describes as the 'timelessness to the enunciating frame' is not a forgetting or denial of proper historical sequence. Rather it brings *The Second Sex* close to the postmodern rethinking of history as 'an ironic coexistence of temporalities,'[41] disrupting chronological cause-and-effect to tremendous political advantage by insisting that past history in no way determines the (feminist) future. If history as a feminist foundation is called in question by *The Second Sex*, then so also is identity.

The politics of identity

For Moi, Beauvoir's problematic 'is one of *power*, not one of identity and/or difference.'[42] Beauvoir will not be drawn into characterising a prior 'female specificity', whether founded in maternity, ways of knowing, or sexuality. Since such a specificity has been seen as grounding for a feminist politics,[43] this has led in some quarters of the women's movement to a dismissal of the political value of *The Second Sex*. Yet the lack of agreement amongst post-1968 feminists about the meanings of 'sex', 'gender' and 'woman' suggests a need for rethinking their usefulness as categories of identity.[44] As Butler argues, one of the strengths of Beauvoir's analysis is precisely its refusal to name the category 'woman': to figure liberation as a gain in *identity*. This does not mean, however, that *The Second Sex* does not speak to the problematic of identity.[45] Butler, for example, explains how Beauvoir subverts identity as ontology, by drawing out the implications of Beauvoir's argument that 'to become' a gender means 'both to submit to a cultural situation and to create one'.[46] In Butler's terms, Beauvoir can be understood as saying that the cultural compulsion to become a woman comes not from 'sex' – from the material body – but from language, even though, as Butler argues in *Gender Trouble*, Beauvoir did not fully realise the radical consequences of her central theory that 'One is not born a woman, rather one becomes one.'[47]

Several essays in this volume take up and extend these radical consequences in terms of psychoanalytic or language-based accounts of subjectivity. Working through Nathalie Sarraute's anti-essentialist fictions to Beauvoir's constructionism, Sage –

like Butler – gestures towards a notion of performativity at work in the re-production of female subjectivity: 'This is how essences are "born", over and over again. ... Repetition is *of the essence*: it is how essences reproduce themselves' (pp. 100–1). Sage argues that Beauvoir's scepticism about classic realism, like Sarraute's, is a scepticism about essences: writing itself cannot reproduce essences, cannot name a thing beyond itself. Patriarchal femininity is an effect of its reproduction in fictions. Likewise, Mackenzie argues that Woman as other is also woman as an effect of language: of the structures of myth that construct her as absolute alterity. Atack also works with Beauvoir's insight of the self/other relationship as fundamental by exploring her construction of gendered subjectivity, especially how unconscious identity is dependent on structures of alienation. Thus, Atack notes how Beauvoir's invocation of Lacan's mirror stage (p. 41; SS297) registers her awareness that subjectivity is based on an illusory sense of wholeness and on alienation, something as true for *men* as for women. In other words, men do not have the magically uncomplicated subjectivity that critics of *The Second Sex*'s transcendent penis-politics have assumed Beauvoir to be celebrating.[48]

If *The Second Sex* nowhere allows a purchase on a prior female identity, it nevertheless addresses the issue of ethical agency. This is explored by Mackenzie, who thus links the text's analysis of oppression (gender relations) to identity politics: how can women achieve the ethical authenticity that the text advocates for them? Feminists should concern themselves with Beauvoir, Mackenzie argues, because she is interested in an 'ethics of action' and in exploring one specific instance of ethical failure: sexual oppression. For Beauvoir, ethical autonomy is predicated on action, not on a static identity. It is an identity that must keep performing itself.[49] In Beauvoir's terms, women have as much right as men to partake of 'freedom', and this must express itself in action, in a 'project'. By demystifying the 'bad faith' which prevents women from realising autonomy, Beauvoir aims to enable them to see more clearly how they can shake it off and confer meaning upon their existence. What is contradictory is that it is Beauvoir's belief in 'embodied consciousness' that makes it more difficult for women than for men to fulfil that project, since their reproductive capacities drag them back to the body. Ultimately, therefore, Beauvoir fails to account for 'an ideal of autonomous agency that is capable of incorporating a recognition of both the speci-ficity and the variety of women's bodily perspectives' (p. 126). Mackenzie's is therefore a specialised understanding of Beauvoir's inability to recognise the political value of female specificity, but one that carefully works through the double bind for women of the embodiedness of ethical agency.

Though Beauvoir's insistence on the bodily dimension of ethics is problematic, she nevertheless offers a way out of the impasse of oppression. Beauvoir argues that it is only through their conscious taking up of subjectivity (in existential terms, their becoming transcendent) that women can break out of the deadlock of the self/other opposition that produces an asymme-try of power relations (SS16–17). However, given her conviction that 'The category of the *Other* is as primordial as consciousness itself' (SS16), this entails that women's production of themselves as subjects – as the One – will be *over and against* an Other-object.[50] Ward Jouve's fictionalised polemics proposes: what if *women* are these others in opposition to whom women achieve subjectivity? Won't such a subjectivity simply repeat the patri-archal structure of what Allison Weir calls 'sacrificial logics': female identity as 'always and only the product of a repression or domination'?[51]

For Ward Jouve's Paula, the unconscious is just as important as consciousness in the construction of female subjectivity (p. 189) and must be a significant part of Beauvoir's textual 'meaning'. Paula admits that her troubled relations with female others also involve her *desires* (for example, she wants them to take control). By invoking Torok's controversial essay about penis-envy (pp. 196–7),[52] she suggests that a reading against the grain of *The Second Sex* hints at a psychoanalytic understanding of female sexual development that involves complex trajectories of desire. Paula thus shifts the site of the self/other debate away from its Hegelian roots in the master-slave dialectic towards the part played by the unconscious in setting up structures, and in our continued investment in those structures *in spite of ourselves*. The feminist *canard* raised by Paula – that Beauvoir's repeated endorsement of the penis as superior is just fuelled by penis-envy, and that she turns her fantasies into universals (p. 188) –

could thus be written another way: 'knowledge will not put an end to desire.'[53] Furthermore, by making Beauvoir's argument wash out of *The Second Sex* and over a group of women who are differentiated socially, politically and in terms of their sexuality, Ward Jouve implies that readers, like writers, are also complex subjects of desire: they too have 'bees in their bonnets' (p. 189). *The Second Sex*'s otherwise modernist project of demystification is thus set astray by desire, in a manner that divides it against itself but which also prevents the text from fossilising into a feminist archaeological remain. Its issues continue to provoke, haunt, and disturb Ward Jouve's debating women.

But if identity involves difference, it does not have to be predicated on hierarchy. Ward Jouve's Anne raises – but does not resolve – the postmodern question of difference without mastery ('isn't it terribly reductive to want two *only* to register as inferior?': p. 205). Horton's essay also addresses the question of mastery, reading *The Second Sex* not for a theory of female identity but for its specific understanding of the traditionally masterful and rational subject of philosophy. Arguing that the subject of *The Second Sex* is situated, as Horton felicitously puts it, in the 'tension-ridden "spaces" between freedom and the social influences around her or him' (p. 164), his essay proposes that this subject is neither fully disseminated nor fully Cartesian. Philosophy has sidelined *The Second Sex*, Horton claims, because Beauvoir's text works from within the Enlightenment tradition to destabilise the Enlightenment subject that is the foundation of philosophy. One way in which it does this is to insist that bodies are not universal but are differentially marked by gender.

The body

Beauvoir's body politics has had a bad feminist press. *The Second Sex*'s descriptions of female sexuality as holes and slime have all been subject to worst case readings, confirming Beauvoir as a hopeless misogynist, mortgaged to what Atack describes as 'the Sartrean "hiérarchie ontologico-charnelle" [ontologico-corporeal hierarchy], where the negative metaphors of the in-itself align viscosity with femininity' (p. 34).[54] Since Beauvoir's account is structured, as Mackenzie explains, according to Hegel's distinction between life (mere maintenance of the species, reproduction) and self-consciousness (individual autonomy) the (reproductive) female body cannot be active. Its events cannot be a 'project', nor can it be, as the penis is for men, an instrument of transcendence (SS97). Beauvoir's female body is doomed to passivity. Ward Jouve further critiques Beauvoir for her eurocentrism: for inscribing female sexuality within a western economy of suffering (p. 204).[55]

Yet the body is central to *The Second Sex*'s argument about oppression. As Mackenzie argues, it is precisely Beauvoir's notion of embodiment — of the joining of the social to the philosophical or ethical — that radically questions and reveals the limits of the Sartrean notion of bad faith and consciousness. This would suggest that Beauvoirian corporeality and its differences are in need of urgent rethinking. Several essays in this volume continue the recent feminist project of reading Beauvoir's representations of the female body deconstructively,[56] discerning this time a devastatingly ironic and politically tactical writer. In infamous passages such as the description of feminine sex desire as 'the soft throbbing of a mollusc' (SS407), Atack argues, Beauvoir is ironically repeating and citing phallogocentric language, and thus beginning to deconstruct the metanarratives of the body that have mired women in facticity. In Butler's terms, Beauvoir uses and repeats dominant cultural metanarratives of gender with subversive intent, by displacing them 'from the contexts in which they have been deployed as instruments of oppressive power.'[57] By making such descriptions part of a complex call for women to resignify their bodies and their lives in terms of 'values', Beauvoir is emphatic that women's *experience* of their bodies may repeat the cultural metanarratives of gender but that this in no way defines how those metanarratives might be *rewritten*. In her words, 'To be present in the world implies strictly that there exists a body which is at once a material thing in the world and a point of view towards this world; but nothing requires that this body have this or that particular structure' (SS39).[58]

By stressing the rhetorical and citational aspects of Beauvoir's so-called repulsive descriptions, the essays by Atack, Sage and Ward Jouve firmly uncouple those descriptions from the ontological, arguing rather that the material reality of women's bodies is an effect of (man-made) language. Though Beauvoir would not have put it in those terms, *The Second Sex* nevertheless admits of such an understanding. In the following passage, for example, there is an acknowledgement that language writes us: 'Man "gets stiff", but woman "gets wet" [more accurately, 'wets']; *in the very word* there are childhood memories of bed-wetting, of guilty and involuntary yielding to the need to urinate' (SS407) (emphasis mine). Mackenzie, too, understands *The Second Sex*'s body politics in more complex and conflicted terms than is usually allowed by noting a similarity between Beauvoir's analysis of female experience of abjection and contemporary psychoanalytic feminist interpretations of anorexia and hysteria as revolt against oppression (p. 145).

Beauvoir is deeply concerned with the relationship between modes of consciousness and the phenomenological body, which is why, as she explains, she begins *The Second Sex* with the data of biology: 'For, the body being the instrument of our grasp upon the world, the world is bound to seem a very different thing when apprehended in one manner or another. This accounts for our lengthy study of the biological facts; they are one of the keys to our understanding of woman. But I deny that they establish for her a fixed and inevitable destiny. They are insufficient for setting up a hierarchy of the sexes; they fail to explain why woman is the Other; they do not condemn her to remain in this subordinate role for ever' (SS65). Unlike Sartre, Beauvoir considers consciousness and thought to be inseparable from the phenomenological body, and she is dependent for this on Merleau-Ponty, as is Lyotard: 'Thought is inseparable from the phenomenological body: although gendered body is separated from thought, and launches thought'.[59] To read Beauvoir and Lyotard in tandem is to see them confronting a similar problematic, insofar as their understanding of the body is not rooted in ontological difference or in the Cartesian notion of body as mere 'container' for thought. On the one hand Beauvoir explores the relationship between self-consciousness and the gendered phenomenological body, but at the same time she tries to articulate the difference of gendered bodies – the differend of gender – with a set of power relations that are not already given, not inscribed in or on the body.

Beauvoir's is an attempt to write a 'situated' philosophy, to explain the asymmetrical power relations instituted by sexual difference not as natural but as the result of women's 'total situation' (SS83). Even more than Lyotard, she is trying to write what cannot yet be thought because woman only 'experiences' her consciousness and phenomenological body in ways that are already underwritten by asymmetrical power relations and which cannot therefore be a guide to what woman *might* become: 'Woman is not a completed reality, but rather a becoming, and it is in her becoming that she should be compared with man; that is to say, her *possibilities* should be defined' (SS66). Beauvoir's task is nothing less than to write a feminist politics for the twentieth century that is cognisant of the postmodern problematic of putting into phrases something which cannot yet be because there are no (generic, universal) rules which could legitimate it.

There are of course major differences between Lyotard and Beauvoir. Lyotard thinks of the body, *qua* sexually-differentiated corporeality, as giving rise to thought, as enabling (without being a foundation), whereas Beauvoir thinks of the body as 'a limiting factor for our projects' (SS66). And she does believe in 'the human project', which Lyotard does not: his is an attempt to write an 'inhuman' philosophy. But 'project' is separate from 'teleology'. Beauvoir stresses how 'the human species is for ever in a state of changing, for ever becoming' (SS65), and that this becoming can never be known in advance. What's more, while Lyotard valorises possibility – a state somewhere between activity and passivity, a state that is receptive without teleological motive – Beauvoir contends that all positive values are active: a 'pro-ject' is a throwing forward of the self.

Yet the challenge of Beauvoir's radical uncoupling of patriarchal femininity from the body and from future consciousness is that she is concerned with the here and now of cultural inscriptions of powerlessness at the same time that she tries to formulate a politics of future possibilities, of what woman might become. If for Lyotard thinking takes place as a result of the differend of gender – 'Thought is inseparable from the phenomenological body; although gendered body is separated from thought, and launches thought' – then Beauvoir is endlessly trying to project thought forward – a difficult thinking – by drawing on narrative techniques that attempt to articulate the perception of gendered body as launching thought. Lyotard's essay does not only make gender visible within the postmodern but finds gender a philosophical question. It claims a space of non-knowledge, of non-mastery, in order to open up future modes of the as-yet-unthought, but *The Second Sex* as a whole can be read as an attempt to do just that in the name of a feminist politics. If we take Lyotard unironically,[60] then his description of embodied consciousness as 'transcendence in immanence' suggests to me an uncanny return of Beauvoir's existentialism as a philosophical framework for thinking through the relationship between corporeality, thought and ethics. By constantly posing the question of the unrepresentable, Beauvoir's postmodern understanding, however problematic, of history, identity and the body has important implications for a feminist future.

The future?

Jane Heath thinks it may be possible to discern, 'in the dense and often difficult final pages of *Le Deuxième Sexe* the adumbrations of Kristeva's utopia', namely 'the outlines of diversity, of differences'.[61] What kind of utopia might this be? Not that imagined by Ward Jouve's Paula. Expressing a nostalgic, wistful desire for unity and transcendence in relation to the future for feminist politics, she claims that *The Second Sex* partakes of that same desire for unity. Observing that in the nineteen fifties and sixties there was a belief – certainly amongst Beauvoir and Sartre – that through the de-colonisation period there would be access to transcendence, and that with this would come 'political independence, new nationhood, access to a true self', she declares that 'a version of the same hope animates the ending of *The Second Sex*.' But she then notes, 'Alas! We see things rather differently today, don't we? Look at Algeria – Rwanda ...' (p. 202). Against this liberal feminism, Jo maintains her Marxist stance, equally problematic for feminism: 'Let's not go for simplistic analyses! What about the sequels left by colonialism – ancient structures destroyed, irksome privileges left standing, inappropriate structures in place, under-development – not to mention economic colonialism, the new imperialism of world capital creating new divisions, new forms of powerlessness ...' (p. 202). Both Paula and Jo, from their different political convictions, are dismayed by the uncertainty of the later twentieth-century, by its aftermath of third-world revolutions and the legacy of late capitalism.

Anne on the other hand tries to nudge them towards a politics that will break out of the impasse. Instead of viewing difference as inevitably involving hierarchical power, she asks 'Isn't it terribly reductive to want two *only* to register as inferior?' (p. 205) Difference, she suggests, can be rethought in order to produce a different feminist politics, one that escapes the logic of hierarchy: 'If we allow them to signify, can they not lead us to all sorts of insights?' Anne's question raises an issue that is of supreme importance to *The Second Sex* and to a feminist politics, namely what might such a politics be? how could we make it differently? Anne situates the politics of the text in a utopia of imagining an uncertain future but she latches on to the political importance of that uncertainty. This is in fact just what Beauvoir's text advocates: 'in order to explain her limitations, it is to women's situation that we must turn and not to a mysterious essence – the future lies wide open' (SS723; DS2,480, trans Heath[62]). Women must take it upon themselves to shape their future, and since this will not be dependent on any previous structures it will therefore necessarily be uncertain.

This does not necessarily equal a politics of indecision. In Elam's words, which apply not to *The Second Sex* but to a postmodern feminism,

> [o]n the contrary, it would be a politics flexible enough to remain open to new modes of political calculation, a politics that would not judge events on the basis of a set of pre-existing criteria ... feminism is perhaps the clearest instance of a force that has retained its political drive precisely through a refusal to be pinned down to certainties. ... Feminism is a politics of uncertainty because it insists that we do not yet know what women can be, and that it is always men who have wanted to have the question of woman decisively answered once and for all, as Tiresias found to his cost.[63]

Existentialism may be outdated, but in Beauvoir's hands it is transformed into a way of thinking through an ethics of action which, as Mackenzie argues, stresses 'the particularity of each moral agent and each moral situation.' This understanding of the extreme localisation of every action is akin to de Certeau's notion of the 'tactic' as opposed to the 'strategy',[64] in which there can be no pre-givens that determine the value of political action in any given situation. Strategies are associated with fixity, directing themselves towards the outside in the pursuit of set goals. Tactics, on the other hand, are the watchful, mobile responses of those who do not occupy a fixed place and who do not calculate in advance.

Interdisciplinary space

This volume contains essays that might be identified as coming from the disciplines of French Literature, English Literature, Cultural History, Women's Studies, and Philosophy. Most, though not all, of the writers might also identify themselves as feminist.[65] Although, as the editor, I would have liked contributions from other disciplines, especially from a biologist, an economist, a socio-linguist or an anthropologist, in order to open up a productive otherness within current cultural appropriations of *The Second Sex*, nevertheless the essays here have sufficiently put different disciplinary approaches into dialogue with each other. This is not in order to assert their essential 'sameness' but to reveal their incommensurability.[66] However, one feature of this volume is that there is a relatively high incidence of shared 'language games' amongst the contributions. This is not to claim, of course, that these essays take similar approaches, but they do show something of the extent to which certain areas of the academy have become interdisciplinary, mingling rhetorical analysis with literary history and cultural politics. At least half of the essays here come out of literary studies, not only because this discipline has been the one in which feminism made the earliest inroads within the academy, but also because, significantly, it concerns itself – like *The Second Sex* – with representation.

The demarcation of the disciplines now is subject to a great deal of slippage: Hegel talks to literary critics; philosophers scrutinise the metaphorical content of their writings, historians find themselves not telling the 'truth' about the past but writing narratives. As several essays here emphasise (Atack, Sage, Mackenzie), *The Second Sex* partakes of this slippage in exhilarating and productive ways, precisely because, as Mackenzie argues, Beauvoir uses existing categories not only to produce new formulations of existing theories but also to reveal their limits. Sage claims for *The Second Sex* the status of a work of 'original' *fiction*. More radically, Ward Jouve rewrites feminist theory as literature, implicitly posing a question at the heart of 'interdisciplinarity' and its institutional inscriptions (and one raised in acute form in *The Second Sex* itself): in what forms can knowledge be produced? what is worthy of the name of theory and what is not? can literature be written – or read – as theory? and vice versa?

What reading across disciplines can do is to show up versions of blindness and insight (which is not at all the same thing as saying that some disciplines have got it 'right' and others have got it 'wrong'). Thus where Diana Coole dismisses *The Second Sex* as having nothing to contribute to the discipline of political philosophy because it is not concerned with 'consciousness',[67] Mackenzie's essay argues that the book is deeply concerned with this category in its central understanding of ethical agency as embodied consciousness.

The question of what constitutes the interdisciplinary runs the risk of essentialising disciplinary categories unless we remember that there are differences *within* singular disciplines that divide them against themselves. Horton's essay, for example, plays off different traditions *within* philosophy, using Beauvoir's text as a lever against the tradition of analytic philosophy and against Radcliffe Richards' so-called feminist appropriation of that tradition. Radcliffe Richards might appear something of a straw woman in this debate, if it were not for the fact that she allows Horton to make a useful point about the blindness of analytic philosophy, since her reading of Beauvoir so patently misses the point. A further implication of Horton's thinking is that to work only within the binary of metaphysics/empiricism means missing what is most valuable in Beauvoir's work: its acknowledgement that the category 'woman' is discursively defined. Similarly, as Horton demonstrates, the category 'reason' is discursively defined, and cannot therefore present itself as transcendent, although this does not entail a wholesale rejection of the analytic tradition (p. 176). There is an important sense in which generic differences, internal differences and incommensurabilities, both within Beauvoir's text and within responses to it, are vital in order for readers to go on thinking productively about *The Second Sex*.

For this reason, any revaluation of *The Second Sex* must avoid the temptation to place it centre-stage, to make it either a foundational text or a point of origin for a feminist politics in the twentieth century. Rodgers notes how the influence of *The Second Sex* 'continues to haunt' the texts written by 'most of the French feminists best known in Great Britain' (p. 67). And in Atack's words, *The Second Sex* 'still stalks the horizons of our philosophical and cultural understandings' (p. 56). The metaphors suggest a text that is neither central nor marginal, but rather one that understands itself as simultaneously central and marginal, on the boundaries ('horizons') but also self-imposing ('stalks'). Overtly presenting a modernist narrative of liberation, *The Second Sex* is nevertheless postmodern in the sense that it continues to open up a series of problems present to modernity: identity, history, gender, representation. The readings in this volume recognise Beauvoir's text as not only presenting an emancipatory narrative but as insisting on thinking through the difficult politics of emancipation in the as-yet-unfinished future past of feminism.

Notes

1 Awarded in a 1996 British promotion jointly organised by the *Observer* newspaper and Waterstone's Booksellers.

2 Will Self, 'Cult books 1966/1996: my generation', Observer *Life* Magazine, 21 January 1996, 32–3: 32.

3 Michèle le Doeuff, *Hipparchia's Choice: An Essay Concerning Women, Philosophy, etc.*, trans. Trista Selous (Oxford: Basil Blackwell, 1991), p. 57. In 1975 Yvette Roudy named *The Second Sex* the 'woman's bible': Yvette Roudy, 'La seconde révolution des Américaines', *L'Arc* 61, *Simone de Beauvoir et la lutte des femmes* (1975), 68, quoted in Rodgers's essay in this volume, p. 61. All page references to essays in this volume appear parenthetically in the text.

4 The first feminist study of *The Second Sex* in French (by Geneviève Gennari) appeared in 1958, but in Britain and America feminism did not hit Beauvoir studies until after 1973. On the book's impact in France amongst feminists who, whilst supportive of Beauvoir, did not find it helpful for a feminist activism, see Le Doeuff, *Hipparchia's Choice*, pp. 101 and 120.

5 Linked by Bill Readings and Bennet Schaber to the time of the postmodern
   'event', which also occurs 'both too soon and too late.' *Nachträglichkeit*
   'occurs too soon to be understood, and is understood too late to be recov-
   ered. To follow Freud, it only enters consciousness as a re-transcription':
   'Introduction: The question mark in the midst of modernity', in Bill
   Readings and Bennet Schaber (eds), *Postmodernism Across the Ages*
   (Syracuse: Syracuse University Press, 1993), pp. 1–28: p. 9.

6 Diane Elam, *Romancing the Postmodern* (London and New York: Routledge,
   1992), pp. 3 and 10.

7 Charles Jencks claims that postmodernism began in about 1960: see Elam,
   Romancing, p. 9. For a placing of Beauvoir's work before postmodernism,
   see Sonia Kruks, 'Gender and subjectivity: Simone de Beauvoir and
   contemporary feminism', *Signs: Journal of Women in Culture and Society*,
   18:1 (1992), 89–110: 91–2. But Kruks is one of the few feminists to claim
   that 'rather than consigning [Beauvoir] to ancestor worship ... I want to
   argue that Beauvoir remains highly relevant to current theoretical
   concerns' (p. 95). On the 'outdatedness' of existentialism, see Michèle Le
   Doeuff, 'Simone de Beauvoir and existentialism', *Feminist Studies*, 6 (1980),
   277–89: 278 and also Le Doeuff, *Hipparchia's Choice*, pp. 55–6. Toril Moi
   ironically notes that the book has been regarded as the work of a 'theoretical dinosaur': *Simone de Beauvoir: The Making of an Intellectual Woman*
   (Oxford: Basil Blackwell, 1994), p. 182. See also Toril Moi, *Feminist Theory
   and Simone de Beauvoir*, The Bucknell Lectures (Oxford: Basil Blackwell,
   1990), p. 108.

8 For a summary of the feminist foundations called in question by postmodernism, see Judith Butler, 'A sceptical feminist postscript to the postmodern', in Readings and Schaber (eds), *Postmodernism Across the Ages*,
   pp. 233–7 and her 'Contingent foundations: feminism and the question of
   "postmodernism"', in Judith Butler and Joan W. Scott (eds), *Feminists
   Theorize the Political* (New York and London: Routledge, 1992), pp. 3–21.

9 Diana H. Coole, *Women in Political Theory: From Ancient Misogyny to
   Contemporary Feminism* (Brighton: Harvester Wheatsheaf, 1988; 2nd edn
   1993), p. 3 (1993). See also p. 190 (1993): 'If the postmodern suggests socio-
   cultural shifts towards a decline of the centre and eruption from the
   margins – where excluded others insist on speaking and where those who
   were included now insist on their difference and the right to a different
   voice – then feminism has itself become postmodern due to its own internal logic. It was, after all, women's insistence on their difference from men
   that began the erosion of normative and universalist concepts like humanity, while the fragmentation of the women's movement against itself arose
   from assertions of difference within it against the falsely unifying claims
   which misrepresented women's own diversity. This was not then an
   extrinsic effect of postmodernism, but feminism's becoming postmodern.'
   For a sceptical view of the idea that feminism is inherently postmodern
   because it challenges Enlightenment thinking, see Kruks, 'Gender and
   subjectivity', 89. However, Kruks at times comes close to using *The Second
   Sex* to rescue feminism from postmodernism by arguing that Beauvoir can

still affirm political agency. On this count, also see Horton's essay in this volume.

10 Jean-François Lyotard, *The Postmodern Condition: A Report on Knowledge* [1979], trans. Geoff Bennington and Brian Massumi (Manchester: Manchester University Press, 1984), p. 79. Elam, *Romancing*, p. 9: 'postmodernism is *not* simply that which comes after modernism. … but is a series of problems present to modernism in its continuing infancy.'

11 Lyotard, *Postmodern Condition*, p. 81: 'L'artiste et l'écrivain travaillent donc sans règles, et pour établir les règles de ce qui *aura été fait*': Jean-François Lyotard, *Le Postmoderne expliqué aux enfants* (Paris: Editions Galilée, 1988), p. 27. See also Elam, *Romancing*, p. 95: 'The future anterior insists upon the fact that what passes for our "present" is not a fullness or a presence, since it is always marked as the potential past of our own future.'

12 Lyotard, *Postmodern Condition*, p. 81.

13 For Lyotard, the essay – as practised by Montaigne in the seventeenth century – is postmodern: *Postmodern Condition*, p. 81.

14 Alice Jardine, 'Interview with Simone de Beauvoir', *Signs: Journal of Women in Culture and Society*, 5:2 (1979), 224–36: 236. Although I have been unable to find the original French transcription of this interview, it is reasonable to assume that Beauvoir's tense was the future anterior: 'aura fait'.

15 For Toril Moi, Beauvoir is 'surely the greatest feminist theorist of our time': *Sexual/Textual Politics* (London and New York: Methuen, 1985), p. 91. For a summary of the reception of Beauvoir's work, including hostile reactions from French critics in particular, see Toril Moi, 'Politics and the intellectual woman: clichés and commonplaces in the reception of Simone de Beauvoir', in *Simone de Beauvoir*, pp. 73–92; an earlier version of this appeared in Moi's *Feminist Theory and Simone de Beauvoir*. For a consideration of the negative reception of Beauvoir within a wider framework of gendered reception theory, see Elizabeth Fallaize, 'Reception problems for women writers: the case of Simone de Beauvoir', in Diane Knight and Judith Still (eds), *Women and Representation* (Nottingham: Women Teaching French Occasional Papers 3, 1995), pp. 43–56. For a historical survey of feminist re-interpretations, see Jo-Ann Pilardi, 'Feminists read *The Second Sex*', in Simons (ed.), *Feminist Interpretations*, pp. 29–43. In Britain and America, Kate Millett's *Sexual Politics* (New York: Doubleday, 1970; repr. London: Virago, 1977) is often seen as the first book of modern feminist criticism, partly because literary studies was the discipline in which feminism made its earliest inroads within the academy, and because feminist literary criticism was often elided with feminist theory. *The Second Sex* is excluded from this Anglo-American institutional history because it is not predominantly a work of literary criticism, cf. Jane Gallop, 'Reading the mother tongue: psychoanalytic feminist criticism', *Critical Inquiry*, 14 (1987), 314–29: 314. On *The Second Sex*'s exclusion from the history of political philosophy, see Margaret A. Simons, '*The Second Sex*: From

Marxism to radical feminism', in Margaret A. Simons (ed.), *Feminist Interpretations of Simone de Beauvoir* (University Park: Penn State Press, 1995), pp. 243–262.

16 See Susan Stanford Friedman, 'Making history: reflections on feminism, narrative, and desire', in Diane Elam and Robyn Wiegman (eds), *Feminism Beside Itself* (New York and London: Routledge, 1995), pp. 11–54: p. 38.

17 Rachel Bowlby, 'Flight reservations', *The Oxford Literary Review*, 10 (1988), 61–72: 68. See also Alice A. Jardine: 'any generic description of either French or American feminisms would immediately homogenize, colonialize and neutralize the specificities of struggles that are often of quite epic proportions': *Gynesis: Configurations of Woman and Modernity* (Ithaca and London: Cornell University Press, 1985), p. 15.

18 Fallaize, 'Reception problems', p. 49; Moi, *Simone de Beauvoir*, p. 68.

19 I am very grateful to Dr Nora Sellei, Department of English Literature, L. Kossuth University, Debrecen, Hungary, for this information.

20 As Friedman explains, there cannot be, since there is no 'definitive narrative of feminism' but rather 'the potential for many localized narratives of feminism, none of which can claim to represent the totality of feminist history': Friedman, 'Making history', p. 41.

21 The difficult politics of this history-making is altogether different from the difficulty of filling in the blanks of women's history, as expressed, for example, by Elaine Showalter, *A Literature of Their Own: British Women Novelists from Brontë to Lessing* (Princeton: Princeton University Press, 1977), p. 10: 'each generation of women writers has found itself, in a sense, without a history, forced to rediscover the past anew, forging again and again the consciousness of their sex.'

22 Susan Gubar, 'Feminist misogyny: Mary Wollstonecraft and the paradox of "It takes one to know one"', in Elam and Wiegman (eds), *Feminism Beside Itself*, pp. 133–54: p. 146. This is not at all the same thing as the view that *The Second Sex* is itself misogynist, as has been claimed by some feminists, most noticeably by Suzanne Lilar, *Le Malentendu du Deuxième sexe* (Paris: PUF, 1969), p. 9.

23 Gubar, 'Feminist misogyny', p. 142.

24 Interestingly, Moi claims that it is not 'unusual for intellectual women to have a difficult time with their [actual] mothers': *Simone de Beauvoir*, p. 3.

25 See Dorothy Kaufmann McCall, 'Simone de Beauvoir: questions of difference and generation', *Yale French Studies*, 72 (1986), 121–131. On the recourse to family structures to legitimate feminist work, see Linda R. Williams, 'Happy Families? Feminist reproduction and matrilineal thought', in Isobel Armstrong (ed.), *New Feminist Discourses* (London and New York: Routledge, 1992), pp. 48–64.

26 Gallop, 'Mother tongue', 318–19.

27 Gallop, 'Mother tongue', 327.

28 Le Doeuff, *Hipparchia's Choice*, p. 106.

29 'It is not merely as a body, but rather as a body subject to taboos, to laws, that the subject is conscious of himself and attains fulfilment – it is with reference to certain values that he evaluates himself' (SS68).

30 Elam, *Romancing*, p. 22.

31 Friedman, 'Making history', p. 14. On history as a foundation for feminism, see Butler, 'A sceptical feminist postscript', p. 234: 'If we take, say, history to be the condition *without which* feminism cannot proceed because feminism cannot be *political* without history as its foundation, then history must remain what is unquestioned and taken for granted, a foundationalist premise insulated from inquiry and contest.'

32 Beauvoir uses both quotations again within the text, where they are translated by Parshley: see SS21 and SS112. The point Atack makes is that their function as epigraphs frames the text in a very specific way. On differences between Parshley's translation and *Le Deuxième Sexe*, see the references in Horton's essay, n. 5.

33 Jean-François Lyotard, *The Differend: Phrases in Dispute*, trans. Georges van den Abbeele (Manchester: Manchester University Press, 1988), p. xi. For Lyotard, as for Beauvoir, gender is an 'irremediable differend': see 'Can thought go on without a body?', in *The Inhuman: Reflections on Time* [1988], trans. Geoff Bennington and Rachel Bowlby (Stanford: Stanford University Press, 1991), pp. 8–23: p. 22.

34 Cf. Lyotard, *The Differend*, p. 27: 'a Martinican is a French citizen; he or she can bring a complaint against whatever impinges upon his or her rights as a French citizen. But the wrong he or she deems to suffer from the fact of being a French citizen is not a matter for litigation under French law.' To paraphrase this in terms of gender: If woman is already defined as a human being ('French citizen'), then she has no grounds for saying that she is 'wronged' by this definition, since there is no possible place outside of this definition from where she could be judged, since the definition is supposed to be all-inclusive. For an understanding of Beauvoir's recognition of this double bind as a problem of phallogocentric language, see Judith Butler, *Gender Trouble, Feminism and the Subversion of Identity* (London and New York: Routledge, 1990), p. 12.

35 Lyotard, 'Can thought go on?', p. 21.

36 Lyotard, *The Differend*, p.13: 'The differend is the unstable state and instant of language wherein something which must be able to be put into phrases cannot yet be.'

37 'Like Aristotle, Hegel attributes to women an imperfect and immature rationality which excludes them from political acts, by drawing on a whole philosophy ... the way he constructs the category "woman" makes the very notion of her liberation nonsensical. History leaves her behind before it reaches its zenith. For ultimately it is man who is freedom/spirit and woman who represents the necessity/nature which is to be conceptually appropriated. Her repetitive reproductive cycle is to be rendered rational by the work of (male) self-consciousness, in which historical agency is located': Coole, *Women in Political Theory*, p. 144 (1993).

38 'Hegel's works together constitute a massive system, a grand narrative, recounting the emergence of reason. ... Through a dialectical interplay, contradictions between the world and our understanding of it gradually engender more universal knowledge and integral truths, until the totality emerges as fully rational. Alienation is eliminated and history ends, reconciled as spirit': Coole, *Women in Political Theory*, p. 139 (1993).

39 Le Doeuff, *Hipparchia's Choice*, p. 91.

40 See Hayden White, 'The question of narrative in contemporary historical theory', in *The Content of the Form: Narrative Discourse and Historical Representation* (Baltimore and London: Johns Hopkins University Press, 1987), pp. 26–57.

41 Elam, *Romancing*, p. 3.

42 Moi, *Simone de Beauvoir*, p. 184.

43 A classic instance is provided by Hélène Cixous's essay 'The laugh of the Medusa', which ironically first appeared in a special issue of a journal dedicated to Beauvoir's activism: 'Le rire de la Méduse', *L'Arc*, 61, *Simone de Beauvoir et la lutte des femmes* (1975), 39–54, trans. Keith Cohen and Paula Cohen in Elaine Marks and Isabelle de Courtivron (eds), *New French Feminisms: An Anthology* (Brighton: Harvester Wheatsheaf, 1981), pp. 245–64. Moi implicitly endorses this form of identity politics in her declaration that 'the deepest political flaw of *The Second Sex* consists in Beauvoir's failure to grasp the progressive potential of "femininity" as a political discourse': *Simone de Beauvoir*, p. 211.

44 Butler, 'Contingent foundations', p. 15.

45 Moi produces a brilliant reading of what she understands as Beauvoir's theory of female subjectivity under patriarchy in which alienation comes to constitute sexual difference as women are 'caught in an ambiguous contradiction between their own transcendent consciousness and their identification with an alienated and patriarchal image of themselves'; in other words, women's subjectivity is the product of a double structure of alienation: *Simone de Beauvoir*, p. 164. For the view that Beauvoir also transformed Sartre's notion of intersubjective relations – the Look – into a 'reciprocity' expressed and mediated through *institutions*, see Sonia Kruks, 'Simone de Beauvoir: teaching Sartre about freedom', in Simons (ed.), *Feminist Interpretations*, pp. 79–95.

46 Judith Butler, 'Sex and gender in Simone de Beauvoir's *Second Sex*', *Yale French Studies*, 72 (1986), 35–50: 48. In this essay Butler is concerned to effect a *rapprochement* between Beauvoir's existentialist notion of gender as 'project' (something to be actively and seemingly voluntaristically taken on by the subject) and an understanding of gender as 'construct' (the variable cultural interpretation of sex).

47 Butler, *Gender Trouble*, p. 112. The translation is Atack's (p. 43), not Parshley's (SS295).

48 For the view that that the only subjectivity *The Second Sex* recognises is masculine, since, according to its fundamental self/other distinction, woman

is always the differentiating other which constructs the male subject, see Allison Weir, *Sacrificial Logics: Feminist Theory and the Critique of Identity* (New York and London: Routledge, 1996).

49   Cf. SS24: 'But the significance of the verb *to be* must be rightly understood here; it is in bad faith to give it a static value when it really has the dynamic Hegelian sense of "to have become". Yes, women on the whole *are* today inferior to men; that is, their situation affords them fewer possibilities. The question is: should that state of affairs continue?' Butler raises the question of a politics of agency that is not dependent on the essentialist category 'woman'. See 'Contingent foundations', p. 16. 'Paradoxically, it may be that only through releasing the category of women from a fixed referent that something like "agency" becomes possible. For if the term permits of a resignification, if its referent is not fixed, then possibilities for new configurations of the term become possible.'

50   Weir, *Sacrificial Logics*, p. 15.

51   Weir, *Sacrificial Logics*, p. 3. Weir is deeply critical of Beauvoir's model of identity: see pp. 23–25.

52   For a critique of the heteronormativity of Torok's essay – one echoed in Jo's response (this volume, p. 197), see Judith Butler, *Bodies That Matter* (New York and London: Routledge, 1993), pp. 264–5.

53   Elam, *Romancing*, p. 146.

54   Lilar's early study, *Le Malentendu*, is one of the most hostile. Rodgers's essay in this volume gives further examples from French feminists. Mary Evans, discussing a passage on female biological 'instability' (SS28), comments that 'Present-day readers may find it almost impossible to believe that this passage was written by a feminist': *Simone de Beauvoir: A Feminist Mandarin* (London and New York: Tavistock, 1985), p. 65. For summaries of negative reactions to *The Second Sex*'s representation of the body, see Kruks, 'Gender and subjectivity', 106, and Pilardi, 'Feminists read *The Second Sex*', 35–7. For a cogent rereading of Beauvoir's representations of maternity, see Linda M.G. Zerilli, 'A process without a subject: Simone de Beauvoir and Julia Kristeva on maternity', *Signs: Journal of Women in Culture and Society*, 18:1 (1992), 111–35. See also Le Doeuff, 'Simone de Beauvoir and existentialism', 280.

55   For an essay that addresses in broadly biographical terms the charges against Beauvoir of ethnocentrism and false universality, see Julien Murphy, 'Beauvoir and the Algerian War: toward a postcolonial ethics', in Simons (ed.), *Feminist Interpretations*, pp. 263–97.

56   For example, Zerilli, 'A process without a subject'.

57   Butler, 'Contingent foundations, p. 17.

58   Butler understands Beauvoir's 'body as situation' as 'a *field of interpretive possibilities*': 'Sex and gender', 45.

59   Lyotard, 'Can thought go on?', p. 23. Cf. Moi, *Simone de Beauvoir*, p. 170. Parshley's translation of the section title 'L'expérience vécue' as 'Woman's life today' misses altogether Beauvoir's phenomenological project.

60 One of the problems of Lyotard's essay is its equivocal tone. When, for example, the 'He' speaker declares (p. 8) that 'You philosophers ask questions without answers, questions that have to remain unanswered to deserve being called philosophical', it is unclear whether Lyotard includes himself in the category of 'philosophers', or even if 'Lyotard' is present in the essay at all, thus putting the whole argument under ironic erasure.

61 Jane Heath, *Simone de Beauvoir* (Hemel Hempstead: Harvester Wheatsheaf, 1989), p. 5

62 Heath, *Simone de Beauvoir*, p. 14.

63 Elam, *Romancing*, pp. 21–3. See also Butler, 'A sceptical feminist postscript', pp. 234–5: 'And is it not – frightening as it may seem – *desirable* that feminism should not know its future, and that its meaning be open to revision?'

64 Michel de Certeau, '"Making do": uses and tactics', in *The Practice of Everyday Life*, trans. Steven Rendall (Berkeley, Los Angeles and London: University of California Press, 1984), pp. 29–44: pp. 35–7. 'I call a *strategy* the calculation (or manipulation) of power relationships that becomes possible as soon as a subject with will and power (a business, an army, a scientific institution) can be isolated. It postulates a *place* that can be delimited as its *own* and serve as the base from which relations with an exteriority composed of targets or threats ... can be managed. ... By contrast with a strategy ..., a *tactic* is a calculated action determined by the absence of a proper locus. No delimitation of an exteriority, then, provides it with the condition necessary for autonomy. The space of a tactic is the space of the other.'

65 On feminism opening up disciplines often sealed from one another, and on feminism's investment in disciplinary boundary-shifting, see Moi, *Feminist Theory*, p. 104: 'Interdisciplinarity seems to me to come with an increased awareness of the need for new theoretizations, new conceptualizations of old problems, and of course feminism would be in the forefront of wanting such new conceptualizations, but we're not the only ones.'

66 This is to take a line suggested by Lyotard's concept of 'the differend' that concerns the incommensurability of different 'language games' or 'phrase regimens' (of cognition, the Idea, etc.), ethical, juridical, political, historical, in which different outcomes are at stake. As Lyotard says in *The Differend*, 'a universal rule of judgment between heterogeneous genres is lacking in general' (p. xi). Cf. 'Inside a genre of discourse ... linkings obey rules that determine the stakes and ends. But between one genre and another, no such rules are known, nor a generalized end' (ibid., p. 30).

67 See Coole, *Women in Political Theory*, p. 179 (1993): 'although it [*The Second Sex*] called for a socialist programme similar to [Alexandra] Kollontai's, its main interest lay in explaining the creation of a gendered subjectivity and the designation of woman as man's Other. Second–wave feminism was, however, really born in the context of the New Left and student and civil rights movements of the 1960s, sharing that decade's enthusiasm for a cultural revolution which again put the state of consciousness to the fore.'

2

Writing from the centre: ironies of otherness and marginality[1]

MARGARET ATACK

In 1966, Francis Jeanson included interviews with Simone de Beauvoir in his book devoted to her work; in the course of the first there was a lengthy discussion of feminism, in which Beauvoir not only identified herself as a feminist but also offered definitions of feminism which would be endorsed as uncontroversial today. 'Feminism is a way of living individually, and a way of struggling collectively.'[2] Their exchange makes for interesting reading, not only because it rather complicates the scenario that she only declared herself a feminist in the early 1970s, once the Women's Liberation Movement had established itself, but also because of the uncanny sense it creates for the reader of reliving the past. The terms of reference within which feminism is discussed will be irrevocably changed by the new ideological and cultural post-1968 landscape. But it certainly makes it clear that given the logic of these pronouncements, she could hardly fail to welcome the emergence of a dynamic collective struggle by and for women. Jeanson asks her whether she is surprised by the reactions and judgements of herself based on readings of her feminism: 'It is true there are many false interpretations of my feminism. But the interpretations which I consider false are those which are not *radically* feminist: no-one has ever betrayed my thought by *pulling* me towards ... absolute feminism, if you like.'[3] What Beauvoir refutes absolutely is 'feminine specificity', which she defines as meaning that 'woman (whatever the culture, civilisation, education, or world structures) can never be the same as man ('le semblable de l'homme').[4] A few years later, 'feminine specificity' will be associated primarily with *écriture féminine*,[5] and Beauvoir will remain adamant that this constitutes a retrograde step for women.

The Second Sex featured prominently in this discussion. Then as now, it was an anchoring text, an emblematic text in favour of women. While Beauvoir later criticises its idealism, preferring to substitute the Sartrean notion of 'scarcity' elaborated in the *Critique of Dialectical Reason* as an explanation of the dimension of otherness, rather than seeing it motivated solely by the dynamics of structures of consciousness,[6] she can hardly have envisaged the extent to which it would be criticised as at best inadequate, at worst an anti-feminist volume.

'Beauvoir was a male identified woman, everybody knows that'[7]

Susan Suleiman's reasons for describing Beauvoir as 'male identified' are that the authors she lists as important to her were male, and that she identifies with the penile pen by creating the character of the male writer in *The Mandarins*. Yet again the feminist philosopher *par excellence* is judged to be on the side of men rather than of women. Other examples are not difficult to find: 'Beauvoir's answer to "the woman question" was the adoption by women of male habits and values. … She offers to contemporary feminism a confusing message: reject subordination as a woman by rejecting traditional femininity and taking on male assumptions and values.'[8] Nicole Ward Jouve argues that Beauvoir writes of women as if she herself were not one: 'She is no longer down among the women, she's escaped the condition.'[9] The theoretical work of Hélène Cixous and others is judged to be specifically breaking with Beauvoir. 'As long as the metaphor for writing is tied to the externally visible, there can be no feminine equivalent of the penile pen. Which is why French feminists after Beauvoir have sought other empowering metaphors, not based on the externally visible: Cixous' "white ink" may be understood as an attempt to counteract, and counterweigh, the penile pen.'[10] The biology section of *The Second Sex* has been particularly controversial, and frequently seen as enshrining a sexual hierarchy of male activity and female passivity. What these readings are effectively saying is that the text is founded and written in self-delusion. Beauvoir thought she was pro-women, producing original analysis from a woman's point of view. In fact she's anti-women, in thrall to a philosophical system alien to their interests. She thought she was investigating a situation from an autobiographical impulse – in order to write her autobiography. In fact she is denying her own identity as a woman. She is philosophically institutionalising that which she is apparently writing against. She is misrecognising her own oppression. She is suggesting that the way forward for women is the adoption of male values. This is in spite of the fact that women have long found it a compelling book to read, and still do. On the other hand, such critical views of its value for women appear confirmed if one considers its absence from contemporary feminist thought. It may rate a passing mention; it is certainly not used.

Not all feminist criticism has been so negative. Among recent examples, both Michèle Le Doeuff and Toril Moi are seeking to demonstrate the productive nature of Beauvoir's thought, in spite of what they argue are the limitations of the ontological categories she is working within. Both are considering the history and trajectory of a text written in the pre-feminist, pre-women's movement days and both are making a major contribution to moving the debate forwards.[11]

Le Doeuff's argument is that existentialism cannot theorise oppression. *The Second Sex* is written within a 'problematics of consciousness', with the result that gender relations are predicated on purely intersubjective relations. Beauvoir is therefore writing with a framework of intersubjectivity and moral fault rather than oppression. Questions around bad faith are crucial here, stressing the individual's ethical failure and inauthenticity. It is only later, Le Doeuff argues, that Beauvoir, via a feminist movement, moves from an analysis of interpersonal relations within the word to an analysis of the world itself – with a view to changing it of course.

In this discussion of the philosophical structures which Beauvoir is mobilising, there are two major areas of investigation supporting the argument that the text is theoretically limited: Beauvoir writes herself as subordinate to Sartre, as the disciple, and therefore perpetuates the canonical philosophical position founded on the exclusion of women (an analogous argument to the psychoanalytic one, that psychoanalysis is founded on the ever insoluble enigma of woman/dark continent constituting the structural heart of the discipline). Secondly, she is importing Sartrean ontology (subject and other) which relies on an association between the in-itself, femininity and negativity. The work of both Le Doeuff and Moi is informed by a broadly postmodernist analysis of language, philosophy and epistemology, which scrutinises the boundaries of the literal and figural – the internal differences established between statements of truth and metaphorical illustration – and the processes by which discourses legitimate their own truths. Beauvoir's attempt to analyse woman as subject is undermined, they argue, by the very philosophy within which this attempt is cast, since subjecthood in *The Second Sex* is predicated as masculine. The feminine and immanence are metonymically locked together by the Sartrean 'hiérarchie ontologico-charnelle',[12] where the negative metaphors of the in-itself align viscosity with femininity. Moi further argues that the project, the mode of being of the for-itself which knows the permanent instability of transcendence and is always throwing itself forwards (pro-ject) towards its goals, is by virtue of these metaphors predicated upon ejaculation and therefore necessarily phallic. For Moi, the strong points of Beauvoir's analysis come from the fact that she is writing on two levels, philosophical and social, and does not fully articulate the transitional points between them. The pro-woman discourse can then operate quasi-independently of the philosophical constraints.

What emerges from this is the importance of deciding on the nature of the relationship between Beauvoir's and Sartre's philoophies, and the particular configuration of each. Beauvoir was well aware of the less than enthusiastic reception in feminist circles of her views on his greater importance as a philosopher, and remained adamant that she did not have to reproduce Sartre in order to retain her self-respect: 'In order to maintain my rights before Sartre, should I have tried to prove that I too could write the *Critique of Dialectical Reason*? That is not what I had wanted to do from when I was young, that is not what I was capable of doing, and it's never stopped me from feeling perfectly independent,

intellectually and as a writer.'[13] While it is undoubtedly the case
that Sartre's ontology is sexualised and hierarchical, it is one
particular part of *Being and Nothingness* which is regularly quoted
to support the argument that Beauvoir is mobilising a philosophical schema which elides consciousness and masculinity. This
comes from the final section,[14] where Sartre even uses the adjective
'feminine' as one of the characteristics of the Viscous (the slimy
state of the in-itself which is always threatening to engulf, devour
and smother the for-itself), in conjunction with the imagery of
holes sucking in and destroying transcendence, and irresistibly
recalls Beauvoir's criticism of Levinas, that the feminine under-
pins the structure as a whole.[15] None the less, it is often compared
to Beauvoir's own description of female sexuality:

> Feminine sex desire is the soft throbbing of a mollusc. Whereas
> man is impetuous, woman is only impatient; her expectation can
> become ardent without ceasing to be passive; man dives upon his
> prey like the eagle and the hawk; woman lies in wait like the
> carnivorous plant, the bog, in which insects and children are swal-
> lowed up. She is absorption, suction, humus, pitch and glue, a
> passive influx, insinuating and viscous: thus, at least, she vaguely
> feels herself to be. (SS407)

The reservation I have about equating these accounts is that
this does not engage with the full range of the work of each
writer, and in order to say that Sartre and Beauvoir are operating
in the same phantasmic universe in relation to being, sexuality
and gender, it would have to do so. In the above passage,
Beauvoir is writing about sexuality, not consciousness. One may
deplore her reproduction of the passive/active binary in relation
to gendered sexual behaviour, but it does not in itself reify femininity as a particular mode of being. Furthermore, the experience
of passivity is fundamental and as threatening, in her view, for
men as it is for women: 'Man feels the same disgust at involuntary nocturnal emissions; to eject a fluid, urine or semen, does not
humiliate: it is an active operation; but it is humiliating if the
liquid flows out passively' (SS407). 'We can never separate the
immanent and the transcendant aspects of living experience:
what I fear or desire is always an embodiment of my own
existence, but nothing happens to me except through that which
is not me. The not-me ('le non-moi') is implicated in nocturnal

emissions, in an erection, if not as the precise shape of woman, at
least as Nature and Life: the individual is possessed by an alien
magic' (SS193–4 (translation adapted)). 'Man aspires to make
Spirit triumph over Life, action over passivity; his consciousness
keeps nature at a distance, his will shapes her, but in his sex
organ he finds himself again beset with life, nature and passivity' (SS194). 'Man glories in the phallus when he thinks of it as
transcendence and activity, as a means for taking possession of
the other; but he is ashamed of it when he sees it as merely
passive flesh through which he is the plaything of the dark forces
of life' (SS195). 'He wishes to possess her: behold him the possessed himself. Odour, moisture, fatigue, ennui – a whole library
of books has described this gloomy passion of a consciousness
made flesh' (SS196).

   There is undeniably a different dynamic for Sartre. In her
pioneering study of language and sexuality in Sartre's philosophy, *À propos de Sartre et de l'amour*,[16] Suzanne Lilar demonstrates the powerful and complex emotional schemas involved.
She argues that the problematic of love in Sartre is in fact a problematic of purity, not only because of the importance accorded to
a biblical and theological vocabulary, but because of an overrid-
ing metaphysics of the pure as opposed to the impure, expressed
very importantly through the masculine/feminine opposition.
She also quotes from the final section of *Being and Nothingness*,
but shows how far this dynamic underlies the creation of female
characters throughout Sartre's *oeuvre*. On the one hand are the
'swamp-women', malodorous, fat, overwhelmingly and negatively female, such as the pregnant Marcelle in *The Age of Reason*.
On the other hand are the virginal, asexual, adolescent-like, pre-
feminine women. Impurity then is female: unhealthy, smelly,
opaque like stagnant water, passive, dirty, sexual, viscous. Purity
is male, mineral, clean and healthy, free, sovereign, the realm of
consciousness. Consciousness falling towards the troubling realm
of physicality and sexuality experiences a moral fall into evil.
And the female is animal, like a leech sucking consciousness
down. What is important in this scenario is that this obsessional
framework can be traced right across Sartre's work, generating
characterisation. It would be very difficult to say the same of
Beauvoir's work.

Andrew Leak has extended and developed Lilar's work within a psychoanalytic frame, and like Le Doeuff considers that ontology obeys a sexual hierarchy in Sartre. However, he also showed how far the metaphorisation is organised by fear of castration and homosexuality. Male/female is an important aspect, but male/male sexual relations are at the centre of the problematic. One has only to consider the passages of *Being and Nothingness* where the amorous/sexual relationship of self and Other is written in unescapably homosexual terms (I/he since *l'Autre* is masculine), grammatically correct but installing ambiguity, especially as the conclusion of one particular passage involving a lengthy dramatisation of desire is to 'make oneself mucous' ('se faire muqueuse'), which everyone would agree is feminised in Sartre.[17] Allan Stoekl also gives an account of the importance of repression of homosexuality to male bonding and the homosocial group in *The Roads to Freedom*.[18]

Beauvoir is clearly working with existentialist philosophy, but her 'philosophical imaginary' should not be subsumed under his. One does not need to 'bracket out' the philosophical framework to make *The Second Sex* function as a progressive text for women, and indeed, it is theoretically unsatisfactory to have to do so. Linda Zerilli and Sonia Kruks present strong arguments for a reappraisal of the text and the ambiguities and complexities of its analysis of women and discourse.[19] In 'A process without a subject: Simone de Beauvoir and Julia Kristeva on maternity', Zerilli even concludes that *The Second Sex* destroys the possibility of any definition of woman.[20] Secondly, the structure of consciousness is an important part of the text, but there are other points within existentialism which deserve more attention than they have received and which are central to it: imagination and representation.

The importance of *The Second Sex* lies in the way that thematically and structurally it helps us think about the gendering of subjectivity, and the position of women in discourse. The arguments it mobilises are powerfully exciting ones for considering women's writing, women's experience, the relationship between ideology, culture and discourse. The relationships of self to self, and of self to other (personal and non- or trans-personal) on which the former relies, are necessarily mediated through representation and imagination. To repeat a key notion quoted earlier: 'Nothing happens to me *except through what is not me*' ('Rien ne m'arrive *qu'à travers ce qui n'est pas moi*'), or what she also refers to as the 'not-me'. Even in her notorious description of female sexuality quoted above, Beauvoir stresses the convergence of representations of male sexuality with women's intimate experience of their own body — reading both in the same direction; and while it is not an example of the ironic writing I discuss later, in the sense that it is not part of the exposition of a myth, none the less the density of the writing inevitably carries with it an awareness of those very representations. Beauvoir was reproached time and again for her 'excessive' style, but the point is that there is no 'dehumanised' factual ground of sober description when dealing with human endeavour. Sexuality cannot be reduced to biology alone. In other words, the question of the metanarrative of gender is a constant concern: 'Woman is thoroughly indoctrinated with common notions ('représentations') that endow masculine passion with splendour and make a shameful abdication of feminine sex feeling: woman's intimate experience confirms the fact of this asymmetry.' (SS406) That which constitutes the 'not-me' of gender: history, politics, biology, class, myth, society, and relationship to the other, is the special terrain of philosophical investigation in *The Second Sex*. Within that investigation of representation and imagination and the narratives of gender, the relationship between centrality and marginality proves to be a very intricate configuration.

Problematics

The complexities of male/female, universal/gender, centrality/ marginality, human/female, are at the heart of *The Second Sex*. Lorna Sage has written that '[Beauvoir]'s best work wrestled with … this dizzying overlap between the human situation and the woman's situation.'[21] Suleiman appraises this quite negatively: 'In the last decade of her life, Beauvoir even spoke occasionally of what in *The Second Sex* she would have called impossible: a kind of feminine universal. "I think that a woman is at the same time universal and a woman, just as a man is universal and a male," she told Alice Jardine in an interview in 1977, as if forgetting that everything she had written in *The Second Sex* suggested the contrary.'[22] It is not at all clear to me that Beauvoir forgot anything at all; the double structure of both universal and particular at the same time sums up very accurately one of the lessons of the text. Sage refers to Beauvoir's 'yearning towards universality and her fascinated reflexiveness' as a 'fertile contradiction';[23] Moi is on not dissimilar ground when she advances the theory that *The Second Sex* itself is born of the indeed very fertile contradiction of Beauvoir writing of marginality from a position of centrality.[24] What I want to argue is that *The Second Sex* does offer the possibility of thinking beyond a static dichotomy, in part I believe because its subject is paradoxically not women or woman but a relationship and gender. *The Second Sex* stakes a claim to the universalism of its object of study in its very title, which sets aside 'le sexe', the term by which women are marked as gendered (*le sexe* can frequently mean the female sex) as opposed to the universalist, gender-free, male, and offers an ironic subversion of that opposition: women may be 'second', but if men are 'first', they are also 'sexed'; an example of the ironic stratagems she deployed with such skill, in its neutral numbering it suggests the possibility of a parity within gender difference, a classification rather than a value. The double structure of the title with its multiple meanings and its ironic positioning in relation to a structure which it silently points to and negates, is a microcosm of the reflection pursued on the kind of positioning woman can adopt in discourse in order to write about that relationship.

One can identify three trajectories through the text in relation to the subject/other, male/female relationship – a political trajectory, a psychological trajectory and a philosophical one. This has important consequences for the question of the personal in discourse. There is at times a tendency on the part of contemporary critics to conflate under the general heading of the 'subject in discourse' different theoretical lines with very different levels of effectivity. In *The Second Sex*, theoretical arguments on philosophical subjects are constantly entwined with arguments about abstract and concrete political and social rights and equalities. These questions do not, it seems to me, elide in any simplistic

way with the trajectory of the philosophical subject and its relationship to the other. I also want to problematise another two
relationships which are usually conflated, that of the philosoph-
ical/existential subject and the dynamic of male/female relationships, with a view to the consequence this would have for the
notion of writing as a woman. One needs to make a distinction
between 'Myths', the centre of the philosophical elaboration,
and 'The Formative Years' or 'Situation', which also mobilise a
range of social and sociological myths in order to denounce their
naturalising effect.

A significant leitmotiv of Beauvoir's work, both fictional and
non-fictional, is the limits of individual freedom in relation to the
constraints of situation. Being is always being-in-situation.
Individual consciousness is not an autonomous unit, and non-
individual factors are structuring dimensions of being itself.
Existentialism consistently presents itself as a philosophy of freedom, that is, taking the theoretical consequences of the absence
of pre-given futures. Beauvoir writes against all forms of structural constraints on outcomes – be they determinist, essentialist
or teleological. We are not determined by our natures or by pre-
existing religious or social scripts. There is no final and glorious
end to history or politics. There are, for example, no grand narratives or metanarratives of progress. In exploring gender, the
same logic is observed, for one of the major lessons of Beauvoir's
work is the way gender can function as one of the grand narratives. There is no essence of woman or man to explain (for which
read justify) the situation Beauvoir saw around her. 'One is not
born a woman' is not the first phrase of this type in *The Second
Sex*. At one point in the first volume we read: 'one is not born a
genius: one becomes a genius' (SS164). As Beauvoir always
stresses, to become is to make oneself into. In other words, we are
not born anything; we are not made into anything either. One
cannot replace a discredited biological female nature with a
notion of socially constructed oppressive womanhood as something just *done* to women. Society does not substitute for god.
Choice, identification and, crucially, desire play their roles in
motivation of individual agency. But because being is being-in-
situation, and because the individual has no more power or
choice over the existence or otherwise of the myths of feminin-

ity than she or he has over the historical moment they are born
into, then inevitably what is brought into focus is the interface
between the individual and the collective, public and private.

To conflate subject and subjectivity in political, philosophical and psychological discourse, is to obscure the complexity of
different relationships in different discourses. Different structures of relationship between the individual and the collective
sustain different subjectivities, which in turn should problematise the question of what 'speaking/writing as a woman' means,
when so often it merely begs the question of authenticity and also
operates within Beauvoir's philosophical problematic, namely
the active assumption of the myth of femininity and its powerful
incarnation of the female as an oppositional force. This is
precisely the terrain Beauvoir is setting out to investigate, the
mechanisms by which the individual internalises and identifies
with beliefs and processes which are neither discovered nor
owned by the individual. She attempts this at several levels: at
the level of psychological dynamic; at the level of social and
political organisation; and at the level of existential theory about
the meaning of life.

The subject/other relationship in *The Second Sex* is frequently
referred to in criticism as if it were a static relationship; man is
subject, woman is other, this is the fault-line to be traced through
humanity with an unequivocal distribution of the sexes to either
side of it. Now, it is certainly true that *The Second Sex* makes
statements of this kind, but only on the basis that this is a
misrecognition on the part of both men and women of the reality
of the situation. The subject/other dynamic is precisely that, a
dynamic which is in constant flux, demands constant reaffirma-
tion both collectively and individually, has to be continually
reinvented because it can ultimately never satisfy, never be
established for once and for all (which is why the processes of
identification and belief are so important). Otherness is a necessary dimension of subjectivity for all consciousness (we should
not forget the invocation of Lacan's mirror stage in this connection) (SS297). In a sense, what Beauvoir is writing against is the
way gender socialisation gives the *illusion* of permanency and
security, falsely naturalising a hierarchical difference, effectively
offering a belief in the (illusory) metanarrative of gender as secu-

rity to both sexes. Hence the role of bad faith for which Beauvoir
is so often chastised. Desire is central to the very dynamics of
existence, and bad faith is a variant of desire. One must be able
to theorise the possibility of alternatives to any situation. Consciousness cannot be coterminous with a situation, however
oppressive. This means that one must be able to explain the
absence of revolt in an oppressive situation as well as a desire for
change. Unless we are to be automata, governed by circumstances, there can be no pure victims.[25]

All consciousness, in the existentialist scenario, is tempted
by a denial of freedom and its attendant anguish in a variety of
ways – among which are the desire to seek an endorsement of
one's own superior position via another, or the desire to identify
with a pre-given identity and set of characteristics. The logic is a
famous one, that of the torturer–victim relationship. The torturer
seeks to impose recognition of his power through torture, but is
condemned to failure: if the victim submits it is meaningless,
because one cannot force freely given consent; and if the victim
dies, the torturer is put on the treadmill of constant repetition
with other victims. His extreme quest is founded in the extreme
anxiety of knowledge of powerlessness – which his ever-
repeated failure can only endorse.[26] It is an endless circularity,
and men and women are caught in the same dance, futilely
attempting to deny contingency, powerlessness and freedom, as
well as the complexity of the self/other relationship of each for
the other. It seems simplified as far as women are concerned,
because the structure of powerlessness is replicated in the
economic, social and political institutions of the world we live in.
Beauvoir's argument in raising the banner of optimism at the
level of individual identification with these categories and the
psycho-dynamics of gender relations, is that firstly the very
complexity of the scenario allows for shifts at different points
within it – and secondly there is a very real sense in which the
whole edifice is built on the sand of nothingness, which is where
the psychological dynamic converges with the philosophical
project. We are dealing with material realities, but they are
neither immutable, nor natural, nor socially essential.

The multiplicity of ways in which individuals are brought to
identify with and act in function of the socially constructed,

collective, transindividual narrative of gender identity forms the substance of the second volume. It is no accident that this is where we meet 'one is not born a woman, rather one becomes one', its opening sentence. The political investigation of the text is also exploring the relationship between individual and collective, between private and public, in the changing context of political discourse and their institutions. Matrimonial regimes, the legal status of women in relation to property, the inclusion or exclusion of women from the conceptualisation of the political subject, all have important effects not only on the material possibilities open to women, but also on the nature of collective, cultural identities.

The chapter on history is one focus for this political investigation, as well as being a quest for the origins of women's otherness in history. It establishes the shifts at the level of political discourse in identities offered to women, whose political history is indeed the history of the creation of a political identity for women in the universal identity of citizenship. Political identity shifts from family to State. Patriarchal definitions of social identity in relation to the family are replaced by the *état civil*. Women's socio-political status is no longer exhausted by, nor coterminous with, subject positions of wives and daughters. The creation of abstract legal and political rights is crucial and allows the focus to shift to the gap between abstract rights and concrete inequalities. Both in the case study of the Republics of Ancient Rome and in more recent times, an abstract subject position in relation to the State represents progress from the enslavement of political status denied, but as long as it remains abstract it still traps women in powerlessness.

This is not just contextual analysis on Beauvoir's part. What is the book for if not to improve and act on the material possibilities in women's lives? Therefore the political project, which engenders the debate around theoretical possibilities and concrete change, is at the heart of the book.[27] Feminist theory necessarily engages with political theory – in part because of the classic gap (in theory and in practice) between the universalism of republican and human rights and gender-specific practices, in part because of the theoretical quagmire of equality versus difference. The importance of abstract subject positions of legal and political status cannot be underestimated, because this also has an impact on the nature and possiblities of representation, in the widest sense of the term, in the public sphere.

The third trajectory is the philosophical one. The section entitled 'Myths', and particularly the first chapter within that section, is an extraordinarily complex discussion of the myth of femininity which goes way beyond the question of the social construction of gender, operating primarily through the social processes of identification with social myths. In contrast to this, 'Myths' relates the cultural myth and identity of women to the existential trajectory of life itself. The myth of women, for men and women, is born not of oppression, but of the existential anguish before the meaninglessness of life familiar from the writings of Camus, Malraux, and Sartre in the 1930s and 1940s. To my knowledge it is the only contemporeanous extended commentary on this symbolisation of the human condition and the use of gender representation within its dynamic, from a woman's point of view, or, perhaps more importantly, from a feminist philosopher's point of view. If one thinks of some of the major texts of that apprehension of meaninglessness, Malraux's *Man's Estate*, Sartre's *Iron in the Soul*, Camus's *The Plague*, gender relations and femininity are indeed central to the narrative of that anguish: the myriad threats and displaced enactments of castration in Malraux's work (one is reminded of Annie Leclerc's very apposite observations on the crises of the 'human' condition being channelled through metaphors of masculinity),[28] the articulation of desire and impotence through the dramatic development of *The Plague*; the narrative continuum between threats to the nation, to human civilisation and to masculine sexual identity in *Iron in The Soul*. In all these cases the primary crisis is that of a male consciousness, equated with consciousness itself, and women are part of and subordinate to the sexual/textual politics of that crisis lived through the male. This is the terrain of 'Myths', and it shares the logic of the torturer–victim dynamic: men can no more win metaphysically than they can psychologically. The perspective has shifted from an interpersonal conflict to a collective cultural response to the human condition in an inhuman world, and in this metaphysical drama, the myth of woman is at the heart.

Beauvoir's analysis owes much to Bachelard, which probably in part explains the closeness to Barthes. Myth is the realm of collective fantasy and identification. Barthes relates mythological thought to the *petit bourgeois* ideology which naturalises its own cultural and historical specificities. The myth of femininity, on the other hand, is the direct expression of the existential anguish which the human condition in the age of modernity provokes.[29] I say 'in the age of modernity', not only because the crises and aspirations which Beauvoir describes are very familiar to any reader of Malraux, Camus, or Tournier, but because she herself explicitly relates them to the kind of dynamic found in Baudelaire. It is crucial to the problematics of gender in *The Second Sex*.

The myth of femininity could be described as the cultural response to the existential crisis. The crisis of modernity is a crisis of value and aspiration to the absolute in an age which has 'abolished' the divinity of man, and left him to his own contingent, finite devices. Baudelaire's poetry expresses the desire for the infinite and the absolute, and the tragic reality of death, finitude and banality. Beauvoir's argument is that the myth of woman is a crucial mediator in this process:

> Man wants to affirm his individual existence and rest with pride on his 'essential difference', but he wishes also to break through the barriers of the ego, to mingle with water, earth, night, with Nothingness, with the Whole. Woman condemns man to finitude, but she also enables him to exceed his own limits; and hence comes the equivocal magic with which she is endowed. (SS180 (translation adapted))

'Woman' is a magical entity, an emblem of the cultural beliefs which are properly kinds of possessions, that is to say in the manner of fetishes and totems, they play a privileged role in cultural identity and mediations with the natural world.

In his *Sartre and 'Les Temps modernes'* Howard Davies emphasised the role of anthropology in defining the intellectual and political parameters of the *Temps modernes* and underlines how Beauvoir extended that journal's project of synthetic anthropology to embrace the largest marginalised group of all: women.[30] Anthropology helps explain the power of the myth of femininity, which is clearly our culture's shaman or totem, the magical centre of things.

[In 'Le Sorcier et sa magie'] Lévi-Strauss discusses the levels of belief that sustain the power of the shaman, his own, that of his patient or victim, and that of the collectivity. He finds that the actions of the shaman are validated by the consensus, but only in such a way that neither the sorcerer nor his society are able clearly to demarcate real magic from simulation.[31]

The collective belief in a myth of femininity *possesses* individual men and women. In that sense, shifting the magical power of femininity from its position as centre and horizon of existence is indeed changing the world.

Beauvoir's analysis of the myth of femininity and the ascription of cultural attributes to woman is a virtuoso piece, a *tour de force* of analysis of dynamic contradictions and paradoxes. Her argument is that woman is both ultimate threat, in her necessary recall of birth, contingency, death, flesh and finitude, and also ultimate liberation: in woman, men can realise their dreams of being and existing, for she is the other through whom he seeks to reach himself as being; furthermore, in her life-bearing role, she is one part of Nature, the great infinite abstract idea of nature which alone he cannot reach. Her negative features, of night, earth, nothingness, are therefore her positive ones in their transcendence of the limits of an individual existence. Erotically, she invites copulation with the cosmos in a quest for ecstasy and intoxication recalling Baudelaire, Malraux, Rousseau and Tournier. Yet the malaise and *trouble* (provoking emotional and intellectual confusion) of flesh, and carnality, are not only at the basis of the rites and rituals of menstruation and defloration, but also place a particular price on the virginal. Hand in hand with the value of the pre-sexual, pre-erotic virgin goes that of the artificialities of eroticism. The threat of the purely-natural means that nature humanised and transformed tames her within the limits of the body which defines her. And the most crucial point in it all is that she must accept all this of her own free will – as in the psychological dynamic of the text, so with the mythological dynamic: the victim is being asked to recognise the power of the torturer, to give assent to its own status as object and confirm the other as sovereign subject. She is the external judge by which the subject can *be* a subject.

Given the richness and complexity of the analysis, it is somewhat wryly that one reads Beauvoir's occasional remarks on the difficulty of describing or defining the myth. On the contrary, there is a sense of being defeated by the profusion and proliferation of the subject matter. Introducing the section on the physical metamorphoses which the mythological body of woman undergoes, Beauvoir writes: 'Poets of East and West have metamorphosed woman's body into flowers, fruits, birds. Here again, from the writings of antiquity, the Middle Ages, and modern times, what might well be cited would make an abundant anthology' (SS187). What one must note, particularly in the stylistics of the Beauvoirian analysis, is the very *density* of the myth, the weight of the accumulated layers of attributes: 'She is the whole fauna, the whole flora of the earth; gazelle and doe, lilies and roses, downy peach, sweet-smelling raspberry; she is precious stones, mother-of-pearl, agate, pearl, silk, the azure blue of the sky, the cool water of springs, air, flame, earth and water' (SS187 (translation adapted)). 'Woman becomes plant, panther, diamond, mother-of-pearl, by blending flowers, furs, jewels, shells, feathers with her body' (SS190). 'Treasure, prey, sport and danger, muse, guide, judge, mediator, mirror, Woman is the Other' (SS218 (translation adapted)).

But this heavy density is also pure movement. The movement between self and other, essential and inessential, is unstoppable – and 'ondoyer' (to undulate, waver, ripple) is a term which recurs frequently in order to capture this. Woman knows no stasis:

> It is always difficult to describe a myth; it cannot be grasped or encompassed; it haunts the human consciousness without ever appearing before it in fixed form. The myth is so various [*ondoyant*], so contradictory, that at first its unity is not discerned: Delilah and Judith, Aspasia and Lucretia, Pandora and Athena – woman is at once Eve and the Virgin Mary. She is an idol, a servant, the source of life, a power of darkness; she is the elemental silence of truth, she is artifice, gossip, and falsehood; she is healing presence and sorceress; she is man's prey, his downfall, she is everything that he is not and that he longs for, his negation and his *raison d'être*. (SS175)

Genette's analysis of the 'univers réversible' of the baroque, its perpetual movement, instability, and metamorphoses, is a perfect analogy for the myth of Woman.[32] The mythic world of

Woman is indeed a baroque, reversible world, where nothing is fixed or stable, but where the magical, dynamic processes of masculinity and femininity are played out through the dialectics of real and imaginary, of antithesis and alterity; the mythic world of Woman is a vertiginous hall of mirrors of reflections and doubles, bearing witness to the useless passion invested in the dream of fixing identity and being:

> This, then, is the reason why woman has a double and deceptive visage: she is all that man desires and all that he does not attain. She is the good mediatrix between propitious Nature and man; and she is the temptation of unconquered Nature, counter to all goodness. She incarnates bodily all moral values, from good to evil, and their opposites; she is the substance of action and whatever is an obstacle to it, she is man's grasp on the world and his failure: as such she is the source and origin of all man's reflection on his existence and of whatever expression he is able to give to it; and yet she works to divert him from himself, to make him sink down in silence and in death. She is servant and companion, but he expects her also to be his audience and critic and to confirm him in his sense of being; but she opposes him with her indifference, even with her mockery and laughter. He projects upon her what he desires and what he fears, what he loves and what he hates. And if it is so difficult to say anything specific about her, that is because man seeks the whole of himself in her and because she is All. She is all, that is, on the mode of the inessential; she is all the Other. And, as other, she is other than herself, other than what is expected of her. Being all, she is never quite *this* which she should be; she is everlasting disappointment, the disappointment of existence itself which never succeeds in reaching itself nor in reconciling itself with the totality of existents. (SS229 (translation adapted))

The myth of woman is at the centre of the ontological crisis of the human condition. Both marginal and absolute, Woman is the ever-moving axis of the desire for transcendence, both of the world and not of it: 'She incarnates Society as much as she incarnates Nature; in her is summed up the civilisation and culture of an epoch ... Mallarmé said the crowd is woman' (SS215 (translation adapted)). The very least one can say of all this, is that the social marginality of woman as enshrined in the myth of femininity is a rather complicated affair, and to consider that marginal is the same thing as marginalised is not to give due force to the weight of the argument, that the myth of femininity is rather more than an exercise in reactionary views of woman-hood, but is central to human culture and society.

Structures of irony and strategies of writing

As a mythologist, Beauvoir holds her own against Barthes, and indeed their analyses have much in common. They both have a great debt to Bachelard, for example, which displays itself partic-ularly in the sensitivity to the material and organic qualities of the objects of analysis. For both, the myth is a system of (secondary) meaning, which invests the object, and is certainly not deduced from it. For both, there is a moral agenda in the unmasking of the mechanisms and techniques of *mauvaise foi*. For Barthes, petty bourgeois culture denies its own historical and cultural nature, naturalising its cultural discourses in a fraudu-lent manner. For Beauvoir, the myth of Woman springs from the collective metaphysical flight from the realities of human exis-tence and its indignities of accident, chance, contingency. For each, the analysis of the phenomenon is necessarily taking a distance from it; it is the object of the scrutiny, the mask to which one points. Yet in both cases, there is an empathetic understand-ing of the process transforming brute facts and raw reality into myth, a clear enjoyment of the sensuality and complexity of the elements on display. Cutting them off by the roots in so far as their cultural function is concerned, but also deploying their distinctive features, the discourses are exhibited as discourses, displayed and denounced simultaneously. Which means we are witnessing the classic skills of the ironist, and the mastery of its double discourse. Irony is necessarily mobilising a double struc-ture, in the sense that a particular view is uttered and ridiculed simultaneously. It is an imitation which goes to the heart of an opponent's rhetoric and thought, the better to destroy it.[33]

One of the ironic techniques most frequently deployed by Beauvoir within the text is the use of *discours indirect libre*, where the thoughts of a character are related indirectly, in the sense of not being quoted in quotation marks, but without the narrative distance of the authoritative 'She thought that ....' The result in the case of Flaubert's *Madame Bovary*, for example, is to create an ironic *tour de force* where the boundaries between narrating and narrated voices become impossibly blurred. Beauvoir uses this technique with great energy and confidence throughout, to the extent that one might say the combination of ironic mimicry and plain sarcasm – directed for example at Claude Mauriac in the introduction – plays a key role in the distinctive tone of the work. Unfortunately, as Suhamy points out, it is not enough to be good at irony, your audience has to be good at it too, and Beauvoir's tendency to present the discourses of the other, those she is arguing against, as a voice in the text has not been recognised as it might.[34]

The beginning of the infamous biology chapter offers a good illustration: a complex and highly literary description of negative attributes which at the end of the paragraph are nailed as 'platitudes':

> The word *female* brings up in his mind a saraband of imagery – a vast, round ovum engulfs and castrates the agile spermatozoon; the monstrous and swollen termite queen rules over the enslaved males; the female praying mantis and the spider, satiated with love, crush and devour their partners; the bitch in heat runs through the alleys, trailing behind her a wake of depraved odours; the she-monkey presents her posterior immodestly and then steals away with hypocritical coquetry; and the most superb wild beasts – the tigress, the lioness, the panther – bed down slavishly under the imperial embrace of the male. Females sluggish, eager, artful, stupid, callous, lustful, ferocious, abased – man projects them all at once upon woman. (SS35)

It is unfortunate that the clear distinction in French between the animal and the human carried by *femelle* as opposed to *femme/féminin* is unavoidably blurred in English, giving a different colouring to the chapter and obscuring, for example, the acerbic ironising through the very juxtaposition of anthropomorphic and cliché-ridden descriptions of human sexuality – all the clichés of nymphomania – ascribed to animals/*la femelle* and projected back onto women. Like Flaubert, Beauvoir's target is the frequently crass stupidity of clichés, and their cumulative metanarrative overdetermining of individual subjects and gendered behaviour. 'Woman is vampire, she eats and drinks him, her organ feeds gluttonously upon his. Certain psychoanalysts have attempted to provide scientific support for *these fancies'* (SS201 (my emphasis)) is another example of the *discours indirect libre* which Beauvoir subsequently signals as such. But sometimes it is the context which carries the identification 'voice of the other': in the course of a long discussion of menstruation taboos and the horror it inspires she writes: 'Pliny said that a menstruating woman ruins crops, destroys gardens, kills bees, and so on.' No reader then or now is going to suggest Beauvoir is validating these sentiments by quoting them. And it thus contextualises the previous sentence: 'Since patriarchal times, only evil powers have been attributed to the loathsome liquid flowing out of women's genitals' (SS180 (translation adapted)).[35] One has therefore to be very careful about isolating comments and presuming Beauvoir is directly endorsing them, for she is using the resources of syntax, of sentence rhythm and lexis to carry a distancing effect. These statements are simultaneously *énoncé* and *énonciation*, exposition of the myth as myth, and negative judgement of it. It is not surprising Beauvoir pursued her gift for irony in later writings, with particular success in her final short stories. As with the double structure of centrality and marginality, the double structure of irony is another strand in the active complication of the notion of womanhood. The complexity of the problematics structuring the subject is matched by the textual strategies which also privilege double structures.

The Second Sex opens with its famous comment on the *querelle du féminisme* having caused enough ink to be spilt. The translation reduces this to something rather petty with its 'quarrelling over feminism'. 'Quarrelling over the Ancients and Moderns' would not exactly capture the scope of that crucial seventeenth-century debate either: a *querelle* is an intellectual confrontation, a battle of ideas. Not only does Beauvoir situate her text immediately within a *querelle*, but she writes it as an argumentative, vocative text, a dramatisation of arguments about gender relations and female identity through history. She proceeds to quote men and women, personal testimonies, novels, sociological studies, psychological case studies, philosophers, on the nature and experience of gender, and this may indeed be one reason for its readability and the sense of excitement and urgency it generates, in that, unlike other surveys of 'women in France', it exists in the here and now, in the eternal present of the debate over interpretation (it's *la querelle du féminisme* and not *la querelle de la femme*).

One can approach the mobilisation of these voices in two different ways, from the perspective of experience and from the perspective of writing. There is an overwhelming volume of testimony from women in the form of quotations from novels, autobiographies, psychological case studies and anecdotes, including those from Beauvoir herself. The first word of the text is 'I', so this supposedly impersonal, depersonalised investigation which will enable Beauvoir to write autobiographically begins personally, and continues in that vein. Beauvoir has been criticised because of the plethora of literary illustrations, but the importance of the relationship between individual experience and collective belief supports this particular emphasis. Moreover, there are also frequent and lengthy quotations from psychological and psychoanalytic case studies. *The Second Sex* is a multivocal text which has the immediacy of dialogue and debate, being both résumé of and intervention in its *querelle*. It can be read as a reenactment of the dramas of gender through history, and it forces reflection on the use of history in this way, the sense of timelessness to the enunciating frame which it seems to install. However, within the narratives of experience, there is a hierarchy of authenticity, in women's favour. Women invoke women's experience with an appearance of total immediacy, while men discoursing on women's experience are distanced and devalued by mediation. In both cases, however, what is revealed is a structure of exemplarity. Male voices and female voices are invoked to typify the lived experiences of gender. Even at their most individual, the narratives are traversed by the collective, and exemplify processes not specific to the individual being quoted.

If one considers this polyphonic text as *written* text, then the proliferation of quotations, in conjunction with frequency of aphorism, is an important variant on the processes already highlighted in relation to irony. Quotation is repetition of the already said, the already written.[36] It is hard to think of a more mediated text, where cliché, platitude, received opinions, are constantly ironised. Quotation, implicit or explicit, is its most striking feature, and confirms the importance one should accord to the text as investigation of representation. The hall of mirrors of representation finds its counterpart in the textual echoing chamber where the distinctions between *énonciation* and *énoncé* become difficult if not impossible to locate. It does allow us to point to the way individual narratives are used to maintain the creative tension between centrality and marginality, firstly because women's experience of women's lives, which often bear witness to marginality, is valorised and made central at the expense of men's views on women; secondly because the great question mark over the source of knowledge and identity of the narrating voice which results from an *énonciation/énoncé* confusion (the classic 'qui parle?') frustrates attempts to fix an identified gender position within discourse, be it central or marginal.

Double structures

To understand why double structures have such importance demands a detour through some of the key elements of existentialist philosophy, and particularly the structure which could be summed up as 'the simultaneity of is and is not'. Central to existentialism is the particular nature of being and the argument that there is no human essence or nature determining us. A table has an essence, a table is, it is in the mode of being in-itself, which means its being is coterminous with its essence. Humankind does not have an essence, and in that sense humankind 'is not'. Our essence is created by what we do, it is the consequence of what we do. We will, therefore, be what we will have done. Only at death does this process end. In life, our being has to be brought into being, we *are not* our being. There is a non-coincidence of the self to the self at the heart of being. Similarly consciousness cannot turn itself into a thing. Consciousness is always consciousness of something, it is always projected towards the world, towards what it 'is not'. By definition we could not aim for a goal of any kind if we were incapable of considering what we might do if we attained it, or unaware we currently lack it. In other words, human consciousness is able to 'nihilate' (render to nothingness) its present, to consider itself as what it is not. In contrast, a table, being filled by what it is, its essence, has no critical distance or gap to judge itself and aim for something else. The structures of consciousness and the mode of being of that which is not replicate the structures of imagination and representation. A photograph or painting of a table *is not* a table. Imagination is a structure of consciousness which again involves nihilation of what is. It is no accident that, as has frequently been noted, metaphors of acting, putting on an act, play-acting, playing a role, dominate descriptions of the relations of self and other, and of bad faith in existentialist philosophy. There is therefore a philosophical structure supporting the shifting non-coincidence of the one to the other (be it self/self or self/other relations), and in both the section on bad faith in *Being and Nothingness*, and in *Search for a Method* Sartre uses the example of Hamlet on stage, an imaginary person created by the actor of whom the audience remains aware, to render the simultaneity of the structure. The actor is and is not Hamlet at one and the same time.

This will all be very clearly articulated in its impact on the nature of the individual in Sartre's later works, *Search for a Method*, *The Condemned of Altona*, and, most famously, *Flaubert*, with the elaboration of the concept of the universal singular. This attempts to account for individuality being in permanent dialectical relationship with non-individuality (class, gender, history, etc.). Frantz, in *The Condemned of Altona*, is a composite figure: he is the madness individual to him, his responsibility for torturing partisans, the development of German industry and capital in the post-war period of American dominance, the crisis of the aristocratic manufacturing barons in the pre-war period faced with the rise to power of a class they despised, his relations with his once-powerful father, his place in the family, Protestantism, (and, on a different level, France's military intervention in Algeria). It is a formidable creation fusing 'me and not-me', demonstrating the multiple discourses present in the very possibility of subjectivity and any 'I'. Beauvoir's investigation of the images, myths, discourses, and representations of the non-me of gender and their relationship to the multiplicity of lived experiences is an anticipation of these structures.

The Second Sex is a brilliant text, stylistically dazzling and of immense theoretical complexity. It enables us to think about women and discourse, and feminist theoretical reflection on women, firstly through the complexity of the theoretical subjects in the text and the unravelling of a whole series of relationships between the individual and the collective. The problematic of consciousness (self/other, male/female) is articulated with a problematic of the city (construction of political subjects) and a problematic of myth. To this triple structure must be added the complex dynamics of human society and history: being is always being-in-situation, and the structures of class, history, the body, relationship to others, and gender, are not monolithic for women, or for men either. It is not surprising that Beauvoir saw no merit in notions of *écriture feminine* or *parler-femme*, for in this multidimensional structure supporting gendered human experience, where would one stick the pin of female identity?[37] Beauvoir's own language to describe it is not the language of linear rationality, but a multilayered ironic textuality where the simultaneity of is and is not, the reversals of centrality and marginality, are structuring the writing itself.

Through this complex structure comes the voice of Beauvoir the social and cultural critic — although as we have seen, the density of the multivocal and ironic layers means the subject of *énonciation* uttering the text is frequently obscured. In fact the double structures carry their own political effects in questioning the mastery of the metanarratives and positions of external superiority. It is a pity that the English translation did not retain the two quotations Beauvoir placed in front of her text, for they ironically install suspicions about discourse at its very beginning:

> There is a good principle which created order, light and man and a bad principle which has created chaos, darkness and woman.[38]
> Pythagoras
> Everything which has been written by men about women must be suspect since they are simultaneously judge and litigant.
> Poulain de la Barre

The ironies of centrality and marginality set in motion through this juxtaposition are quite splendid: the double structure of hierarchical binary opposition is met with another double structure which sets a frame (of argument, *interest*, and duplicity) by which the former may be read. Beauvoir, it will be remembered, sets her subject not as men or women, but as the relationship between the two. None the less, she goes on to adopt Poulain de la Barre's pronouncement as her own, showing that occasionally one must take irony at face value.

The political characteristics of *Les Temps modernes*'s project of synthetic anthropology show an awareness of the imperialism of discourse, particularly colonialist discourse, constructing its object of study as its other.[39] Beauvoir addresses the question in her introduction, for a woman writing about women is structurally in the same position as a man writing about women: 'Just how shall we pose the question. And, to begin with, who are we to pose it at all? Men are judge and litigant; but so are women. What we need is an angel, but where shall we find one? Still, an angel would be poorly qualified to speak, being not man and woman at once but rather neither man nor woman' (SS27 (translation adapted)). We cannot step outside discourse, and alterity is fundamental to discourse ('je est un autre'); no writer can romantically coincide with the subject of their discourse, be it themselves. There is no romantic coincidence in discourse with an *être femme* either. Beauvoir's very political solution is to draw attention to the fact that there are no context-free judgements, or naïve identifications, no utopian bisexuality to transcend difference, conflict and contradiction. And in this she remains most modern; as feminist reflection on women and gender relations, *The Second Sex* still stalks the horizons of our philosophical and cultural understandings.

Notes

1 This essay includes some material first presented at the conference held in memory of Andrea Cady and published as part of 'Le Deuxième Sexe: subjects, subjectivities and gender', in D. Berry and A. Hargreaves (eds), *Women in Twentieth-Century Culture and Society: Papers in Memory of Andrea Cady* (European Research Centre, 1993), pp. 1–16.

2 Francis Jeanson, *Simone de Beauvoir ou l'entreprise de vivre* (Paris: Seuil, 1966), p. 264.

3 Ibid., p. 262. Beauvoir refers to this statement in the final volume of her autobiography, arguing that her feminism was nonetheless too theoretical at the time. See Beauvoir, *Tout compte fait* (Paris: Gallimard, 1972), pp. 623–4 folio edition.

4 Ibid., p. 262.

5 A form of writing associated primarily with Hélène Cixous. See Toril Moi, *Sexual/Textual Politics: Feminist Literary Theory* (London: Methuen, 1985), Chapter 6, pp. 102–26; H. Cixous, 'The laugh of the Medusa', in Elaine Marks and Isabelle de Courtivron (eds), *New French Feminisms: An*

Anthology (Brighton: Harvester, 1981), pp. 244–64.

6 It is difficult to see how this would work in practice, though it is probably not generally realised that this will be what she meant when she says she would offer a more materialist analysis if she were writing the book now. See Sylvie le Bon de Beauvoir, '*Le Deuxième Sexe*: l'esprit et la lettre', in *Simone de Beauvoir ou la lutte des femmes, L'Arc*, 61 (1975), p. 57.

7 Susan Rubin Suleiman, 'Simone de Beauvoir and the writing self', in *L'Esprit Créateur*, 29:4 (1989), 45.

8 Mary Evans, *Simone de Beauvoir: A Feminist Mandarin* (London and New York: Tavistock, 1985), p. xi. See also pp. 55–6, 58–9; Anne Whitmarsh, *Simone de Beauvoir and the Limits of Commitment* (Cambridge: Cambridge University Press, 1981), pp. 149–50; Diana H. Coole, *Women in Political Theory* (Brighton: Harvester Wheatsheaf, 1988), pp. 3, 240.

9 Nicole Ward Jouve, *White Woman Speaks with Forked Tongue: Criticism as Autobiography* (London: Routledge, 1991), p. 111.

10 Suleiman, 'Simone de Beauvoir and the writing self', p. 50.

11 Michèle Le Doeuff, *L'Étude et le rouet: des femmes, de la philosophie, etc.* (Paris: Seuil, 1989); trans. Trista Selous as *Hipparchia's Choice: An Essay Concerning Women, Philosophy, etc.* (Oxford: Basil Blackwell, 1991); Toril Moi, *Simone de Beauvoir: The Making of An Intellectual Woman* (Oxford: Basil Blackwell, 1994).

12 Literally, an 'ontologico-corporeal hierarchy': Le Doeuff, *L'Étude et le Rouet*, p. 74.

13 Jeanson, *Simone de Beauvoir ou l'enterprise de vivre*, p. 265.

14 See particularly the existential psychoanalysis section, pp. 643–63, and, on viscosity, pp. 697–708, of *L'Être et le néant* (Paris: Gallimard, 1943).

15 Introduction to *The Second Sex*, p. 16.

16 Suzanne Lilar, *À propos de Sartre et de l'amour* (Paris: Grasset, 1969).

17 Sartre, *L'Être et le néant*, p. 466.

18 Allan Stoekl, *Agonies of the Intellectual: Commitment, Subjectivity and the Performative in the Twentieth-Century French Tradition* (Lincoln and London: University of Nebraska Press, 1992), pp. 118–21.

19 Linda Zerilli, '"I am a woman": female voice and ambiguity in *The Second Sex*', *Women in Politics*, 11:1 (1991), 93–108; Sonia Kruks, 'Gender and subjectivity: Simone de Beauvoir and contemporary feminism', 'Special cluster on Simone de Beauvoir', *Signs*, 18:1 (1992), 89–110.

20 Zerilli argues that the 'overarching discursive strategy of *The Second Sex*' is 'to subvert traditional assumptions by enlisting a multitude of female voices. ... To tell different narratives is to throw into question the meta-narrative of motherhood.' She glosses this: 'Beauvoir's strategy disarms by overwhelming the reader with a barrage of competing facts, views, and voices. ... By the end of *The Second Sex*, the reader has not the slightest idea of what a woman is – and that was Beauvoir's amazing achievement.'

Linda M. G. Zerilli, 'A process without a subject: Simone de Beauvoir and Julia Kristeva on maternity', *Signs*, 18:1 (1992), 123.

21 Sage, *Women in the House of Fiction: Post-War Women Novelists* (London: Macmillan, 1992), p. 4.

22 Suleiman, 'Simone de Beauvoir and the writing self ', p. 50.

23 Sage, *Women in the House of Fiction*, p. 2.

24 Moi, *Simone de Beauvoir*, p. 68.

25 Cf., the quotation from Sartre placed at the head of the second volume in the original edition: '*Moitié complices, moitié victimes, comme tout le monde*': DS2, 7.

26 'He takes great pride in his sexuality only in so far as it is a means of appropriating the Other – and this dream of possession ends only in failure': SS195 (translation adapted); 'He wishes to possess her: behold him the possessed himself': SS196.

27 See also Moi on *The Second Sex* as utopian writing, *Simone de Beauvoir*, pp. 185–90.

28 Annie Leclerc, *Parole de femme* (Paris: Grasset, 1974).

29 This is not to say that myths of femininity are exclusively related to questions of modernity, and indeed, Beauvoir herself does not present the issue in these terms. My point is that her analysis of these myths is inseparable from her philosophical perspective on human freedom and the death of God.

30 Howard Davies, *Sartre and 'Les Temps modernes'* (Cambridge: Cambridge University Press, 1987), p. 35.

31 Ibid. p. 31.

32 G. Genette, 'L'Univers réversible', *Figures 1* (Paris: Seuil, 1966).

33 Henri Suhamy, *Les Figures de style* (Paris: PUF Que sais-je, 1981), p. 116.

34 See also Zerilli on critics who misread denunciations as Beauvoir's own views: 'A process without a subject', 128.

35 Translation adapted, since 'la louche liqueur qui s'écoule du sexe féminin' is rendered as 'feminine flow': SS180; DS1, 244.

36 See Antoine Compagnon, *La Seconde Main, ou le travail de la citation* (Paris: Seuil, 1979).

37 Linda Zerilli makes a similar point in her excellent article '"I am a woman": female voice and ambiguity in *The Second Sex*', in the course of a rather different argument about the necessity and impossibility of naming the female self.

38 This entry into the subject through the classic binary oppositions is the one Cixous will choose with 'Sorties' (see Marks and de Courtivron (eds), *New French Feminisms*, p. 90).

39 See Davies, *Sartre and 'Les Temps modernes'*.

3

The influence of *The Second Sex* on the French feminist scene

CATHERINE RODGERS

'Flambeau', 'beacon', 'bible of feminism' were the terms used by the press to describe *The Second Sex* when Simone de Beauvoir died in 1986, she herself being portrayed as 'the great figure, the high priestess, the mother of feminism'.[1] This may surprise an Anglo-American reader, who thinks of French feminism as consisting of Hélène Cixous, Julia Kristeva and Luce Irigaray, and as being psychoanalytical, differentialist, deconstructionist and postmodern – hence a world away from Beauvoir's humanist, existentialist and egalitarian feminism.

Toril Moi in *Sexual/Textual Politics* was instrumental in constructing this view of the French feminist scene,[2] so when, in her more recent book on Beauvoir, she briefly surveys French feminist responses to *The Second Sex*,[3] her conclusion, that *The Second Sex* is considered by 'the French feminists' to be 'a theoretical dinosaur',[4] is not surprising, since she has dismissed from her survey the feminists who are closer to Beauvoir's egalitarian feminism.

I intend in this essay to correct this imbalance by looking not only at the reactions of the French differentialist feminists to *The Second Sex*, but also at those of other French feminists: Elisabeth Badinter (a popular, humanist feminist),[5] the reformist group *Choisir* and Gisèle Halimi, the materialist feminists of *Nouvelles Questions Féministes*, and Monique Wittig and political lesbianism.

Most of the relevant texts by French feminist writers were published after 1970, after the beginning of the French feminist movement. However, these feminists had come into contact with *The Second Sex* before that time, often having read it in isolation during their formative years. In order to find out more about their first reactions to *The Second Sex*, and to supplement documentary evidence, I interviewed several of them.[6] In the course of these interviews, they were able to assess the importance this book had had for them,[7] but also for French feminism since 1949. These responses need to be seen in the context of the problems besetting French feminism, which is currently going through a difficult phase. It is being weakened by internal tensions – which is not in itself a new phenomenon – but also by a lack of publishing opportunities and funds, as well as by widespread denigration and a general backlash against feminist ideas.

The first part of the essay deals briefly with the fundamental, but unquantifiable, role *The Second Sex* played between its publication in 1949 and the beginning of the *Mouvement de Libération des Femmes* (MLF). This consists in an examination of the consciousness-raising effect it had on mainly isolated women, some of whom would become the leaders of the MLF, as well as in its appraisal by the few feminist studies that were published at that time. Consideration of *The Second Sex* by the MLF is then briefly examined, before the reactions of individual thinkers are presented. Although French feminists are often, for clarity of exposition, classified into the differentialists and the egalitarians – and to some extent I have organised the presentation of individual thinkers on a loose spectrum going from the most differentialist (Antoinette Fouque) to the most constructionist (Christine Delphy, Monique Wittig) – reactions to *The Second Sex* show a more complex picture, one which highlights the richness and individualistic nature of French feminism, but which also points to the difficulty it experiences in creating a history for itself.

The movement before the movement and first feminist readings

When *The Second Sex* was published in 1949, although it is not true to say that there was no feminism – Claire Duchen found that there 'were organisations and groups and individuals discussing women's rights, analysing women's "condition"'[8] – the feminist debate was limited and Beauvoir herself, not yet a feminist, refused to associate herself with feminist groups she found too bourgeois and conformist. The publication of *The Second Sex*, and especially of the three chapters in *Les Temps modernes*, shocked a pronatalist, moralist France, and virulent reviews of the book dominated the press.[9] However, according to Duchen, the ideas of *The Second Sex* were too new and too threatening for them to be taken up by the women's rights groups in the 1950s; and it seems that *The Second Sex* 'remained without immediate influence on existing feminist organisations and did not lead in the short term to the formation of any new group.'[10]

However, if we look at the testimonies of women published in the press at Beauvoir's death,[11] it becomes apparent that many women read *The Second Sex* on their own, isolated from any organised feminist association. Many record how *The Second Sex* 'opened a door' for them. Elisabeth Badinter, who calls Beauvoir her 'spiritual mother', is one of the most lyrical: 'We were 15 or 16, very dutiful young daughters in the fifth form, when we discovered *The Second Sex* [...] reading it was like growing wings. The message, so clear and right, was heard by my whole generation. Follow me, she was saying, do not be afraid. Set out and conquer the world: it belongs to you.'[12] Several responses to the question put by *Elle*: 'What does Beauvoir represent for you?'[13] attest to the crucial role that *The Second Sex* played: Anne Sylvestre: 'I read *The Second Sex* about 20 years ago. It awakened me completely [...] Beauvoir, in a kind of way, was our mother'; Benoîte Groult: 'She is both my mother and my sister'; Yvette Roudy: 'her work – the woman's bible'; Marie-France Pisier: 'She cleared the way for us [...] we owe her everything'. From the minutes of the meeting organised by Michèle Le Doeuff in December 1989 in memory of Beauvoir – at which an estimated 800 people were present – it is clear that *The Second Sex* gave an interpretative grid for women, that it enabled them to give a name to their oppression and think it through. Very importantly, it constituted for thousands of isolated women, in the words of Le Doeuff, 'the movement before the movement'.[14] Beauvoir herself asserts that: 'at least I helped the women of my time and generation to become aware of themselves and their situation' (*Force of Circumstance* (1978), p. 202 [*La Force des choses* (1963), p. 210].

Little of the impact made by *The Second Sex* during this period is known, as reading was done privately. As Beauvoir put it: 'its success was rather private in character'.[15] Publicly, after its scandalised reception, *The Second Sex* was discussed only in the chapters of the few books published on Beauvoir, and even then the term 'discussed' may be too strong for what amounts to little more than a summary of the main ideas together with disapproval of Beauvoir's denigration of maternity, marriage, and the Church's negative influence on women.[16]

Geneviève Gennari's *Simone de Beauvoir* (1958) is the first feminist study of *The Second Sex*,[17] and while Gennari thinks that *The Second Sex* is 'a necessary book'[18] because it gives women responsibility for their own lives, it gradually becomes obvious that Gennari believes in a biological determination of women, in marriage, and in procreation as 'the creative act *par excellence*'[19] and as a natural vocation for women.

Although more detailed and feminist, Gennari's study is close in tone and content to the other works produced on *The Second Sex* during the 1950s and 1960s. Suzanne Lilar is therefore right when she states in her introduction to *Le Malentendu du Deuxième sexe* that 'Simone de Beauvoir has never seen her theses *seriously* contested' (my emphasis).[20] In contrast to previous studies, *Le Malentendu* is a sophisticated if not always unbiased offensive on *The Second Sex*.[21]

The standpoint from which Lilar makes her attacks on *The Second Sex* is that of 'the intrinsic bisexuality of the living',[22] visible both at the physiological and psychic levels. Far from denying the biological elements in sexual identity, Lilar uses them in order to put forward the bisexual nature of both men and women. Lilar's point is that once androgyny is recognised, the question of the hierarchy of the sexes becomes redundant.

Soon after Lilar's assault, the ideas of *The Second Sex* were to be challenged implicitly by a large part of the feminist movement.

The French feminist movement

The extent to which *The Second Sex* formed a point of reference for the feminist movement is difficult to determine, and opinions vary tremendously.

At Beauvoir's death, most feminists (except Fouque) agreed in recognising the importance Beauvoir and *The Second Sex* had had for them. The occasion would certainly have encouraged positive statements, but the idea that *The Second Sex* was a key text for feminism did circulate before Beauvoir's death. In 1977, Albistur and Armogathe stated that 'All contemporary feminism proceeds from *The Second Sex*.'[23]

The Second Sex is seen by many and by Beauvoir herself as having provided a theoretical framework for the discussion of women's oppression. Monique Remy writes: '*The Second Sex* gave to the struggle for women's rights the theoretical basis which was lacking';[24] Savigneau hails *The Second Sex* as 'the most important theoretical work of contemporary feminism';[25] while in 1975 Claude Sarraute speaks of it as a 'key book, a text book for feminists throughout the world'.[26] Nancy Huston calls French feminists of the 1970s spiritual daughters of Beauvoir:

> Not only do we derive personal inspiration from her writing (in a way, to reread *The Second Sex* today is to rediscover the seeds of almost everything we have been able to write since: more or less every paragraph sown by Simone de Beauvoir flowered later in a book by someone else) but also this work contributed, very concretely, to the creation of the conditions necessary for the advent of neo-feminism: she changed the ideological, and by the same token, institutional context of our age.[27]

Developing the same idea, Françoise Picq stresses that in writing *The Second Sex*, Beauvoir — unwittingly — 'was fashioning the keys'[28] of the future feminist movement; and she adds that during the 1960s 'Beauvoir's analyses, examples and formulations were transmitted, disseminated, propagated'.[29] What is more, for Picq the feminist movement: 'is situated therefore at the meeting point of two systems of analysis. From Simone de Beauvoir comes its awareness of the social inequality between the sexes and the definition of the second as 'Other' ... In Marxism it finds collective struggle, the revolutionary project.'[30]

Picq's analysis is attractive, but is not shared by everybody. Geneviève Fraisse recognises an affiliation between Beauvoir and the feminists of the 1970s, in the sense that both wanted to change tradition; but she adds 'many daft things have been said about *The Second Sex*. In particular that it was the source —

historic, symbolic and theoretical – of contemporary feminism'.[31] For her, what *The Second Sex* is best known for – the denunciation of the belief in a natural essence of woman, and of femininity – is not new to *The Second Sex*, and can be found in earlier texts. What she credits *The Second Sex* with on the other hand is to have given, thanks to the concept of woman as other, 'philosophical status to the question of the difference between the sexes' and to have started an epistemological reflection by introducing 'being a woman as a condition of the possibility of discourse [on women].'

When I asked the women I interviewed whether, from their experience, *The Second Sex* played a role in the movement during the 1970s, their answers varied from granting it 'an absolutely essential role' (Badinter) to a complete denial of influence: 'the women who created the Women's Movement did so without Simone de Beauvoir' (Cixous); and 'the movement did not have Simone de Beauvoir as its starting point at all' (Fouque). Michelle Perrot pointed out the difficulty of separating *The Second Sex* from the rest of Beauvoir's work and from her personality and lifestyle which served as a model for many women. Similarly, Sarah Kofman considered it was a combination of Beauvoir's theoretical writings, including *The Second Sex*, and her affirmation of freedom, of the possibility of transcending any situation, as well as the example she and Sartre provided of a free couple, which influenced her own early life and thought.

What everyone agreed upon is that the text itself was not directly referred to in meetings: it was not discussed, and certainly did not function as a programme. The fact is that the ideas of *The Second Sex* had already been thoroughly assimilated by the 1970s. All the leaders of the movement had read *The Second Sex* earlier in the 1950s or 1960s, and by the time the feminist movement gathered momentum, they had either absorbed Beauvoir's premises, and therefore were ready to radicalise them further (materialist feminists; *Choisir*), or had had time to reject them (the differentialist feminists). In any case, a number of Beauvoir's ideas which were controversial in 1949 had become common claims for all feminists by the 1970s: the right to contraception, abortion, equal pay, and the need for new legislation against sexual harassment and rape. By then, these ideas were no longer linked to *The Second Sex*. They had become so obvious that nobody wondered about their origin. In 1979 Chapsal wrote that *The Second Sex* 'has become a classic to such an extent that, reading it today, it seems made up of self-evident truths'.[32]

Given the multi-faceted nature of French feminism, the limits of a general appraisal of the influence on it of *The Second Sex* are soon reached. A more specific approach, respecting the variety, and indeed divergence of contemporary feminists' views, becomes necessary.

The Second Sex and individual thinkers

Michèle Le Doeuff

Le Doeuff is the only feminist in France since Lilar to publish a detailed study of *The Second Sex*. In *Hipparchia's Choice* and in various articles, she has examined the consequences for *The Second Sex* of Beauvoir's adoption of the existentialist perspective, and the transformations she brought to it.

Existentialism enabled Beauvoir to avoid the traps of essentialism and determinism, but caused her other problems. Firstly, existentialism is full of masculinist biases and some of them find their way into *The Second Sex*.[33] Another problem is the fact that 'no oppression is thinkable in the existentialist system'.[34] As Beauvoir was witnessing the daily domination of women, she multiplied in her text the descriptions of this oppression, and of the mechanisms perpetuating it – which is one of the strengths of *The Second Sex* according to Le Doeuff – but without coming to any final explanation. In taking into account women's situation, their lack of rights and of means to act and affirm themselves, Beauvoir was substantially modifying Sartre's thought.

Information released after *Hipparchia's Choice*, in Beauvoir's recently published correspondence, has enabled Le Doeuff to articulate more clearly the role played by Hegel's *The Phenomenology of Spirit* in Beauvoir's theorising of woman's oppression, and to assert that 'with a postulate such as that of the primacy of my consciousness for me [which is that of Sartre in *Being and Nothingness*] one cannot write *The Second Sex*, which today appears to me as a prolongation of the reading of Hegel.'[35]

Le Doeuff's reading of *The Second Sex* is first and foremost a

philosophical enquiry into the limits and possibilities of a phallocratic philosophical framework when adopted by a feminist.
But she also looks at what *The Second Sex* brought to her as a
woman, how it constituted for her and others 'the movement
before the movement', how its ideas have 'galvanized women's
movements pretty well everywhere and helped them get going'.[36]

While sympathetic to Beauvoir's plight – her isolation in a
phallocratic environment – and admiring her for her 'formidably
astute intelligence',[37] Le Doeuff voices several criticisms of Beauvoir, most being consequences of her liberal humanist outlook.
Beauvoir tended to present herself as unique, neglecting the
achievements of earlier remarkable women, such as Virginia
Woolf; she ignored the possibility of, and in fact the need for,
collective solutions; she was unable to envisage a community of
women; she tended to analyse oppression at the level of interpersonal relationships, without considering sufficiently the
social and institutional factors. This led Beauvoir to lay blame too
quickly on women who seemingly did not seize the chance to
emancipate themselves, not understanding that they might be
prevented from so doing by socio-cultural mechanisms. This is
why *The Second Sex* 'is not a "Little Red Book" for militant feminists'.[38]

Le Doeuff's appraisal of *The Second Sex* is cautious; she recognises: 'my thinking is downstream of Simone de Beauvoir's work:
it would not have been possible without the things that can be
learned from reading *The Second Sex*, nor without many things I
have learned elsewhere'.[39] But she concludes the section of
Hipparchia's Choice on *The Second Sex* by writing:

> 'But what exactly were you looking for in *The Second Sex*? A
> theory, or the voice and support of a big sister?'
>   'What are we looking for in any philosophical text if not the
> theoretical support of a forerunner? Although, of course we may
> not find it.'[40]

It is certainly true that *The Second Sex* disappointed many French
feminists, some bitterly. However, even most of the French
feminists best known in Great Britain, who do not form a
continuity with Beauvoir's work, have felt the need, in interviews or in articles, to separate themselves from the ideas of *The*

Second Sex, as if to exorcise its powerful influence – an influence which, ironically, continues to haunt some of their texts.

Antoinette Fouque

At Beauvoir's death, the most virulent attack on her work came from Fouque in the form of a short article in *Libération*, in which she pitted her perspective on women against Beauvoir's.[41] She accuses Beauvoir of promoting an 'intolerant, assimilating, sterilising universalism, full of hatred and reductive of otherness'. Fouque presents her own position as having its source in 'fruitful differences that, as everybody knows, flow from, are informed by and find their origins in the difference between the sexes'. For Fouque, Beauvoir's death is like a setting free of her own generation, and will 'perhaps speed up women's entry into the twenty-first century'.

Her antagonism could not be stated more bluntly, and Fouque is bitter about the 'shameful, merciless campaign that Beauvoir waged against her', although she recognises the importance of *The Second Sex*. Indeed her analysis of woman's oppression does share some ground with Beauvoir. Like Beauvoir, Fouque criticises Freud for constructing woman as lacking, for having posited a single phallic libido,[42] for having modelled the development of the little girl on that of the little boy ('in psychoanalysis one is not born a woman ... one is born a little boy, or rather a little castrated boy').[43] Like Beauvoir too, she recognises that 'more often than not, what we call "feminine" is only a metaphor, a phantasmatic representation (a making over or a making up) of woman by man.'[44]

However, from this common diagnosis, their prescriptions differ fundamentally. Whereas Beauvoir minimised the significance of physiological difference, by showing sexual difference to be mainly cultural, Fouque makes of sexual difference, and especially procreation, the cornerstone of her theory, something that she grounds in her own experience of pregnancy. For her 'there are two sexes' – the title of her article – and 'one is born a girl or a boy and physiology is a destiny for both girl and boy'. Whereas Beauvoir was wary of reproduction because she saw it as the moment when women became the prey of the species, Fouque stresses that this specificity of women must be the starting point of any reflection on women, and that any denial of this irreducible difference only leads to further oppression: 'an equality incapable of taking differences into account produces only homogenization and assimilation, which is literally sterilizing for women who have chosen, or who desire, solely to be like their so-called kinsmen, their brothers.'[45] Fouque considers that Beauvoir theorised her own personal refusal of reproduction, tried to impose a 'matricidal and motherless feminism', and is 'wedded to a strictly masculine way of thinking'. Far from considering reproduction as a handicap for women, Fouque sees it as a plus: 'there is an asymmetry in procreation which means that women have a burden, a greater responsibility, but perhaps also a greater value in relation to the species.'

For Fouque, in gestation women accomplish a true labour of humanisation. She likes to put forward the myth that it was pregnant women who invented language through their need to communicate with the foetus. For her, gestation and then breast-feeding are not just animal functions, but the site of a symbolic, cultural nurturing. The way a pregnant woman welcomes the foetus within her body, by a 'spiritual as much as carnal grafting'[46] is an ethical model. Because of their ability to give life and nurture it, women have a 'truly ethical relationship with life'.

Gestation, being a state that combines activity and passivity, could also serve as a model for the act of creation. Fouque refuses the separation between procreation and creation, a division invented by men who accord greater value to creation out of jealousy of women's procreative ability. She accuses feminism, and especially Beauvoir, of presenting them as exclusive activities,[47] and finds feminism to be 'a form of sterility, of hysteria'.[48]

Gestation also gives Fouque a lever to undo the supremacy of the phallus in Freudian/Lacanian psychoanalysis. Like Beauvoir, she criticises this supremacy, but rather than rejecting psychoanalysis, attempts to modify it from the inside by positing the existence of a female libido. As she told me, woman must have a libido of her own: 'If we manage to give the phallus its proper place, that is, if it is made to coexist with a female, uterine libido, we will no longer be in a murderous, priapic, violating eroticism. With a good phallic and a good uterine economy, we will have a heterosexual and democratic mode of existence.'

Chantal Chawaf

In a different way, via her poetic fictions, Chawaf approaches Fouque's more theoretical opposition to Beauvoir's feminism. Like Fouque, Chawaf reproaches Beauvoir with having given 'facile solutions to a serious problem, which is that of motherhood'. By refusing maternity, and the necessary dialectic between procreation and creation, Beauvoir: 'brought more grist to misogyny's mill: she belongs to a tendency which has lasted for thousands of years, and which showed no improvement in the 19th, nor even in the 20th century, with the claims of feminism; she does not break with the forces that suffocate and drag women down to a primary and repulsive maternity.'

It is not a matter of sublimating maternity and the body, something that the Christian church has done to the detriment of women, but of translating it into writing, of symbolising the body, sexuality and gestation. Otherwise, the body, and especially female sexuality, becomes a source of anguish – an anguish well captured in Beauvoir's visceral descriptions.

Chawaf agrees with Beauvoir on the often negative role that mothers play towards their daughters; however, for her the solution is not to refuse motherhood, nor to separate mothers and offspring, but to understand why maternity can only be bad in a society cut off from the body, structured uniquely by the father and masculine values, resting on the absence of the mother at the symbolic level. Chawaf commented that Beauvoir is in 'the masculine part of language, in the concept detached from the body' when she writes about maternity and breast-feeding; whereas for Chawaf, as for Fouque, 'breast-feeding can partake of a very strong spirituality'.

Like Beauvoir, Chawaf admits that 'woman is always reminded of her body', but this should be a 'richness of perception'. For this closeness to life to be a source of wealth, mediation must be found between the body and language, a prelanguage which is 'halfway between language and flesh'[49] – which is what Chawaf tries to elaborate in her own texts.

Like Fouque, Chawaf felt the falsity of Beauvoir's statements, which were often at odds with her private life; and she resented her authoritative, intransigent stance, her despising of ordinary women who devote their lives to their families.

Hélène Cixous

Chawaf, in her search for 'linguistic flesh', is putting into practice Cixous's exhortation to women in 'The laugh of the Medusa' to write their bodies and show their 'sexts'.[50] Moi has commented on the absence of reference to Beauvoir in this article,[51] even though it was first published in a special issue of *L'Arc* (1975) devoted to Beauvoir.[52] The absence of references to Beauvoir in Cixous's work is in fact total, and when I met Cixous, I quickly became aware of the complete estrangement between the perspectives of the two authors. Cixous said that she did read *The Second Sex*, when she was fifteen, because at the time Sartre, hence Beauvoir, were being read; however, she quickly added: 'I didn't get anything out of it'. She found then that 'in *The Second Sex* there was no progress, no opening out, no invention, only tremendous repression'. She cannot find anything positive in *The Second Sex*, except perhaps the fact that it was a feminist book and 'to be a feminist is basic'. But otherwise, she refuses to credit Beauvoir with any innovative analysis — 'Beauvoir invents nothing, she copies, she reproduces Sartre and society's clichés' — or with any *écriture*: 'there is no 'writing' (*écriture*)' in *The Second Sex*, which when one knows that for Cixous 'writing is what liberates' may be the worst comment of them all. She sees Beauvoir 'caught in discourse', whereas 'what progresses in leaps and bounds is related to a breaking of language'. She also reproaches Beauvoir for having rejected psychoanalysis. And according to her 'the woman's movement was not Beauvoirist but driven by a capacity for deconstruction and the possibility of using psychoanalysis.'

The gulf between Cixous and Beauvoir could not be summarised better than by Cixous's own words: 'Beauvoir is not an enemy, she is no-one ... nothing.' Feelings were mutual; Beauvoir also had harsh words to say about Cixous:

> I can't read her, understand her. And I think it's wrong to write in a totally esoteric language when you want to talk about things which interest a multitude of women. ... There is something false in this search for a purely feminine writing style.... I consider it almost antifeminist to say that there is a feminine nature which expresses itself differently, that a woman speaks her body more than a man.[53]

This search for an *écriture féminine*, a specificity of women's writing or of the feminine in writing, was a major undertaking of the feminist movement in the 1970s and can be found in many texts, such as Cixous' 'Des femmes en écriture' and 'The laugh of the Medusa', Cixous, Leclerc and Cagnon's *Coming to Writing*, *Sorcières*, Gauthier's 'Lutte de femmes', Leclerc's *Parole de femme*, and the *Le Magazine Littéraire* dossier 'Femmes, une autre écriture?'.

Xavière Gauthier

In 'Femmes, une autre écriture?', Gauthier, the editor of *Sorcières*, looks back on women's achievements. After relegating to the past 'the feminist lineage of *The Second Sex*',[54] she lists the really innovative books, which according to her are: Leclerc's *Parole de femme* (1994), in which 'a woman dares sing of her woman's body as different from man's and in which she glorifies her periods, her pregnancy'; Chawaf's *Retable*, 'which makes us inhabit the darkness, the wetness, the heat of the uterine cavity'; Irigaray's *Speculum of the Other Woman*, which 'finally frees women from the theoretical discourse of men about them and reveals what makes them "other"'; Gauthier and Duras's *Woman to Woman*, where Marguerite Duras identifies 'the difference between the sexes at the very heart of writing'; and Cixous and Clément's *The Newly Born Woman*. Anne-Marie de Vilaine, in the same issue of *Le Magazine Littéraire*, recapitulates what has emerged from the work done by women over the previous decade, concluding that women have been trying to find new values, that they have:

> a double demand for equality and difference, that they call into question power and mastery in concepts or relationships, that they refuse to be defined in relation to the male sex and refuse the fact that 'every other has to be reduced to sameness', that they affirm the spiritual, symbolic dimension of the body and matter and consider *jouissance* as a way of knowing, that they make gaps visible ... that their discourse is not always linear ... that they find strength in the maternal.[55]

Each element of this new feminism clearly inscribes itself against the tenets of *The Second Sex*.

Gauthier's own development is significant. She told me that when she first read *The Second Sex*, she was 'in complete agreement' with its ideas, something she now analyses as a rebellious movement belonging to her adolescence. But she gradually distanced herself from Beauvoir when she understood that the latter's analysis led to the disappearance of women – since, on the one hand there is no feminine nature, and on the other, the feminine that exists must be refused because it is the result of masculine oppression. In 'Lutte de femmes', she criticises women who only seem to seek equality with men in the masculine world:

> believing herself emancipated, she had access to education where she was sung the praises of a language in which everything, verbs and subjects, were masculine. It was then, become mad, that she thought she could turn into a man, be the equal of her masters by adopting their grammar and syntax. Completely alienated from herself, without knowing it, Woman has transformed herself into this Mad Sex that some women have called the 'Second'.[56]

While agreeing that *fémininité* – the feminine imposed by men – had to be rejected, Gauthier as a reaction to Beauvoir's approach, went in search of the 'féminin', or 'femellitude', a neologism she forged after the concept of 'négritude', and founded *Sorcières*. Her starting point is biological data and sexual difference. For her 'one is born a woman', the question then being 'what is one going to become?'. In *Sorcières*, or in a poetic text like *Rose saignée*,[57] she works at the emergence of a feminine specificity in the writing itself.

Annie Leclerc

It is perhaps *Parole de femme* that epitomises best this second wave of feminism, that glorifies women's physical difference and promotes feminine values. Leclerc admitted that *Parole de femme* could be read 'as an "anti-*Second Sex*".'[58]

In *Parole de femme* Leclerc recognises that men have imposed their values on the world and on language: 'nothing exists that has not been made by man: neither thought, nor word ... not even me. Especially not me.'[59] Man has not only imposed his view, he has silenced woman, has reviled her and her activities – in other words, Leclerc would agree that man has made woman the other. But she distances herself from any feminist claims that would want woman to accede to men's prerogatives and powers: 'do not lay claim to those things enjoyed by man, for they are nothing other than the weapons of your oppression ... Do not seek for Man to be recognised in you.'[60] Leclerc mocks the supposedly universal values of courage and heroism, and in particular the Sartrean project. She warns that 'far from attaining the sexual neutrality of concepts ... it is very often philosophy that shows most barefacedly the virility of thought in general.'[61] Instead, a 'woman's word', to be born, will have to originate mainly in the female body, and in *jouissance*.

Most of *Parole de femme* is spent singing the female body, the female sex – 'the place of life's Dionysian revelry'[62] – periods, giving birth, breast feeding. A short extract will suffice to give a flavour of the contrast between Leclerc's text and the clinical or disgusted descriptions in *The Second Sex*:

> Living is happiness. To see and feel the gentle, warm blood flowing from you, flowing from its source once a month is happiness. To be this vagina, an open eye in life's nocturnal fermentation, an ear alive to the pulse, the vibration of the originating magma, a hand tied and untied, a mouth in love with another's flesh. To be this vagina is happiness.[63]

Like Beauvoir, Leclerc cannot accept the universality of penis-envy; and although she recognises its existence in our patriarchal society, she is a long way from considering this 'awkward and ugly instrument'[64] in envious terms, the way Beauvoir does. For Leclerc 'woman's physical superiority is [....] obvious',[65] with her ability to give and sustain life. And she rewrites, in a playful manner, the myth of our origins, toying with the idea that it is out of uterus envy that men have arrogated for themselves all economic, social and political power, belittling women and their tasks. Leclerc does not challenge the sexual division of tasks, but their respective values.

Parole de femme is written in the name of the search for happiness, *jouissance*, life. It is not surprising that in 1986, Leclerc in *La Croix*, besides admitting her liking for Beauvoir – 'Simone de Beauvoir fought throughout her life for what she called women's liberation, basically to remove women from a position of subjection' – also expresses reservations: 'the values Simone de Beauvoir appealed to in her struggle remained basically very masculine ones: she reasoned in terms of self-affirmation, of social recognition, economic independence. I realised quite early on that something else needed doing: we had to give new value to that which is traditionally considered as feminine.'[66]

Luce Irigaray

In 'A personal note: equal or different?' in *Je, tu, nous*, Irigaray analyses her relation to Beauvoir and her ideas. The article starts as a homage to Beauvoir, recognising her work for the liberation of women: 'What woman has not read *The Second Sex*? What woman hasn't found it inspiring? Hasn't as a result, perhaps, become a feminist?'.[67] She praises Beauvoir's courage in recounting her life, thereby offering women a model for greater sexual freedom; and salutes her commitment to feminist causes.

But, after having acknowledged this much, Irigaray stresses the distance between herself and Beauvoir: a painful distance caused in part by Beauvoir's personal coldness towards her at a time when she was vulnerable and was looking up to Beauvoir for personal support in her struggles with institutions and academic life – but a conceptual and unbridgeable distance too. Irigaray mentions here her own psychoanalytical formation which contrasts with Beauvoir's resistance to psychoanalysis, a formation which led her to pose the problem of women's liberation in radically different terms from Beauvoir's: 'my thought on women's liberation has gone beyond simply a quest for equality between the sexes.'[68]

As Naomi Schor states, Beauvoir and Irigaray occupy 'dramatically opposed positions' but they 'share a fundamental grounding conviction: under the social arrangement known as patriarchy the subject is exclusively male.'[69] Irigaray has investigated the modes of exclusion of women from the symbolic order, in particular from philosophical discourse and Freudian psychoanalysis. She has criticised Freud for having described woman's sexuality in male terms – as Beauvoir did.[70] Also like Beauvoir, she has denounced the way capitalism and patriarchy work together to objectify women, to reduce them to the status of commodities exchanged by men. As such, Irigaray, again like Beauvoir in *The Second Sex,* is ready, even if it is on a utopian level, to link the advance of Marxism and women's liberation: 'the realization of Marxism would be the liberation of women, that is to say, the abolition of private property, the family, the state.'[71] Irigaray agrees with Beauvoir in the recognition of the danger that reproduction constitutes for women: 'it's not in the factory that we are most trapped – it is in the reproductive function',[72] and recognises too the negative role that the mother often plays, especially towards her daughter, because 'she reproduces the oppression to which she is subject',[73] something she translates poetically in the first sentence of 'And the one doesn't stir without the other': 'With your milk, mother, I swallowed ice'.[74]

In spite of these points in common with Beauvoir[75] Irigaray strongly rejects her claims for equality, because 'equality signifies becoming totally like men',[76] any attempt at doing away with sexual difference being equivalent to a genocide. She refuses 'to be a human being'[77] because the 'so called universal discourse ... is sexualized and mainly in a masculine way.'[78] In 'L'Autre de la nature' ['Nature's other'] she goes further in suggesting that for women to deny their difference is to play into the hands of phallogocentrism: 'When we renounce our difference in order to conquer equality, are we not accomplices in such a process? In fact, in an escalation of western masculine imperialism?'[79] She explains: 'Refusing the oppression of women does not amount to renouncing our bodies, our sex, our imaginations, our language ... but involves discovering them and asserting their value.'[80]

Irigaray reiterates her criticism of Beauvoir's type of feminism in 'L'Identité féminine: biologie ou conditionnement social?' ['Feminine identity: biology or social conditioning?'], where she bemoans the fact that 'becoming a woman is considered old hat, reactionary, therefore shameful, something to be analysed and surpassed, like the effect of social conditioning.'[81] She views this wish to uncondition oneself in order to 'rejoin a universal neuter that can only be partaken of in a masculine or neuter universe' as 'feminism's most obvious dead end.'[82] Instead she proposes the building of a feminine culture: 'it is quite simply a matter of social justice to balance out this power of the one sex over the other by giving, or giving back, cultural values to female sexuality.'[83] In *J'aime à toi*, Irigaray rewrites Beauvoir's most famous sentence, thus comparing their two perspectives: 'It is a question of demanding a culture, of wanting and of working out a spirituality, a subjectivity and an otherness fitting for this gender: feminine. That is, not as Simone de Beauvoir said: one is not born but becomes a woman (through culture) but rather: I was born a woman, but I have still to become this woman that I am by nature.'[84]

In one sense, Irigaray herself occupies the position of the Other, but as Judith Butler explains in *Gender Trouble*,[85] Irigaray's other is not Beauvoir's. Butler's analysis is confirmed by Irigaray's later article 'The question of the other', where she herself compares her position on the question of alterity to Beauvoir's. Beauvoir, still functioning within a philosophical system where the subject could only be masculine and unique, is led to refuse the place accorded to woman as second, as the other of man. Irigaray not only refuses the fact that woman should be second, but she criticises the very phallocentrism of western philosophy, the fact that 'the other is always seen as the other of the same, the other of the subject itself, rather than an/other subject [...] irreducible to the masculine subject and sharing equivalent dignity'.[86] Already in 1977, Irigaray by saying that the female sex 'is not one' posits a different notion of the subject, indicating at the same time that the female sex cannot be represented within phallogocentrism; and she provides a starting point from which to criticise western metaphysics and its notion of the subject.

In *This Sex which Is not One*, Irigaray puts forward elements for a positive symbolisation of woman's otherness, of her female pleasure; and attempts to make it possible for women to speak a language corresponding to their sexuality and their creativity.

Irigaray insists on the necessity of stressing woman's difference, and of undermining the logic of the same which either presents woman's difference as a lack, as negativity (the Other of Beauvoir) or erases this very difference (Beauvoir's ideal according to Irigaray): 'Equality between men and women cannot be achieved without a *theory of gender as sexed* and a rewriting of the rights and obligations of each sex, *qua different*, in social rights and obligations.'[87]

Irigaray therefore cannot be accused, as Beauvoir can, of wanting women's access to a subjectivity thought of in masculine terms (the humanist, transcendent, active subject), nor of upholding masculine values disguised as universal ones, though she has been accused of essentialism. Contrary to some differentialists, however, she refuses to hang her reappraisal of femininity on procreation: 'To emphasise in this way the privilege of motherhood seems to me a suspect gesture, one with which I do not agree. The reversal of power does not interest me.'[88]

Julia Kristeva

In 'Women's time'[89] Kristeva looks back on feminist achievements and strategies, and draws distinctions between three generations of feminists. Although she does not give any names when she discusses the first generation — suffragettes and existentialist feminists — she obviously has Beauvoir in mind. She acknowledges the social benefits obtained by these early feminists, but criticises them for their rejection of feminine or maternal attributes, judged incompatible with women's insertion in the economic and political sphere,[90] together with their globalising approach to women's problems — women being subsumed under the label of Universal Woman. Kristeva condemns them especially for having made the question of the desire for maternity in women a forbidden question, and for having attempted to make the refusal of maternity a general policy.

Except for these implicit references, the name of Beauvoir in Kristeva's writing is rare. Moi signals rightly that Kristeva only makes allusions to Beauvoir when she moves away from theory towards fiction,[91] and Kristeva to date has made only one direct reference to *The Second Sex* in an interview in *L'Infini*, where she describes *The Second Sex* as an 'ineffaceable lesson of feminine dignity'.[92] When I met Kristeva, she told me that the interest of *The Second Sex* for her 'lies less in what it says than in Simone de Beauvoir's own behaviour'; that is, she prefers to consider *The Second Sex* as part of Beauvoir's overall claim for an autonomous life.

Admitting that *The Second Sex* and its demand for sexual equality was of historical moment, helping generations of women, she adds that 'it would be a mistake for women to keep to those principles, reiterating those militant aspects of phallic equality with men.' Kristeva, like Irigaray, is interested in difference rather than equality. She agrees with 'the idea found throughout the book that the feminine character is formed out of the look of others and a social model which means that one is not born but is made a woman'; but she finds that this analysis takes insufficient account of biological factors and the unconscious. Kristeva agrees with Beauvoir that women are constantly reminded of their body through periods, pregnancy, and the menopause; that through it they are confronted with pain, passivity, and death;

but she does not view this as a handicap, considering that it becomes one only within a phallocratic conception of life: on the contrary, it can give rise to subtle artistic elaborations, as in the works of Duras or Woolf.

As a Freudian psychoanalyst, Kristeva does not dispute Freud's theory of penis-envy for women, and rejects the idea of equality in relation to the unconscious as 'untenable'. But she also refuses the idea that men and women are different subjects: 'if from the outset we begin to differentiate access to subjectivity within language, we handicap women and remove them from the social domain. This is a poor service to render them.' One should only say that the 'configuration within subjectivity is different'; that the feminine configuration has another relation to prelanguage, drives, gestures and smells.

Kristeva opposes Beauvoir most strongly on the question of maternity.[93] She pointed out to me her disagreement with Beauvoir's interpretation of the painting by Piero della Franscesca of the Virgin Mary.[94] While Beauvoir reads into it the humiliation of the Virgin, Kristeva sees it as an expression of ecstasy which is both submissive and omnipotent. Kristeva finds Beauvoir's presentation of maternity in terms of 'masochistic obligation imposed on women' totally outmoded; and suggests that Beauvoir's position on the question has been harmful to feminist thinking on maternity, and to feminism as a whole: 'The feminist movement's second stage, the one that came after Simone de Beauvoir, felt hampered by her thinking and did not go far enough in this re-evaluation of motherhood, causing the deep split between feminism and the mass of women.' Difference for Kristeva is in evidence at the biological and psychological levels, and is necessary for harmony to exist between the sexes. Where only equality has been attempted, as in the socialist countries which have not taken into account woman's specificity, where therefore 'Simone de Beauvoir's ideal of egalitarianism has been realised', it has proven to be a source of slavery for women. For Kristeva: 'it is untenable to insist on this type of uniformity where women all turn into men in order to attain a human ideal stemming from a universalism which is undoubtedly glorious but which effaces difference; and from this point of view *The Second Sex* is dated.' In 'Women's time', Kristeva places herself beyond the second generation of feminists who stress women's radical difference, and rejects the dichotomy Man/Woman as metaphysical.[95] She displaces the sexual difference to within each individual, seeing the individual as being made up of both the masculine and the feminine. She explained to me that: 'one must accept that the feminine, in so far as that means "passive", "second", can be found in both sexes.' This should lead to a de-dramatisation of the fight between men and women, taking women out of the excessive subordination to their devalued image, and 'allow them a mosaic of particulars'.

Elisabeth Badinter

Kristeva occupies an ambivalent place on the French feminist scene, considered as one of the main proponents of French feminism by Anglo-American feminists, and by other French feminists as being outside the feminist scene altogether. Badinter also stands apart. Her ideas are dismissed by most French feminists, but she is by far the best-known to the general public, and is the only one who professes overtly and strongly her links with Beauvoir. She recognises her debt to Beauvoir, both on a personal level and a conceptual one: '*The Second Sex* made a deep impression on me: it has marked the whole course of my life ... it formed the basis of my own ideas and way of life as well as my understanding of the relationship between the sexes.' She does not hesitate to call Beauvoir her 'spiritual mother'. From Beauvoir she derives the culturalist approach which is clearly visible in her main texts. In *The Myth of Motherhood*, for example, Badinter challenges, after Beauvoir, the existence of the maternal instinct. Tracing the evolution of maternal behaviour, she shows that maternal love is neither a constant through time, nor is it equally shared by all women, and that one cannot therefore talk of a maternal instinct. Similarly, at the beginning of *Man/Woman, The One is the Other*, she stresses 'that there is an overtly cultural bias running through this work'.[96] And in *XY, de l'identité masculine*, she shows that 'one is not born, but rather becomes, a man'.[97]

Although Badinter stresses her closeness to Beauvoir's culturalist and humanist approach, their ideas diverge on a number of crucial points. While Beauvoir warned women against the trap of motherhood, and could not envisage a way of combining procreation and emancipation, Badinter recognises that women now want both, necessitating a redistribution of tasks between the sexes and a revival of the paternal role.

In *Man/Woman*, where Badinter studies the relationship between the sexes from a historical perspective, her analysis of the workings of patriarchy is similar to Beauvoir's. Like Beauvoir, and with the help of Lévi-Strauss, she identifies marriage as the linchpin of the patriarchal system. But her analysis differs explicitly from Beauvoir's in her reading of prehistory and of contemporary and future developments. First, Badinter is well aware, unlike Beauvoir, of the elements of wishful thinking and projection which are inevitable in any appraisal of prehistory. Like Beauvoir, she refutes the hypothesis of an original matriarchy, identifying a sexual division of tasks, placing particular importance on the fact that political power has always been retained by men. But their conclusions are different, as Badinter herself stresses: 'it was said a bit too quickly that women were condemned to immanence, while transcendence belonged by right to men';[98] and 'contrary to what Simone de Beauvoir thought, to say that woman is the Other, is not to renounce the reciprocal relationship between the sexes, nor is it to consider her as 'the Inessential'.[99] For Badinter, in prehistory the sexes are in a relationship of difference and complementarity, but also of equality.

In the last part of *Man/Woman*, Badinter puts forward her most controversial and distinctive thesis: that each one of us is androgynous. She asserts that at the biological level there are not two heterogeneous groups, males and females, but rather a continuum of people with varying quantities of female and male elements. She also turns to Freud's theory of psychic bisexuality to substantiate her thesis. Interestingly, she refers here to *Le Malentendu du Deuxième sexe*, siding with Lilar's defence of an intrinsic bisexuality.

Badinter does not so much challenge the stereotypical notions of the masculine and feminine, as rewrite their occurrence in each one of us. Resolutely optimistic, she envisages a fraternal society where tenderness replaces passion and desire, and where sexual difference is no longer paramount. She thus regains, but by a different route, Beauvoir's ideal of an egalitarian society.

Gisèle Halimi and Choisir

Like Badinter, Halimi is well known to the general public – in Halimi's case, for her constant involvement in the political scene, and especially for her widely mediatised role as barrister for the accused in the Bobigny trial.[100] In 1971 she created *Choisir* to organise the defence of the women who signed the *Manifeste des 343*.[101] Beauvoir agreed to support her friend's efforts and became co-founder of *Choisir*. First *Choisir* aimed at obtaining sexual education, free contraception and the right to abortion. Soon however its objectives were widened, as more and more battles were fought in court by Halimi, and won. In 1974 its objectives were to fight:

- for the rights of women over their own bodies and to choose whether or not to have children
- for women to be completely integrated into economic and social life
- for women to be completely integrated into political life
- for the destruction of all the myths relating to the traditional image of women and the creation of new cultural patterns from which all sexism will be excluded
- to give every woman the education and training necessary for the accomplishment of these aims
- against all physical and moral violence perpetuated on them and notably against the crime of rape[102]

Except for the demand for women's inclusion in politics, the aims follow directly from *The Second Sex*. 'One is not born, but rather becomes, a woman' is used as an epigraph to *La Cause des femmes*,[103] signalling Halimi's overall agreement with Beauvoir's thesis.

In her 1978 introduction to *La Cause des femmes*, Halimi reiterates several points put forward by Beauvoir. She criticises Freud for his masculine and essentialist perspective on women, and contests the universality of his ideas;[104] she finds that women are the first to reproduce the schemas of their own alienation;[105] and she agrees with Beauvoir's analysis of the role played by myths in women's objectification and reduction to the Other.[106] She agrees that women often accept their oppression and have recourse to 'the weapon of the weak – bad faith',[107] and that 'procreation remains the essential link in the machinery of this oppression';[108] that woman is oppressed foremost in the family;[109] and that to escape her oppression she must be economically independent.[110] Halimi is virulent against unwanted pregnancy, which she compares to a cancer, and her defence during the Bobigny trial was instrumental in the elaboration of the *Loi Veil* of 1975 legalising abortion. However, she holds a more positive view of maternity as a choice than Beauvoir, having had three children herself.

In the 1992 introduction to *La Cause des femmes*, a definite move away from Beauvoir's feminism, from universalisation towards an affirmation of difference and the specificity of women, is noticeable. She writes: 'The female citizen is not the male citizen and the affirmation of an egalitarian identity engenders a reductive equality.'[111] In *Le Lait de l'oranger*, Halimi concedes that *The Second Sex* provided a theoretical basis for feminism,[112] but she also denounces 'the excesses of the beginning of feminism',[113] the danger that exists in only claiming equality, because 'the world is not androgynous and the egalitarian assimilation of everyone would only come about along the lines of a single model, that of man.'[114] In her 'Plaidoyer pour une démocratie paritaire' ['Plea for equal democratic representation'], she goes further, saying of the concept of universality: 'it acts *objectively* against justice and real equality. Perversely, it turns back against women's claims for equality.'[114]

Otherwise, the main difference between Halimi and the Beauvoir of *The Second Sex* is that Halimi believes in the need for specific political action to change women's situation.[115] She has never thought that the advent of socialism would be enough to liberate women: 'the transition to socialism is ... a necessary condition [of women's liberation] but in no case sufficient.'[116] Women must fight their own battles, through militant action, legal reforms, and above all political parity. Given these convictions, she finds *The Second Sex* lacking, in its omission of recommendations for practical action.

Beauvoir herself soon accused *Choisir* of not being radical enough, perhaps even of being made up of 'wicked reformists' (Halimi's words).[117] Refusing the presidency of *Choisir*, she accepted that of *Questions Féministes* instead.

Questions Féministes (QF), Nouvelles Questions Féministes (NQF), Françoise Armengaud and Christine Delphy

Although as Armengaud, who is on the editorial board of NQF, stressed, QF never wanted to situate themselves as disciples of Beauvoir – there being hardly any references to Beauvoir in past issues of QF and NQF – she agrees that QF's feminism is close to Beauvoir's: 'A more precise link with Simone de Beauvoir occurs at the level of Chapter 3 of *The Second Sex* on historical materialism.' On reading QF and NQF, and the work produced by writers associated with the journal – Colette Guillaumin, Nicole-Claude Mathieu, and in particular Christine Delphy – this constellation of works can be viewed as a radicalisation of *The Second Sex*'s culturalist thesis.

In the first issue of QF in 1977, in the article 'Variation on common themes', the collective define their aims as being those of materialist feminism. They share Beauvoir's non-differentialist, non-essentialist approach. 'Arguments that have recourse to "nature" must be shattered.'[118] QF go further than Beauvoir in the rejection of biology. This rejection is an epistemological choice on their behalf, as Armengaud pointed out. QF consider that only social factors are pertinent to the analysis of women's oppression. For this reason, Delphy criticises *The Second Sex* for its eclecticism, its juxtaposition of various, in fact contradictory, theoretical frameworks; which means, for example, that a certain biologism cohabits with a sociological approach.

Beauvoir considered gender to be the result of education and social expectation, and that it was a social construction. The adherents of QF go further in positing that not only is gender socially constructed, but sex is too. Christine Delphy has expanded this hypothesis in 'Rethinking sex and gender'. She believes that our view of anatomical sex is an effect of the hierarchy between genders. For her: 'gender precedes sex: ... sex itself simply marks a social division; ... it serves to allow social recognition and identification of those who are dominants and those who are dominated.'[119]

Although Beauvoir identified and described the oppression of women in *The Second Sex*, there is little sense of men's responsibility for this oppression. She did not envisage women as constituting a class dominated by the class of men. On the contrary,

Beauvoir argued that women could not constitute a class, nor even a community. QF on the other hand theorises the relation between men and women as a relation of power between two classes, where men are accused of being the oppressors. The conceptual tools used by QF are derived from Marxism. Delphy in 'A materialist feminism is possible'[120] argues for the need to carry out a materialist analysis of women's oppression. She affirms that 'women and men are *social* groups[121] and that 'men are the class which oppresses and exploits women.'[122] In her analysis, Delphy always starts from socio-economic relations and shows how sexist ideology emerges from the relations of production. She is totally opposed to any approach, like Leclerc's in *Parole de femme*, which attempts to change values without modifying the relations of production first, hence her virulent attack on this book in 'Protofeminism and antifeminism'.[123] When one analyses society, one understands that it is not so much capitalists who appropriate women's labour – as socialist feminists (and the early Beauvoir?) who hold capitalism responsible for women's oppression would have us believe – but men: the system to be destroyed is not just capitalism, but patriarchy.[124] An autonomous women's struggle is therefore necessary.[125] The main site of oppression for women, and of inequality between the sexes, is the family, where patriarchal and capitalist exploitation are combined.[126]

The aim of QF is eventually to 'deconstruct the notion of "sex difference"',[127] to go beyond the relevance of anatomical difference in the construction of identity. Their ideal is therefore very close to that of Beauvoir, as expressed in some passages of *The Second Sex* (for example, SS722–3). Like Beauvoir, they want 'access to the neuter, the general';[128] they want to 'reclaim for ourselves all human potentials, including those unduly established as masculine';[129] and they reject the idea of a woman's language as an illusion.

Monique Wittig

In 1980 a rift opened amongst the materialist feminists of QF over the issue of lesbianism. Radical lesbians, amongst them Wittig, claimed that lesbianism was the only viable political choice to make, once the premise that men and women were enemy classes was accepted.

In spite of this break with QF, Wittig's theoretical position retains many elements of QF's analysis. She shares the materialist approach; the idea that it is 'oppression that creates sex'[130] and turns women into sexual beings; that men and women form social classes; the aim to 'destroy politically, philosophically, and symbolically the categories of 'men' and 'women';[131] the claim of the universal for oneself; as well as a distrust of psychoanalysis. However, while patriarchy is the system under attack in NQF — and in *The Second Sex* — Wittig's criticism is aimed more specifically at heterosexuality, which she describes as 'a social system which is based on the oppression of women by men and which produces the doctrine of the difference between the sexes to justify this oppression.'[132] Wittig views heterosexuality as 'a political regime which must be overthrown'.[133] The only way to break away from heterosexuality is to become a lesbian; a lesbian being neither a man, nor a woman, since these categories exist only as creations by heterosexuality to enforce its existence. Being a lesbian is therefore a political choice.

This political understanding of lesbianism is a far cry from Beauvoir's rather confused chapter on the lesbian in *The Second Sex*.[134] Although Beauvoir was prepared to concede that lesbianism was 'an attitude *chosen in a certain situation*' (SS444) and not a perversion or a malediction, her chapter can be regarded as verging on the homophobic, as stated by Armengaud. Not surprisingly, Wittig does not refer to this chapter of *The Second Sex* in *The Straight Mind*. But she does acknowledge Beauvoir's ground-breaking work in her article 'One is not born a Woman'.[135] Significantly, Wittig refers in her title to the first part only of Beauvoir's sentence, leaving out the 'one becomes one', thus indicating more strongly than Beauvoir ever did that this becoming need not happen. In her article she quotes the first five lines of the second volume of *The Second Sex*, lamenting that in spite of the fact that thirty years earlier Beauvoir had already denounced the myth of woman and the danger of asserting difference, many feminists still believe in difference and a biological explanation of women's oppression.

In 'Homo sum',[136] Wittig expands on the necessity of refusing difference. She shows that our civilisation has been dominated by dialectical thought which, because of the failed attempt by Marxism to dynamise the relations of the One to the Other, still has metaphysical, essentialist connotations, with the One dominating and possessing everything. She also rejects the current magnification and celebration of the Other as a trap to maintain women in their oppressed position. In particular, in 'Point of view' she rejects the concept of feminine writing: 'That there is no 'feminine writing' must be said at the outset',[137] because it reduces what is actually production and work by women to a kind of 'secretion natural to "Woman".'[138] Instead, like Beauvoir, Wittig is keen to reclaim the universal which has been appropriated by men, but which belongs to every human being. Gender, which she defines as 'the linguistic index of the political opposition between the sexes and of the domination of women',[139] must be destroyed; and she explains that it is through language that this destruction will be enacted: 'for each time I say "I", I reorganize the world from my point of view and through abstraction I lay claim to universality.'[140] She sees part of her work as a writer as being to destroy the categories of sex and gender: for example, in *Les Guérillères*, by giving to the normally exclusively feminine pronoun 'elles' a universal value, she attempts 'not to feminize the world but to make the categories of sex obsolete in language'.[141]

By taking Beauvoir's 'on ne naît pas femme' not only at the level of 'femme' meaning 'woman' but also 'female', materialist feminists, and especially radical lesbians, have transformed Beauvoir's already revolutionary sentence into an explosive one.

Conclusion

What this rapid survey of some French feminist thinkers reveals is that, while they are generally ready to recognise Beauvoir's commitment to the feminist cause, the historic importance of her work, and on the whole the accurateness of her analysis of women's oppression in a patriarchal system, very few admit to being influenced by *The Second Sex* directly. Apart from Badinter, Sarah Kofman is the only other feminist writer I interviewed who was prepared to acknowledge such an influence. She told me:

> I would have been less sensitive to what I call women's becoming in the texts of Freud and Nietzsche if I had not come to them,

thanks to existentialism, and to Simone de Beauvoir's 'one is not born, but rather becomes a woman,' equipped with a non-essentialist conception of man in general and woman in particular. This sentence oriented my reading of Freud's lectures on femininity.

In *The Enigma of Woman* Kofman echoes Beauvoir in her analysis of Freud's reflection on women: 'One is not a woman, one is not born a woman, one becomes a woman.'[142] Although Sarah Kofman's more recent theoretical position shifted away from her original interest in existentialism, she was still happy to acknowledge *The Second Sex* as an early influence on her work.

But how is it that so few individual feminists are willing to recognise any connection between their work and *The Second Sex*, when at the same time, *The Second Sex* can be cited as a major reference for French feminism by Picq?[143]

The nature of the MLF certainly militated against recognition of Beauvoir. As Le Doeuff told me, the feminist movement in France was 'leftist, against star personalities' and encouraged women to trust their own experience, rather than to consult books. Delphy also referred to the unease the movement felt vis-à-vis someone who was already considered as a monument.[144]

In addition, to declare an interest in *The Second Sex* in the 1970s was to set oneself apart from the fashionable Parisian intellectual scene, whose *maîtres à penser* were no longer Sartre, but Lacan, Foucault and Derrida. Le Doeuff told me that when she started her research on *The Second Sex*, she 'was considered behind the times'.

This ideological shift created a distance between Beauvoir's work and the differentialists. It is hardly surprising that Cixous, Chawaf, Fouque, Gauthier, Irigaray, Kristeva and Leclerc should stress the distance between their ideas and those of *The Second Sex*. For Beauvoir, difference was the source of oppression: her strategy was to minimise difference, and to combat the social and cultural differences between men and women, as in patriarchy these differences have come to constitute a hierarchy. For differentialist feminists, it is woman's very difference which must be the starting point for any reflection, and for change in society, whether this difference is woman's ability to give birth, her libidinal economy, her writing or her closeness to the unconscious. When differentialists refer to Beauvoir, if they do,[145] it is to refute her position: to present it, at worst as harmful, at best as a necessary, but outmoded stage in feminism.

The absence of references to *The Second Sex* in the work of the materialist feminists is more surprising, given the similarity of their premises, and the closeness of Beauvoir to their strategies for action. Delphy explained this absence in her own work by the necessity in sociology of referring only to up-to-date material. It is also the case that, since materialist feminists choose to concentrate on the social mechanisms of the oppression of women, adopting in doing so a materialist perspective, Beauvoir's idealist text, her eclectic approach, and especially the fact she even considers biology, are irksome to them, and as a consequence they tend to ignore her achievements.

The fact that most French feminists do not refer in their work to *The Second Sex* could be taken as encouraging, if considered as a sign of the progress feminism has made since 1949, progress which might make Beauvoir's claims for women seem redundant to today's women.

But there is a more negative aspect to French feminists' reluctance to recognise Beauvoir's contribution to feminist thought. Beauvoir's age, her fame, her having written *The Second Sex* in 1949, her position of authority and her manner, all contributed to making her seem a mother figure to French feminists. But this was not seen positively in the MLF: women, emerging from May 1968, rejected the possessive, castrating image of the mother, and were as a consequence prone to denigrate the work of previous women. They were often unable to evaluate positively the heritage handed down to them, an attitude detrimental to feminism, as Geneviève Prost explains: 'if the "daughters" continue to be intransigent, scornful, even hateful towards the mothers who preceded them and who prepared the way, none of them will have any chance of seeing our claims realised even a little.'[146]

Today, thanks to the work done by writers such as Irigaray, there is a greater awareness of the divisive effect of patriarchal ideology on women, and especially on mothers and daughters. But this does not prevent even leading French feminists from entertaining a rather ambivalent relationship with *The Second Sex* and its author. This ambivalence is testimony to the difficulty of the task, so crucial to feminism, of creating a genealogy of women.

Notes

1 Although it is impossible to measure the influence of a text solely by reference to the number of copies published, 499,849 copies have been published in France of the first volume of *Le Deuxième Sexe,* and 425,715 of the second volume. I would like to thank Sylvie le Bon de Beauvoir and Gallimard for letting me have these figures.

2 Toril Moi, *Sexual/Textual Politics* (London: Methuen, 1985). For a virulent criticism of this portrayal of French feminism, see Christine Delphy, 'The invention of French feminism: An essential move', *Yale French Studies,* 87 (1995), 190–221. While the objections put forward by Delphy are in many ways well-founded, their tone is symptomatic of the deep animosity that still separates the two major currents of French feminism – the differentialist and the egalitarian feminists – and of the power struggles still taking place in Paris, in spite of the fact that the feminist debate is much less in the limelight than it was in the 1970s.

3 Toril Moi, *Simone de Beauvoir: The Making of an Intellectual Woman* (Oxford: Basil Blackwell, 1994), pp. 182–4.

4 Ibid., p. 182.

5 These 'labels' are indications for readers who might be less familiar with these thinkers, but are not meant as strict categories.

6 I interviewed Françoise Armengaud, Elisabeth Badinter, Chantal Chawaf, Hélène Cixous, Christine Delphy, Antoinette Fouque, Xavière Gauthier, Gisèle Halimi, Sarah Kofman, Julia Kristeva, Annie Leclerc, Michèle Le Doeuff, Michelle Perrot, and talked to Luce Irigaray. Quotations without references are from these interviews held during 1993–94.

7 While Toril Moi analyses the psychological mechanisms which underlie the reception of Beauvoir's work, I have tried to concentrate on the continuity or rejection of the ideas of *The Second Sex* in later texts.

8 Claire Duchen, *Women's Rights and Women's Lives in France, 1944–1968* (London: Routledge, 1994), p. 3.

9 Accounts of the reception of *The Second Sex* are to be found in Moi, *Simone de Beauvoir,* pp. 78–85; Claude Francis and Fernand Gonthier, *Simone de Beauvoir* (Paris: Perrin, 1985), pp. 274–7; and Simone de Beauvoir, *Force of Circumstance,* trans. R. Howard (New York: Putnam, 1976, and Harmondsworth: Penguin Books, 1978), pp. 203–11; originally published as *La Force des choses* (Paris: Gallimard, Coll. Folio, 1963), pp. 195–203. Subsequent page references to de Beauvoir's work are in parentheses in the text.

10 J. Rabaut, *Histoires des féminismes français* (Paris: Stock, 1978), p. 319. Unless otherwise stated, when there is an existing English translation of a French work from which I quote, I give the quotation from the translation; when there is no easily available translation, I give my own translation. Where it is necessary to make the distinction within the text or notes, page references to the English translations (where appropriate) are in round brackets; those to the French texts in square brackets.

11   Collections of testimonies can be found in *Elle*, 'Enquête «Que représente pour vous Simone de Beauvoir?»', 28 avril 1986, 77–9; Gallimard's press pack; *Simone de Beauvoir Studies*, 3 (1985–86), and 'Elles sont pour, Simone de Beauvoir, de la mémoire aux projets: rencontre du 16 décembre 1989', copy in Marguerite Durand library, Paris.

12   Elisabeth Badinter, 'Femmes, vous lui devez tout', *Le Nouvel Observateur*, 18–24 avril 1986, 39.

13   *Elle*, 'Enquête «Que représente pour vous Simone de Beauvoir?»'.

14   Michèle Le Doeuff, *Hipparchia's Choice: An Essay Concerning Women, Philosophy, etc.*, trans. Trista Selous (Oxford: Basil Blackwell, 1991), p. 57; originally published as *L'Étude et le rouet, des femmes, de la philosophie, etc.* (Paris: Seuil, 1989), pp. 70–1.

15   Hélène V. Wenzel, 'Interview with Simone de Beauvoir', *Yale French Studies*, 72 (1986), 7.

16   See Moi, *Simone de Beauvoir*, Chapter 3, for analysis.

17   Geneviève Gennari, *Simone de Beauvoir* (Paris: Editions Universitaires, 1958).

18   Ibid., p. 103.

19   Ibid., p. 96.

20   Suzanne Lilar, *Le Malentendu du Deuxième sexe* (Paris: PUF, 1969), p. 7.

21   Cf. J. Prasteau, 'Suzanne contre Simone, Lilar contre Beauvoir', *Le Figaro Littéraire*, 29.9–5.10 (1969), 25, which dramatises Beauvoir and Lilar's opposition as 'an impending duel between women'.

22   Ibid., p. 20.

23   Maïté Albistur and Daniel Armogathe, *Histoire du féminisme français du moyen âge à nos jours* (Paris: des femmes, 1977), p. 606.

24   Monique Remy, *De l'utopie à l'intégration, Histoire des mouvements de femmes* (Paris: L'Harmattan, 1990), p. 29.

25   Josyane Savigneau, 'La Mort de Simone de Beauvoir, une mère symbolique', *Le Monde*, 16 avril 1986, 19.

26   Claude Sarraute, 'Féminisme=humanisme', *Le Monde*, 6–7 avril 1975.

27   Nancy Huston, 'Les Enfants de Simone de Beauvoir', *La Vie en rose* (mars, 1984), 41–4: 41.

28   Françoise Picq, *Libération des femmes, les années-mouvement* (Paris: Seuil, 1993), p. 24.

29   Ibid., p. 26.

30   Ibid., p. 29.

31   Geneviève Fraisse, *Révolution*, 18 avril 1986.

32   M. Chapsal, 'Simone de Beauvoir, une femme qui parle parmi les femmes', *Elle*, 12 février 1979.

33   All the more so in that, as Le Doeuff pointed out to me, the sexism of existentialism reinforced the already misogynist religious discourses that

Beauvoir would have been exposed to in her youth.

34 Le Doeuff, *Hipparchia's Choice*, (1991), p. 60; [1989], p. 74.

35 Michèle Le Doeuff, 'Simone de Beauvoir: les ambiguïtés d'un ralliement', *Le Magazine Littéraire*, 320 (1994), 58–61: 61. Trans. by Margaret A. Simons as 'Simone de Beauvoir: falling into (ambiguous) line', in Margaret A. Simons (ed.), *Feminist Interpretations of Simone de Beauvoir* (University Park: Penn State Press, 1995), pp. 59–65: 64.

36 Le Doeuff, *Hipparchia's Choice*, (1991), p. 57; [1989], p. 70.

37 Ibid., (1991), p.106; [1989], p. 123.

38 Ibid., (1991), p. 120; [1989], p. 138.

39 Ibid., (1991), p. 170; [1989], p. 190.

40 Ibid., (1991), p. 133); [1989]: p. 152.

41 Antoinette Fouque, 'Moi et elle', *Libération*, 15.4. (1986).

42 Antoinette Fouque, 'Il y a deux sexes', in M. Negrón (ed.), *Lectures de la différence sexuelle* (Paris: des femmes, 1994), pp. 283–317: 288.

43 Ibid., p. 288. Fouque points out ironically here that both Freud and Beauvoir insist on the becoming of women.

44 Ibid., p. 291

45 Ibid., p. 300.

46 Ibid., p. 315.

47 'Paroles avec Antoinette Fouque [entretien avec Isabelle Huppert]', *Cahiers du Cinéma*, 477 (1994), 36–49: 43.

48 Fouque, 'Il y a deux sexes', p. 45.

49 Chantal Chawaf, *Le Corps et le verbe, la langue en sens inverse* (Paris: Presses de la Renaissance, 1992), p. 130.

50 Hélène Cixous, 'The laugh of the Medusa', in Elaine Marks and Isabelle de Courtivron (eds), *New French Feminisms: An Anthology*, trans. Keith Cohen and Paula Cohen (Brighton: Harvester, 1981), pp. 245–64: 255; translation of 'Le Rire de la Méduse', *L'Arc*, 61 (1975), 39–54: 46.

51 Moi, *Simone de Beauvoir*, (1994), p. 182.

52 Moi explains this absence as 'an effort to snub Beauvoir, a deliberate challenge to the *doyenne* of French feminism, and more specifically, as Cixous's bid for power' (Toril Moi, 'Appropriating Bourdieu: feminist theory and Pierre Bourdieu's sociology of culture', *New Literary History*, 22 (1991), 1017–49: 1041), and she analyses Cixous's move as an attempt to displace the Oedipal mother.

53 Alice Jardine, 'Interview with Simone de Beauvoir', *Signs*, 5:2 (1979), 224–36: 229–30.

54 Xavière Gauthier, 'Femmes, une autre écriture?', *Le Magazine Littéraire*, 180 (1982), 17.

55 Anne-Marie de Vilaine, 'Le Corps de la théorie', in 'Femmes, une autre écri-

ture?', (1982), 25–8: 28.

56 Xavière Gauthier, 'Lutte de femmes', *Tel Quel*, 58 (1974), 93–7: 96.

57 Xavière Gauthier, *Rose saignée* (Paris: des femmes, 1974).

58 In a personal letter. Annie Leclerc, *Parole de femme* (Paris: Grasset & Fasquelle, 1974).

59 Leclerc, *Parole*, p. 5.

60 Ibid., p. 10.

61 Ibid., p. 124.

62 Ibid., p. 11.

63 Ibid., p. 39.

64 Ibid., p. 109.

65 Ibid., p. 99.

66 Annie Leclerc, 'Patronne des femmes?', *La Croix*, 16.4. (1986) [Gallimard Press Pack]

67 Luce Irigaray, *Je, Tu, Nous, Towards a Culture of Difference,* trans. A. Martin (London: Routledge, 1993), p. 9. Translation of *Je, tu, nous, Pour une culture de la différence* (Paris: Grasset & Fasquelle, 1990), p. 9.

68 Ibid., p. 11 [p. 11].

69 Naomi Schor, 'This essentialism which is not one: coming to grips with Irigaray', *Differences*, 1:2 (1989), 38–58: 43.

70 Luce Irigaray, *Ce sexe qui n'en est pas un* (Paris: Minuit, 1977), pp. 79–80. Trans. by Catherine Porter with Carolyn Burke as *This Sex which Is not One* (Ithaca: Cornell University Press, 1985). Beauvoir approved of Irigaray's trying to construct a feminist psychoanalysis, cf., Jardine, 'Inteview', p. 228.

71 Luce Irigaray, 'Interview', in E. Hoffman Baruch, *Women Analyse Women: In France, England, and the United States* (London: Harvester Wheatsheaf, 1988), pp. 149–64: 151.

72 Ibid., p. 151.

73 Ibid., p. 156.

74 Luce Irigaray, 'And the one doesn't stir without the other', *Signs*, 7:1 (1981), 60–7: 60. Translation by H. V. Wenzel of *Et l'une ne bouge pas sans l'autre* (Paris: Minuit, 1979): p. 7.

75 Margaret Whitford in *Luce Irigaray: Philosophy in the Feminine* (London: Routledge, 1991) states in a note that although Irigaray does not mention Beauvoir except in 'Equal or different' she suspects that 'a comparison would reveal more debt than she [Irigaray] acknowledges'(p. 216).

76 Irigaray, 'Inteview', (1988), p. 153.

77 Ibid., p. 160.

78 Ibid., p. 161.

79 Luce Irigaray, F. Clédat, X. Gauthier, and A.-M. Vilaine, 'L'Autre de la nature', *Sorcières*, 20 (1980), 14–25: 16.

80 Ibid., p. 16.

81 Luce Irigaray, 'L'Identité féminine, biologie ou conditionnement social?' in Gisèle Halimi (ed.), *Femmes, moitié de la terre, moitié du pouvoir* (Paris: Gallimard, 1994), pp. 101–8: p. 104.

82 Ibid., p. 106.

83 Irigaray, *Je, tu, nous*, p. 13; [1990], p. 13.

84 Luce Irigaray, *J'aime à toi* (Paris: Grasset, 1992), p. 168.

85 Judith Butler, *Gender Trouble, Feminism and the Subversion of Identity* (London and New York: Routledge, 1990), pp. 8–13.

86 Luce Irigaray, 'The question of the other', *Yale French Studies*, 87 (1995), 7–19: 8.

87 Irigaray, *Je, tu, nous*, p. 13; [1990], p. 14.

88 Irigaray *et al.*, 'L'Autre de la nature', p. 25.

89 Julia Kristeva, 'Women's time', *Signs*, 7 (1981), 13–35; repr. in *The Kristeva Reader*, ed. Toril Moi (Oxford: Basil Blackwell, 1986), pp. 187–213; translation by Alice Jardine and Harry Blake of 'Le Temps des femmes', *33/44: Cahiers de recherche de sciences des textes et documents*, 5 (Winter, 1979), 5–19; repr. in Julia Kristeva, *Les Nouvelles Maladies de l'âme* (Paris: Fayard, 1993), pp. 297–331.

90 Ibid., in Kristeva, *Les Nouvelles Maladies*, p. 193; in Moi (ed.), *The Kristeva Reader*, p. 306.

91 Julia Kristeva, 'Stabat mater', in Moi (ed.), *The Kristeva Reader*, pp. 160–86: 183.

92 Julia Kristeva, 'À propos des *Samouraïs* (entretien)', *L'Infini*, 30 (été, 1990), 65. I would like to thank John Lechte for this information.

93 A detailed and sophisticated comparison between Beauvoir and Kristeva's conceptualisation of maternity can be found in the article by Linda Zerilli 'A process without a subject: Simone de Beauvoir and Julia Kristeva on maternity', *Signs*, 18: 1 (1992), 111–35. In particular Zerilli stresses the political strength of Beauvoir's position over Kristeva's in challenging the eternal maternal, and reproaches the latter with having caricatured Beauvoir's analysis in 'Women's time', while actually several elements of Kristeva's critique of maternity in patriarchy can already be found in *The Second Sex*: the radical splitting of the female subject in pregnancy, the denunciation of the illusion of creativity in pregnancy, the mechanisms by which men veil the horror that gestation and their origins arouse in them.

94 The picture is reproduced on the front cover of Moi (ed.), *The Kristeva Reader*. The disagreement was already expressed in Kristeva, 'Stabat mater', in Moi, *The Kristeva Reader*, p. 171.

95 Kristeva, 'Women's time', in Moi (ed.), *The Kristeva Reader*, p. 209; 'Le Temps des femmes', in *Les Nouvelles Maladies*, p. 328.

96 Elisabeth Badinter, *Man/Woman, The One is the Other* (London: Collins Harvill, 1989), p. xv; translation by Barbara Wright of *L'Un est l'autre, des relations entre hommes et femmes* (Paris: Odile Jacob, 1986), p. 14.

97 Elisabeth Badinter, *XY, de l'identité masculine* (Paris: Odile Jacob, 1992), p. 50.

98 Badinter, *Man/Woman*, p. 53.

99 Ibid., p. 60.

100 Trial in 1972 of three women accused of having procured an abortion for the daughter of one of them. Halimi defended the women and attacked the repressive law of 1920 criminalising abortion. Her action and that of *Choisir* is documented in Gisèle Halimi, *La Cause des femmes* (Paris: Gallimard, 1992).

101 343 well-known women (among them Simone de Beauvoir) signed a text in which they admitted to having had an abortion, demanded free access to birth-control methods and freedom of abortion. The petition was published in *Le Nouvel Observateur*, 5 avril (1971), thus bringing contraception and abortion to the centre of public debate.

102 Gisèle Halimi, *La Cause des femmes*, p. 297.

103 Ibid. The book was first published in 1973. Subsequent page references in notes are to the 1992 edition.

104 Ibid., p. 16.

105 Ibid., p. 17.

106 Ibid., p. 18.

107 Ibid., p. xv.

108 Ibid., p. 167.

109 Ibid., p. 166.

110 Ibid., p. 211.

111 Ibid., p. xxii.

112 Gisèle Halimi, *Le Lait de l'oranger* (Paris: Gallimard, 1988), p. 316.

113 Ibid., p. 288.

114 At the same time she refutes Badinter's thesis, insisting that 'the *one* is not the *other*' (p. 288).

114 Gisèle Halimi, 'Plaidoyer pour une démocratie paritaire', in Gisèle Halimi (ed.), *Femmes, moitié de la terre*, pp. 11–22: 16.

115 Simone Veil's evolution is similar: she too was 'excited' (Halimi (ed.), *Femmes, moitié de la terre*, p. 265) when she first read *The Second Sex* in the late 1960s or early 1970s, but finds she is no longer in agreement with Beauvoir, believing now in the affirmation of difference.

116 Halimi, *La Cause des femmes*, p. 203.

117 Halimi, *Le Lait de l'oranger*, p. 326.

118 'Variations sur des thèmes communs', *Questions Féministes*, 1 (Nov., 1977),

pp 3–19. Trans. as 'Variations on common themes' in Marks and de Courtivron (eds), *New French Feminisms*, pp. 212–30: 214.

119 Christine Delphy, 'Rethinking sex and gender', *Women's Studies International Forum*, 16:1 (1993), 1–9: 5.

120 In Christine Delphy, *Close to Home: A Materialist Analysis of Women's Oppression*, trans. and ed. by Diana Leonard (London: Hutchinson, 1984).

121 Ibid., p. 24.

122 Ibid., p. 179.

123 Ibid.

124 Ibid., p. 140.

125 Ibid., p. 58.

126 Christine Delphy and Diana Leonard, *Familiar Exploitation, A New Analysis of Marriage in Contemporary Western Societies* (Cambridge: Polity Press, 1992).

127 'Variations on common themes', p. 214.

128 Ibid., p. 222.

129 Ibid., p. 222.

130 Monique Wittig, *The Straight Mind and Other Essays* (Boston: Beacon and London: Harvester Wheatsheaf, 1992), p. 2.

131 Ibid., p. xiii–xiv.

132 Ibid., p. 20.

133 Ibid., p. ix.

134 Beauvoir never publicly acknowledged a lesbian identity in spite of sexual bonds with women, and *The Second Sex*, even if it recognises the possibility of an authentic lesbian choice, is written within the general framework of heterosexuality. To say, as Margaret Simons does, that 'Beauvoir's feminist philosophy disrupts the boundaries of heterosexual and lesbian identity' (Margaret A. Simons, 'Lesbian connections, Simone de Beauvoir and feminism', *Signs*, 18:1 (1992), 136–61: 160) may be a rather overstated reading.

135 As Butler points out, by subscribing to the idea that it is oppression that creates sex, Wittig actually rewrites Beauvoir's sentence. For her, not only is one not born a woman, but one is not born female either: Judith Butler, *Gender Trouble, Feminism and the Subversion of Identity* (London and New York: Routledge, 1990), p. 113.

136 'Homo sum', in Wittig, *The Straight Mind*.

137 Wittig, *The Straight Mind*, p. 59.

138 Ibid., p. 60.

139 Ibid., p. 77.

140 Ibid., p. 81.

141 Ibid., p. 85.

142 Sarah Kofman, *The Enigma of Woman: Woman in Freud's Writings* (London: Cornell University Press, 1985), p. 122; translated by Catherine Porter from *L'Énigme de la femme, la femme dans les textes de Freud* (Paris: Editions Galilée, 1980), p. 146.

143 Picq, *Libération des femmes*. Or by M.-J. Dhavernas: '*The Second Sex* is certainly the work that most left its mark on the generation of feminists who experienced May 1968' and 'the essential ideas which it contains have become part of the common store of feminism' (*Le Monde* (15 avril 1986))?

144 Delphy also pointed out that it was easier for French feminists to recognise the influence of American feminists such as Betty Friedan, and for American feminists to acknowledge Beauvoir's work.

145 This article, by concentrating on passages in French feminists' works where there are open or veiled references to *The Second Sex*, may even have given a biased idea of its importance for them.

146 Geneviève Prost, 'Merci Simone', *Paris Féministes*, 26 (1986), 13–14: 14. Le Doeuff pointed out to me that if many feminists found it difficult to accept a spiritual mother, such reluctance did not seem to apply as far as spiritual fathers were concerned, the influence of Lacan, Freud and Derrida being easily recognised. One could also add that Beauvoir herself behaved similarly, that she tended to minimise the work of previous women, while being quite happy to acknowledge Sartre's influence.

4

Simone de Beauvoir:
transcending fictions

LORNA SAGE

Art is not a mirage

'Through literature,' Simone de Beauvoir wrote, 'one justifies the world by creating it anew, in the purity of the imaginary, and by the same token, one justifies one's own existence.'[1] It may sound at this distance in time a safely vague, uplifting declaration of faith, but it was not. Indeed, she meant it as a kind of parody of other people's religions of art. Writing affirms human liberty, for Beauvoir, but only writing that has sloughed off the bad faith of sublimity and spilt religion. In this essay I want to look again at Beauvoir the writer as an iconoclast and a utopian. She has been mistaken for a realist, in part because of her open hostility to self-reflexive, experimental writing, but in fact she is, I shall argue, best understood as an anti-realist – a writer who systematically destabilised the relations between past and present, work and world, on which realism depends. She has more in common with the *nouveau roman*, and a novelist like Nathalie Sarraute, than might at first appear. She too is preoccupied with the writer's role – though in her case this leads her into autobiography, sexual politics and the obsessive demolition of cultural fictions. Her main creation was herself-as-writer: writing became for her a process of retreating ahead of herself, living for the future.

In *When Things of the Spirit Come First* (her early sequence of apprentice 'tales' eventually published forty years on, in 1979) she is savagely knowing at the expense of pretentious Chantal, who writes a diary designed to bear witness to her superior

sensibility. An example: Chantal describes her search for lodgings
in a provincial city where she's about to take up a teaching job:

> ... after I had looked at five dreary places ... I found this old house,
> whose massive outer doors seemed less to bar the entrance to a
> dwelling than the way into a soul. An exceedingly distinguished
> white-haired lady led me very graciously though the garden, and
> then through her apartment; even before I had seen my room I was
> entirely won over. These walls contain all that is most touching in
> provincial France: the mellow surface of the old furniture, the
> books in their rare bindings ... in every corner of this house the
> vanished past has left an impalpable scent − one that gives the
> present the rare and heady bouquet of a very old wine .... I feel
> more ardently than ever, that in spite of everything Life is
> wonderful.[2]

She is making herself imaginatively at home, snuggling down
into a nest of stock responses which if she were English would
have been woven out of Dickensian echoes, but in France suggest
Balzac, with several generations of quotation in between. Chantal,
in fact, has a taste for the modern − Proust, Rilke, Katherine
Mansfield − but she contrives to turn everything she reads into
a script for day-dreaming. She's well-insulated against the raw real.

Chantal lies to herself as well as to others (this is her diary,
after all), and she does it in the name of something ineffable she
calls 'Life' − which is, of course, emphatically not what Beauvoir
means by 'existence' ('one justifies one's own existence').
Looking back on the time when she wrote these stories, Beauvoir
said that Chantal (though based mainly on a hated colleague) bore
a resemblance to her own young self: 'If the bad habits which I
attributed to Chantal irked me so much, that was because ... I had
slipped into them myself.'[3] Like Chantal, she says, she'd embell-
ished her own life history, too, in those days. And she believed
in 'Life' back then: 'Sartre and I were seeking some kind of
"salvation" ... we were, in fact, a couple of mystics. Sartre had
an unqualified faith in Beauty, which he treated as inseparable
from Art; while I attached supreme importance to Life' (*The
Prime of Life*, p. 26). Literature had to free itself from those
nostalgic fakes, those dead Ideas or essences (Beauty, Art, Life) if
it was to become a real vocation, a proper project.

The last story in *Things of the Spirit* was, Beauvoir said, the best (though she did not think she was saying much). It is certainly the nearest to a portrait of the artist, and it stages at the end a kind of anti-revelation. The world around the narrator, Marguerite, is stripped of its 'bouquet', and hence its bad magic: 'it was as though a spell were fading. Suddenly, instead of symbolic scenery, I saw around me a host of objects that seemed to exist in their own right. All along the pavement little cafés came into being ...' (p. 201) This is the public world (Chantal nestles indoors), the world where you look on, write (all her life Beauvoir would write at café tables), share the space. Interestingly enough, Beauvoir privileges this character with a retrospective view of herself. Marguerite judges that her awakening may sound all too epiphanic: 'At the time I attributed too much importance to what I may call this kind of revelation; it was not a conversion of a spiritual nature that could rid me of spirituality .... all I have wished to do was to show how I was brought to try to look things straight in the face, without accepting oracles or ready-made values' (p. 201). At this point she ceases in effect to be a character at all, and merges with her author – recognisably the same writer who will say in her 1979 Preface, at seventy, 'In the end, her eyes are opened, she tosses mysteries, mirages and myths overboard and looks the world in the face ...' (p. 8). You trade in Life for the world, the old cosy writing that lent significance and soul to things for a new world of existence, where people and things are on a level, the realm of what she and Sartre called contingency.

So writing begins with a process of demystification. The early stories, clumsy as they were, mapped out many of Beauvoir's abiding themes, and even some of her later strategies. The quest for a point of vantage on one's self is the same one that will inspire her to write the story of herself as a writer in the autobiographies; and the obligation 'you try to look things straight in the face' stays with her to the bitter end. She became the kind of writer she was because she feared fictions ('mysteries, mirages and myths'), and she feared them because she saw them not as securely separate from the way people lived their lives, but as interwoven with our whole understanding of ourselves as characters. If she put real people into her novels, that was because she habitually assumed that people lived in and with fictions. In other words, the boundary between books and the world was permeable: 'To write a novel,' she wrote in 1966, 'is somehow to destroy the real world.'[4] Her whole life's work, and *The Second Sex* in particular, depends on the conviction that people are constructs: we come from the matrix of the culture at large, not from God, or nature, or (even) Mother.

If Beauvoir had found a publisher for *Things of the Spirit* in the late 1930s, it would have been part of the same literary moment as Sartre's novel *Nausea* (1938) and Nathalie Sarraute's first book, her collection of cunningly unclassifiable short fictions, *Tropisms* (1939). In the event the war put iconoclasm on hold, in any case. But it is worth reflecting on the common ground they shared, which was not yet the site of *literary* war between the self-consciousness of the *nouveau roman* and existentialist 'commitment'. Until the great falling-out in the 1950s it was enough that (as Beauvoir said) Sarraute 'was hostile to all essentialism' (*Force of Circumstance*, p. 27). Her attacks on mystery and false consciousness were very recognisable – though she was from the start a much more fastidious and consistent craftswoman than Beauvoir. One of her favourite tricks was to dive under the surface patina of the 'real' to discover the way it is processed and pre-digested for us. Witness this description of a chorus of bourgeois ladies at work in a teashop, from Tropism X:

> '... he won't marry her. What he needs is a good housewife; he does not realise it himself. Certainly not; I mean it. What he needs is a good housewife .... Housewife .... Housewife ....' They had always heard it said, they knew it: the sentiments, love, life, these were their domain ....
>
> And they talked and talked ... continually rolling between their fingers this unsatisfactory, mean substance that they had extracted from their lives (what they called 'life', their domain), kneading it, pulling it, rolling it until it ceased to form anything between their fingers but a little pile, a little grey pellet.[5]

This is how essences are 'born', over and over again. Beauvoir in *The Second Sex*, in her marvellously bleak chapter on 'Women's situation and character', says: 'it is not matter she comes to grips with, but Life, and Life cannot be mastered through the use of tools, one can only submit to its secret laws. The world does not seem to woman "an assemblage of implements" intermediate between her will and her goals, as Heidegger defines it' (SS609). She goes on to remark that pregnancy and cooking teach woman a fatal patience: 'time has for her no element of novelty' (SS610). Repetition is *of the essence*: it is how essences reproduce themselves.

In making this connection between Beauvoir and Sarraute I am trying to place Beauvoir not merely as an enemy of mystification, but also as an anti-realist. She may invoke 'objects', 'matter', 'things' and 'existence' as writing's proper material, but that makes her as much a sceptic about *classic* realism as Sarraute. Novels in the great nineteenth-century tradition, with their elaborate strategies for creating perspective, continuity and typicality, and finding the universal in the particular, depend on precisely the kind of metaphysical or magical underpinning Beauvoir wanted to demolish. Compare Roland Barthes (the very early Barthes, who in 1953 sounds still rather existentialist) on the nineteenth-century novel: 'the true is supposed to contain a germ of the universal, or to put it differently, an essence capable of fecundating by mere reproduction, several orders of things among which some differ by their remoteness and some by their fictional character'.[6] In her hands, fictional narratives veered back towards earlier eighteenth-century and Enlightenment modes of mimicry, and first persons jostled third persons on the page. As Sarraute said in her brilliant 1950 essay 'The age of suspicion', the distinctive sign of contemporaneity was the way writers and readers had drawn closer together. The writer's urgency to make it new – to unmake convention – became the more-or-less openly admitted theme of the narratives of now. For Beauvoir, pursuing the author's vocation became itself a vocation. She lacked the subtlety and skill and sheer passion for (and against) words of Sarraute. She was in love with the idea not of making something (the *nouveau roman* was a problematic literary object, shot through with auto-destructive irony, yet it was clearly obsessively crafted) but of self-invention, 'transcendence'. So when she broke the rules of the traditional novel form – as she did in her two most ambitious fictions, *She Came to Stay* (1943) and *The Mandarins* (1954) – it was not in order to make the *novel* new, but in order to say something about the role of the writer. In the first, she committed a barefaced authorial murder that was in no sense in her character's character: 'by releasing Françoise through the agency of a crime ... I regained my personal autonomy', she said in the autobiography (*The Prime of Life*, p. 340); anything was preferable to having her *alter ego* submit to being 'just a woman' (p. 600). In *The Mandarins* she gives the authorial role to (third person) Henri, and allows her (first person) heroine Anne nowhere to speak from, and no access to writing. As Susan Rubin Suleiman points out, in an interesting essay on Beauvoir's writing self, the narrative structure is anomalous: 'Anne's narrative discourse is impossible ... Here, then, is a curious chiasmus: Anne who is the subject of enunciation, neither speaks her narrative, nor writes it.'[7] Beauvoir readily sacrifices formal logic and decorum in order to make her escape from her own novels, in short.

Transcendence she describes in *The Second Sex* as 'escape towards some objective, through enterprise' (SS171). The world of transcendence is wide open, has a 'sky' (SS174); whereas the girl growing up discovers that society does not want her to become 'an autonomous and transcendent subject': 'The sphere to which she belongs is everywhere enclosed, limited, dominated, by the male universe ... there will always be a ceiling over her head, walls that will block her way' (SS324–5).

This metaphorically housebound woman is so thoroughly domesticated by the culture that she can – like Chantal – believe herself emancipated, a free spirit. She is, perhaps, never more self-deceived than when she sees herself as having a special intimacy with poetry, and with nature: 'Poetry is supposed to catch what exists beyond the prose of everyday; and woman is an eminently poetic reality since man projects into her all that he does not resolve to be' (SS213). All sorts of 'spiritual hocuspocus' (*The Prime of Life*, p. 222) are generated in the attempt to disguise this state of affairs, and from time to time in *The Second Sex* Beauvoir tries on the 'line', in a spirit of gross mockery: 'Society enslaves Nature; but Nature dominates it. The Spirit flames out beyond Life; but it ceases to burn when Life no longer supports it. Woman is justified by this equivocation in finding more verity in a garden than in a city, in a malady than in an idea, in a birth than in a revolution' (SS629). Women carry ideas, they are in fact conscripted by the culture at large (by men, that is) as signs and exchanged like messages (this was famously pointed out by Lévi-Strauss),[8] and when they use signs themselves, they often do so in bad faith, without a real vocation: 'for the vast majority of women an art, a profession, is only a means: in practising it they are not engaged in genuine projects' (SS585). Women read as if they were playing solitaire, and write or paint without disturbing the stereotypes that shape their lives. No wonder Beauvoir so distrusted not only traditional forms of fiction, but any pursuit of art that seemed (as of course avant-garde experiments like Sarraute's did) to cultivate a *mystery*.

The archetypal non-project, though, is 'embodying' meanings. Women are regularly endowed with allegorical significance, they are vessels or containers for abstract ideas. Or perhaps one should say, as Beauvoir does, that mythic Woman does this kind of higher housework: 'She is the soul of the house, of the family, of the home. And she is the soul of such larger groups, also, as the city, state and nation. ... in ... statues that represent France, Rome and Germania ... the Church, the Synagogue, the Republic, Humanity are women; so also are Peace, War, Liberty, the Revolution, Victory ...' (SS209–211). But still, and always, she is inside a 'house' built of fictions. Liberty may be a woman, woman incarnates the 'mystic mana' of (say) Democracy, while women are unfree, unrepresented. This is the territory Marina Warner explored in *Monuments and Maidens* in 1985, with – appropriately enough – a chapter on the public statuary of Paris, a city particularly rich in stone sirens and civic saints.

Stone is the right stuff, because it emphasises the way woman is construed as timeless – that is, exiled from history. Myth turns you to stone, 'the Eternal Feminine, unique and changeless'. (SS283) And yet of course, there is nothing actually fixed about woman's meaning: she can and does embody quite opposed symbolic values, she is a wandering signifier – 'woman incarnates no stable concept' (SS175). Beauvoir reels off whole lists of woman's allegorical roles: 'Renown and glory are women; and Mallarmé said: "The crowd is a woman"' (SS215). And she develops her own distinctive brand of mock-modernist poetry as she celebrates woman's wonderful versatility – 'She is the

triumph of victory ... she is the vertigo of ruin ... There is a whole
world of significance which exists only through woman ... she is
the source and origin of all man's reflection on his existence'
(SS228–9). The most important words in such sentences are not
the grand nouns like victory or ruin (which are mini-allegories,
fictions, false constants), but the verb to be, and the flat-sound-
ing 'existence'. Woman *is*, man reflects on his *existence*: woman
is ontologically compromised, she 'is' in bad faith. But what
about that 'is' in the last sentence – 'she is the source ... Of all
man's reflection' – is that a false construction too? Certainly it is
a compromised 'is', since it relates, not to a quality of being, but
a state of affairs, a situation that we can change; it is inessential.
Beauvoir, as her commentators have noted, does sometimes make
essentialist oppositions sound terminally true, as if she forgets,
or loses faith in, her theoretical confidence that women are in fact
part of history's processes. For now, however, I want to point to
her over-riding, destructive euphoria. If you want access to the
present and the future, you find it in the (anti-) art of demystification – 'it is by denying Woman that we can help women to
assume the status of human beings' (SS232–3).

It is not, then, excessively paradoxical to argue that *The
Second Sex* comes closer to fulfilling literature's project, for
Beauvoir – 'one justifies the world by creating it anew' – than her
novels. Toril Moi is, I think, making a very similar point when
she says that *The Second Sex* is 'the direct result of ... her autobiographical impulse'.[9] Taking over from the patriarchal author-
gods who exiled women from history, Beauvoir declares: 'I shall
place woman in a world of values and give her behaviour a
dimension of liberty. I believe that she has the power to choose
between the assertion of her transcendence and her alienation as
object ...' (SS82). In other words, 'It is not nature that defines
woman' (SS69), but culture. Many of Beauvoir's most eloquent
and memorable sentences make negative assertions of this kind:
most famously the one that says one is not born a woman, but
becomes a woman. Other examples: 'man is not a natural species:
he is a historical idea' (SS66); 'one is not born a genius, one
becomes a genius' (SS164); 'essence does not precede existence:
in pure subjectivity, the human being *is not anything*' (SS287); (on
lesbian relationships), 'Because they are not sanctioned by an

institution or by custom ... they are all the more sincere' (SS439); and, heroically and finally (though one could cull many more), 'There is no such thing as an "unnatural mother"' (SS538). The spirit of contradiction animates and inspires her prose whenever 'nature' threatens, or when nature's bourgeois apologists and their traditions are in question, particularly marriage and the family – 'The family is not a closed community ... the couple is a social unit' (SS542). She will go out of her way, on odd occasions, to mock nice middle-class ladies by treating their domestic pieties as vices. Thus, we are told of a woman who 'took to orderly housekeeping as others take to drink' (SS471); and later on, describing women's confinement in various separate spheres she learnedly and maliciously alludes to 'a dull gynaeceum' – which she glosses as 'brothel or middle-class home' (SS614).

In practice her solemn definitions of a literature that sides with change – 'Literature assumes sense and dignity when it makes its appeal to persons engaged in projects ... integrated with the movement of human transcendence' (SS605) – are realised in this eager iconoclasm, which is a form of utopian anti-art. It is perhaps worth remembering that in the autobiography she says that she liked 'hermetic poems, surrealist films, abstract art, illuminated manuscripts and ancient tapestries, African masks' and had 'a passion for watching puppet shows' (*The Prime of Life*, pp. 40–1). During her visit to the United States in 1947 she dined with Marcel Duchamp one evening, after lecturing at the New School in New York; and a party given in her honour was attended by Kurt Weill, Le Corbusier, and Charlie Chaplin.[10] Her avant-garde credentials were in good order at the time she began work on *The Second Sex*. She was conscious, too, that although she was seen in the United States as a spokesperson for existentialism, her sex rendered her, still, an anomaly – 'an existentialist *woman* was more than they could tolerate' (*Letters to Sartre*, p. 415). This, as it turned out, was to be the time when she 'chose herself' – when she decided that her American love-affair with Nelson Algren was not to change her life radically; when she returned to Paris, Sartre, and the role of the New Woman; and when she entered on middle age. She would note ironically that many a middle-aged woman 'suddenly undertakes to save her lost existence' (SS589). Hers had not been 'lost', of course. But it was only now that she justified herself, in her own terms, by uncreating mythical Woman.

Born, again

Woman she sees as impregnated with generality and timelessness: myth makes the 'real' woman, and in particular myth makes the mother. It is on the topic of motherhood that Beauvoir is most herself — that is, most radical, outrageous and inventive. Motherhood is the original of women's oppression, and of the many forms of mystical *mauvaise foi* with which they attempt to disguise it from themselves. It is woman's 'misfortune to have been biologically destined for the repetition of Life' (SS96), she is in bondage to the species. It is on this note that the book begins and ends: 'It is her duty to assure the monotonous repetition of life in all its mindless factuality. It is natural for woman to repeat, to begin again without even inventing, for time to seem to her to go round and round without ever leading anywhere' (SS615–16). In fact, here, she is describing housework, not childbearing, but you can see how the language picks up on *repetition*. When she says 'it is natural', here, she means that women's character follows from their situation, which seems (but only seems) to assimilate individual lives to a general pattern. (Her distrust of realism in its nineteenth-century form finds weighty confirmation here, too. Realist representations, looked at from her angle, are a way of reproducing the world as it is, adding to its plausibility and seeming finality.) Mother is the mythic being — the false universal — that upholds the binary oppositions that oppress actual women: immanence/transcendence, essence/existence, natural/historical, and so on. And since myths are not safely locked away in books, but work in and through our lives, then mother is a menace. You have to give birth to yourself, become self-made, and make mother redundant, in order to *exist*.

So her chapter on 'The Mother' starts, logically enough, with abortion. The gothic brutality of the gesture is still shocking: or perhaps it would be truer to say that it has become shocking in a different way from the one Beauvoir had in mind. She was intent on demystifying and secularising maternity, in a Roman Catholic culture that outlawed not only abortion but contraception. She

wanted to separate sex-for-pleasure and reproduction. All of
which now seems too obvious for words, but is not, by any
means. Feminism itself has encouraged a certain amnesia on this
issue, by making new myths of motherhood, as if the old, bad
magic had been safely exorcised. As Elaine Marks says,
Beauvoir's line on motherhood made her suspect in her turn to a
younger generation: 'The most famous French women theorists
of the past fifteen years – Hélène Cixous, Luce Irigaray, and Julia
Kristeva – have been adding to the sacred untouchable quality of
the figure of the mother within our patriarchal Judeo-Christian
tradition .... in their search for a feminine specificity, they have
once again magnified mother and motherhood'.[11] Marks could
have found matriarchal attitudes closer to home, too, of course,
notably in the work of Adrienne Rich. Since Marks's essay was
published in 1987 gender studies have developed in directions
that make more sense of Beauvoir again – towards notions of
(gay) self-fashioning, and a critique of ahistorical or nostalgic
views of the sexual character. The self-creation of transsexuals,
the discussions of the politics of fertility that surround test-tube
babies, surrogate motherhood, cloning and male 'pregnancy', all
underline the fact that the human body, and particularly the
woman's body, is less a secret garden than a public thoroughfare
scrawled over with slogans.

   Not that younger feminist writers all found Beauvoir's demystificatory savagery alienating. Fiction writers in particular – so
many of them now un-writers, or re-writers – sympathised with
her strategies. Angela Carter, in her 1977 novel *The Passion of
New Eve*, and her polemical anatomy of powerlessness, *The
Sadeian Woman* (1979), was very much in the Beauvoir tradition:
'The nature of actual modes of sexual intercourse is determined
by historical changes in less intimate human relations, just as the
actual nature of men and women is capable of infinite modula-
tions as social structures change ....'[12] Indeed, in ironically enlisting Sade as an ally Carter was realising a project Beauvoir only
sketched in her 1953 essay titled 'Must we burn Sade?'.[13]
Beauvoir's use of Montherlant in *The Second Sex* follows the same
unscrupulous pattern: his attacks on motherhood would be fine,
she says, if only he were not actually myth-making in his turn:
'If Montherlant had really deflated the myth of the eternal femi-

nine, it would be in order to congratulate him on the achievement: it is by denying Woman that we can help women ...
(SS232–3). The affinities between Carter and Beauvoir are less
obvious than they might be because Carter in her fiction adopted
the old magical motifs and turned them on their heads carnival-
style, rather than abusing and banishing them as did Beauvoir.
Margaret Atwood, too, re-engages with the themes of *The Second
Sex*. Her 1973 novel *Surfacing* was bewitched by exactly the
mystique of motherhood Beauvoir attacked: 'The animals have
no need for speech, why talk when you are a word I lean against
a tree I am a tree leaning .... I am not an animal or a tree, I am the
thing in which the trees and animals move and grow, I am a
place.'[14] This nameless and pregnant narrator is an allegory of
threatened Nature – in other words, very much the product of
later twentieth-century culture, though neither she (nor her
author) saw it that way at the time. Atwood produced her own
revisionist treatment of the same myth (*as myth* this time) in her
dystopian fable *The Handmaid's Tale* (1985). Her earlier fertility-
fiction becomes a nightmare, set in a born-again biblical theoc-
racy where women 'are' wombs – 'I sink down into my body as
into a swamp, fenland.'[15] To be a place, a space, is to become, in
this book, a carrier of the state's meanings. In Atwood's dystopia
female literacy is being denied and abolished, women are words,
they do not use them – or at least not in elaborate or public ways.

It is no accident that such revisionist writers home in on the
Mother, and start to sound like Beauvoir. Woman in her role as
Mother, *The Second Sex* argues, is symbolically gravid with timeless feminine wisdom, and so becomes deeply dangerous – 'the
daughter is for the mother at once her double and another person
... she saddles her child with her own destiny: a way of proudly
laying claim to her own femininity and also a way of revenging
herself for it' (SS309). And, as often, Beauvoir underlines her
point about how exotic, perverse and disreputable bourgeois
traditions are, by adding with an anthropologist's solemnity,
'The same process is to be found in pederasts, gamblers, drug
addicts, in all who at once take pride in belonging to a certain
confraternity and feel humiliated by the association' (SS309).
Mothers hand on the habit, in short. Or as she puts it later, the
child is 'already dreaming of Bluebeard and the holy martyrs'

(SS371); or, again with a very straight face – 'The great danger which threatens the infant in our culture lies in the fact that the mother to whom it is confided in all its helplessness is almost always a discontented woman' (SS528). This is why the young women in Beauvoir's novels are almost hysterical with hatred for their mothers, or for anyone who represents the same kind of equivocal female authority, and – what is often even more puzzling – why the author lets them get away with a level of routine vileness of temper that seems out of proportion to any particular provocation they are offered. They are, it seems, inspired by an intuitive loathing of their elders' bad faith; and those elders, conscious of their guilt, quail before them. At such moments, even when the grown-ups (Françoise in *She Came to Stay*, or Anne in *The Mandarins*) are versions of Beauvoir herself, she sides with the 'daughter'.

Mothers give birth to their daughters twice over, in her world. The first, physical birth is relatively innocent, although pregnancy taints the mother with generality – 'in the mother-to-be the antithesis of subject and object cease to exist; she and the child with which she is swollen make up together an equivocal pair .... Ensnared by nature the pregnant woman is plant and animal ....' (SS512). Women can salvage their sense of themselves as subjects, nonetheless. 'Mme de Staël', we're told briskly, 'carried on a pregnancy as readily as a conversation' (SS517). It is the second birth that traumatises both mother and daughter: that is, the shaping of the daughter into a woman, in the process of which mother becomes the medium for the wide world's cramping pressures. In Beauvoir's account she turns into a figure much resembling the wicked step-mother in fairy-tales:

> Sometimes the child's gaiety, heedlessness, games, laughter, are enough to exasperate her .... why should her daughter, this other woman, enjoy advantages denied to her? .... The older the child gets, the more does resentment gnaw at the mother's heart; each year brings her nearer her decline ... it seems to the mother that she is robbed of this future which opens before her daughter .... She keeps the girl in the house, watches her, tyrannizes over her .... (SS535–6)

The eery feeling that we're in the land of fable is not inappropriate, since this is a *generic* role the mother is playing, not a particular person's part. An earlier passage spells this out even more clearly – 'the young bride ... at her mother's side ... seems no longer like an individual, but like a phase of a species ... her individual and separate existence merges into universal life' (SS206). The mother is also rather like the bad fairy who lays a curse on the unfortunate princess – the curse of repetition, woman's 'nature', the big sleep in which she embodies 'the harmony of nature and society' (SS206). This is what incites all revolutionaries against the figure of the mother, says Beauvoir: 'in flouting her they reject the status quo it is intended to impose upon them ...' (SS206). To become a woman is to be programmed 'to conserve the world as given' (SS95) in your turn.

And conversely, to make it new is to break the chain, by refusing to reproduce the world; to desecrate the shrines and expose the mysteries as conjuring tricks and old wives' tales. Beauvoir's sardonic eloquence in telling tales of mothers and daughters gives these passages a power she seldom musters when dealing with the same themes in her fiction, where she is at once less polemical and less inventive – though she does achieve similarly vivid effects by different means in the autobiographical writing. It is when she is smashing time-honoured icons that she feels her own separate identity as a writer most intensely. She may pile up enormous quantities of material in *The Second Sex*, but this has, formally speaking, the effect of oxymoron – vandalism-by-accretion – since the material is all there to demolish received wisdom. Or to put it another way: attacking the myth of motherhood, she has orphaned herself, cut herself off from the past. Now she is faced with the vertiginous prospect of writing for her life, authoring herself.

If a woman starts to see round the corners of the conventional picture – starts to let things slip deliberately out of perspective – the results are not going to be pleasant, even for a constitutional optimist like Beauvoir. Sartre in *Nausea* has his anti-hero Roquentin look in the mirror and see not a face but a meaningless puffy assemblage of colours and textures, a Frankenstein mask; and when he contemplates the ocean, his mental eye penetrates the glassy surface to the seething (pre-human, post-human) marine life underneath. The year before the publication of *The Second Sex* he had written a Preface to Nathalie Sarraute's first novel – *Portrait of a Man Unknown* (1948), a kind of anti-portrait of the artist – in which he congratulated her on her 'protoplasmic vision of our interior universe': 'roll away the stone of the commonplace and we find running discharges, slobbering, mucous, hesitant, amoeba-like movements .... these viscous, live solutions.'[16] Sartre was doubtless recognising the language of 'sliminess' he had employed in *Being and Nothingness* to describe the 'in-itself' – 'It is a soft, yielding action, a moist and feminine sucking.'[17] Sarraute, as he says admiringly, has found a richer vocabulary for this new sub-textual stuff than he had. She describes 'inner' life – the life that is usually decently 'clothed' and contained in a realistically-described character – in skinless detail. Her narrator in *Portrait of a Man Unknown* much enjoys the ghoulish sport of picking people apart, looking inside their skins – 'to find the crack, the tiny crevice, the weak point as delicate as a baby's fontanelle .... And all that remains of the firm, rosy, velvety flesh of these "live" persons is a shapeless gray covering from which all blood has been drained away' (pp. 68–9). This new life is a *decomposing* life, a life that does not – as the conventional picture does – deny the presence of death; this 'protoplasm' is a metaphor for the stuff of life we share with the things around us, grey matter that resists the projects of consciousness.

Beauvoir uses the same imagery in *The Second Sex*, and applies it to the bodily situation of women. Nonetheless it is important to recognise that this is a style of literary discourse – a discourse about the horror of the new (in both senses, the horror belonging to the new, the revulsion caused by it) generated out of deliberate efforts of defamiliarisation. So it is not merely a symptom of Beauvoir's personal psychopathology, nor a private, perverse language shared solely with Sartre. If you suspend the habit of seeing embryonic existence as Life, this is the prospect that opens before you:

> This quivering jelly which is elaborated in the womb (the womb, secret and sealed like the tomb) evokes too clearly the soft viscosity of carrion for [man] not to turn shuddering away. Wherever life is in the making – germination, fermentation – it arouses disgust because it is made only in being destroyed; the slimy embryo begins the cycle that is completed only in the putrefaction of death. (SS178)

Like Sarraute (and Sartre) Beauvoir is producing a counter-myth about a levelling of material processes, eliding the distinctions between human and non-human, decomposing and composing.

Still, it is not clear in this passage how far she means us to see 'disgust' as a squeamish male reaction or as a *human* response to a contingent world that forces on us a sense of absurdity. The problem is even more pressing when one comes to a later and more famous passage about women and slime:

> Man 'gets stiff', but woman 'gets wet' .... If the body leaks – as an ancient wall or a dead body may leak it seems to liquefy rather than to eject fluid: a horrid decomposition.
>
> Feminine sex desire is the soft throbbing of a mollusc .... woman lies in wait like the carnivorous plant, the bog, in which insects and children are swallowed up. She is absorption, suction, humus, pitch and glue, a passive influx, insinuating and viscous: thus, at least she vaguely feels herself to be. Hence it is that there is in her not only resistance to the subjugating intentions of the male, but also conflict within herself. (SS407)

The question of *who she is speaking for*, so often unresolved, is here for once directly addressed – no doubt a measure of Beauvoir's embarrassment. It is woman who feels herself to 'be' this slimy, sucking, bog, 'vaguely', graphic though the list is. This, however, does not really sort out the question of bad faith entirely, since it may well be that she only experiences herself this way as a result of internalising cultural propaganda. So we can, if we like, absolve Beauvoir of an essentialist picture of women's bodies as inessential and absurd. But perhaps there is not much point in the manoeuvre, since so far as 'feeling' goes ('thus ... she vaguely feels herself to be'), this present-tense woman (whatever the future may hold) is self-divided, and contemplates her own genitals with fascinated horror. Indeed, most readers probably read 'I' for 'she', and take this passage as an example of what Beauvoir now feels 'free' to say, having ditched the reticence and mysticism with which women were conventionally supposed to veil their sexual parts from themselves.

The swamp imagery conjures up the surreal prospect of genitals with 'a life of their own' (also a presage of death). Sartre's Roquentin in *Nausea* had had a sea-food hallucination too, once his body stopped seeming to him like a tool. Beauvoir in the autobiography describes, from an amused distance in time, some mescalin-induced horrors he suffered, and which fed his depression, on turning thirty, at the idea of becoming 'a mere passive object' (*The Prime of Life*, p. 212) – 'behind him, past the corner of his eye, swarmed crabs, polyps and grimacing Things' (p. 205). The slime passage in *The Second Sex*, which is so riveting and awkward precisely because it is neither distanced nor 'owned' by Beauvoir, is followed, unsurprisingly perhaps, by twenty-odd pages of very uneven writing. There is a bad-tempered and chauvinist attack on the American practice of 'safe' sex before marriage (she probably means what was known as 'heavy petting'), which she thinks leaves girls technically deflowered but also uninitiated. Then, as if to prove her own credentials as a 'real' woman, she produces a praise of carnality which seems entirely to have forgotten the horrors (above) of mollusc moisture: 'True sexual maturity is to be found only in the woman who fully accepts carnality in sex desire and pleasure', who will be someone 'of ardent temperament' (SS411) naturally, as opposed to those frigid Anglo-Saxons. This – not the horror-writing about slime – is the sort of thing that reveals Beauvoir at her most vulnerable to her own favourite charge of bad faith. But then again, a few more pages on, she is writing like a paid-up and conscious utopian:

> The erotic experience is one that most poignantly discloses to human beings the ambiguity of their condition; in it they are aware of themselves as flesh and spirit, as the other and as subject .... the very difficulty of [woman's] position protects her against the traps into which the male readily falls .... he hesitates to see himself fully as flesh. Woman lives her love in more genuine fashion. (SS423)

The sense of ambiguity as (this time fairly certainly) *human* – as a situation to be lived and not a symptom – represents a significant move into different territory. Difference does not mean, necessarily, a self/other (or true self/false self) divide, but multiplies and divides inside one's life.

Beauvoir and Sartre habitually talked of themselves as 'one'. Toril Moi goes so far as to say that 'the myth of the unity between herself and Sartre functions as one of the most fundamental elements in her own sense of identity .... the one untouchable dogma of her life.'[18] I am not convinced – or not exactly. For

Beauvoir this 'one' had continually to be invented. It was Sartre who, she says, encouraged her to use her own life as material for her writing. They are seated (where else?) at a café table in Paris at the end of the summer:

> 'Look,' he said with sudden vehemence, 'why don't you put *yourself* into your writing ...?' The blood flushed up in my cheeks; it was a hot day and as usual the place was full of smoke and noise. I felt as though someone had banged me hard on the head. To put my raw, undigested self into a book, to lose perspective, compromise myself – no, I couldn't do it, I found the whole idea terrifying .... It seemed to me that from the moment I began to nourish literature with the stuff of my own personality, it would become something as serious as happiness or death. (*The Prime of Life*, p. 315)

This was the moment writing became a real project, we are invited to infer; and the fruit of the decision to put herself ('raw, undigested') onto the page, *She Came to Stay*, 'embodied my future. I moved towards this goal with effortless speed ....' (*The Prime of Life*, p. 345) The imagery announces the inception of her first published book as if it were a brain-child – she is giving birth to herself. It is worth noting also, however, that the scene from the autobiography is itself embodying the process it talks about – living in public, a sort of communal creation, a running commentary on a writing life. I suggested above that it was in *The Second Sex*, rather than the novels, that she realised her project of originality most fully. Perhaps, however, it would be truer to say that it was in writing across the boundaries of genre that she found her *métier*, and that *The Second Sex* was the book that confirmed her in this sense of her vocation.

Elaine Marks, in the essay already quoted, has some very suggestive and apposite things to say about Beauvoir's interpretation of her role as a writer:

> Simone de Beauvoir has consistently broken with decorum and has written directly about those topics one does not write or speak about today except in the discourse of empirical social science, of jokes, or through metaphor. It could, therefore, be maintained that the originality of Simone de Beauvoir's discourse is precisely this act of trespassing. She has not obeyed the taboos placed by the institutionalisation of specialised discourses on the body, sexuality,

ageing, and God; she has not remained within the acceptable boundaries marked by level of style or genre that tell a reader this is a poetic text, a scientific text, a philosophical text.[19]

This negative originality – 'She has not obeyed ...' – creates an enhanced sense of *playing* the writer, living writing, not only producing books, but producing more writing about the earlier self that produced them .... This way one keeps one jump ahead of oneself; and one keeps, too, a privileged, ever-shifting point of view. Beauvoir lays her own experience on the line, ageing becomes her topic (for example) because she will not accept the indignity of inhabiting the ready-made character lying in wait for an old woman. And in her account of the decomposition and death of part of herself, in Sartre, she deconstructs the myth of the great man who's all mind.

Behind the scenes

Where in all this is transcendence? Beauvoir's eternal return to her own situation and character (the novels made of fictionalised fact, the autobiographies, the interviews, the private letters made public) starts to look oddly like the kind of sub-art she castigates. For example: give any discontented woman a chance, she says nastily, near the end of *The Second Sex*, and she'll turn into a fake artist or a pseudo-writer: 'Woman's situation inclines her to seek salvation in literature and art .... With a little ambition, she will be found writing her memoirs, making her biography into a novel, breathing forth her feelings in poems' (SS713). Although Beauvoir had not yet written any memoirs, she had certainly turned a lurid episode from her biography into a first novel. The final mocking gesture above, about 'breathing forth ... feelings', insulates her from this feminine art sunk in immanence and bad faith, of course, since she is entirely innocent of poetry. But why is she sailing so close to the wind here, almost daring herself and her reader to make the connection between her iconoclastic refusal to write decorously separate, invented fictions, and the self-expressive not-quite-fiction indulged in by middle-class women with time on their hands? Did she still think at this stage that she would write positively utopian, speculative fictions? Possibly, given that she had had a stab at it in *All Men are Mortal* in 1946. Or was she engaged, as I rather suspect, in the vertiginous game of revealing how very little ground there was on which to stand in *good* faith? In fact, it is almost as though good faith consists in doing the same things, but with the awareness of their provisonality, particularity, and in-built irony.

As early as 1939, in a letter to Sartre, she produced what she referred to jokily as 'a whole dissertation on this privileged character one always accords to *oneself*' (*Letters*, p. 126). It is a fascinating example of her thinking under pressure and on the run, and explains a good deal about the function, for her, of their oneness. the setting is the latest of their three-cornered intrigues:

> when you love someone trustingly ... you take each tender act, each word, not as *true* but rather as a signifying object: a given bit of reality with respect to which the question of truth isn't posed. By contrast, however, the tender acts or words of the said beloved person with a third party (let's say with Wanda) appear like constructed objects – they're 'bracketed off'. The difference is not that you think in one case: 'He's telling me the truth' and in the other: 'He's lying to her.' You may very well concede that he isn't lying to the other person, but truth itself is disarmed here, appearing almost a matter of luck – since it could be false. Whereas in your own case you do not even have that reflective idea of *truth* – the bracketing does not occur. This explains how far illusion can go ....
> (*Letters to Sartre*, p. 106)

Without a metaphysical guarantee of Truth, shorn of pure reference, the only way she can see of getting beyond fictions is in *dialogue*, an exchange of words that transcends words (Socrates would have agreed). She concludes, in the letter – absurdly and heroically – 'When I say we're as one ... it means we're beneath reflection.' This last phrase is a splendid way of describing how she manages to keep her future, real self out of the picture, out of the question. Sartre is her double, her witness, pooling perceptions and judgements with him she has a place to stand in utopia. So she can author her fate by retreating ahead of it.

Such an argument implies that bodily separateness, and gender difference, are themselves at some level fictions. To a whole generation of feminists this looked like nonsense. However, a more recent reader like Judith Butler readily makes sense of it: 'the body is a *field of interpretive possibilities*, the locus of a dialectical process of interpreting anew a historical set of interpretations which have become imprinted on the flesh'.[20] You can understand Beauvoir's insistence on the necessity for transcendence, Butler argues, if you understand gender as 'an active style of living one's body in the world'.[21] The body 'wears' our 'cultural history':[22] in other words, the body is eminently interpretable, and (conversely) consciousness is not the flesh. Beauvoir had acknowledged as much: 'The fact is that every human existence involves transcendence and immanence at the same time' (SS449). To say this is also to acknowledge that from now on we have to make up difference as we go along. For Butler this is of course a central tenet — one is freed, or doomed, to inhabit one's images and language 'performatively'. Having nowhere else to stand but at a temporary point in a whole series of interpretations has become second nature.[23] For Beauvoir, it was, I think, nearly always a bleak and reluctant adventure, though it was what made her know herself a writer and alive.

In old age, she said, woman often acquires willy-nilly an ironic, unillusioned gaze: 'she has seen in man not the image on public view but the contingent individual, the creature of circumstance, that each man in the absence of his peers shows himself to be' (SS606). This is a woman who has been behind the scenes. In the event, a quarter of a century on, it was Sartre who declined first, and whose body leaked and decomposed. Her report from behind the scenes of his last years, *Adieux* (1981), caused scandal by its references to the absurd indignities of age, and particularly his incontinence. In a sense, however, she was paying tribute to the notion of themselves they had so long sustained, as people who could face the worst without false consolations. She talks about the precautions taken to prevent journalists and photographers spying on his last, comatose hours in hospital, wanting not only to protect him, but to take charge of the horrible truth *herself*: 'I made as if to lie down beside him under the sheet. A nurse stopped me. "No. take care … the gangrene. It was then that I understood the real nature of the bedsores. I lay on top of the sheet and I slept a little.'[24] In the same volume she published transcriptions of the taped conversations between the two of them that had taken the place of reading and writing for him as he grew blind. Some of his ruminations have a particular relevance to the project of transcending fictions: 'There's one thing I've always thought – I spoke about it to some extent in *Nausea* – and that is the idea that you don't have experience, that you don't grow older. The slow accumulation of events and experiences that gradually create a character is one of the myths of the late nineteenth century and of empiricism. I don't think it really exists' (*Adieux*, p. 324). Beauvoir likewise was always wary of the narrative habits that make for reconciliation, and smuggle back into material lives a metaphysical notion of wholeness, a kind of afterlife spelling fulfilment.

So she remained an anti-realist. Her strategies as a writer were all to do with banishing the mellowing perspective and the soulful and structuring typicality of classic realist writing. She reported, blow by blow, from the battlefront of her life, and the books were themselves part of the battle. So her encounters with literariness are not the kind that lead you 'on' into formal experimentation, but the kind that lead you 'back' into the character of authorship in our time. The fictions Beauvoir was interested in did not flourish solely between the covers of books, but in the culture at large, which continues – for example – to think of 'genius' as male (Beauvoir: 'One is not born a genius, one becomes a genius'), and mystify the (phallic) magic of making it new. Christine Brooke-Rose, after a long career as an experimental writer, and a lifetime's discreet silence on such matters, made the same points from a very different angle in her essay 'Illiterations': it was, she said wryly, almost as difficult as getting women into the priesthood, getting the right quality of attention for women's writing that invented new tricks.[25]

Beauvoir (as with Sarraute) would have been unsympathetic; would have thought that formal experimentation was a distraction from the real business of tracking down the lies that shape people's lives. She became very brisk about this towards the end of her own life. Her biographer Deirdre Bair reports a throwaway line on Virginia Woolf: 'Yes, Woolf is among the writers whose works I admire and sometimes reread, but only her feminist writings because I don't agree with her novels. They don't have any centre. There isn't any thesis.'[26] Nonetheless, from her own very different angle, and from behind the scenes, she was converging on the same mental territory when she asked Sartre in their late conversations about how the old dichotomies of active/passive (and by implication masculine and feminine) applied to his experience of writing: 'as I work with my pen, and as I write,' he replied, 'I have not really refused passivity .... there is an element of passivity in my work' (*Adieux*, p. 326). Indeed, one might argue that, as against received notions like 'The Death of the Author', Beauvoir's demystificatory exploration of the *life* of the author emerges with considerable credit for prescience as we survey a period in which biography and autobiography – and particularly literary biography, and authors' autobiographies – have so proliferated.

Beauvoir wanted to think that the life of the writer was a representative life, that it stood for the project of self-choice and human freedom. But does the burgeoning of such 'lives' bear her out? Often it looks very much as though (auto)biography is the refuge for the comforting realist assumptions exiled for the most part from 'serious' fiction. Phyllis Rose, in her Introduction to *The Penguin Book of Women's Lives*, quotes a confession from a biography-addict, Kennedy Fraser: 'For several years in my early thirties, I would sit in my armchair reading books about these other lives .... I felt very lonely then, self-absorbed, shut off. I needed all this murmured chorus, this continuum of true-life stories to pull me through. They were like mothers and sisters to me ....'[27] She would read 'furtively', she says, 'as if I were afraid that someone might look through the window and find me out.' Beauvoir would have been horrified, one imagines, to be hailed (as she is by Phyllis Rose) as one of these 'mothers of the literature of women's lives',[28] if what it meant was feeding the closeted, self-regarding character of the unreconciled-but-inactive woman, the woman insulated, the woman in bad faith. On the other hand, Kennedy Fraser, looking back on her sedentary self, knows very well what she was up to – she is looking in through that window, coolly, her eyes unsealed, a self-writer in something of the Beauvoir mould, though a good deal more amenable and forgiving.

In the end, it is Beauvoir's intransigence that is so impressive, for better and for worse. Instead of recanting when, reluctantly, sometime during the 1940s it seems, she accepted that by putting *oneself* out of the picture – 'beneath reflection' – was indeed a mental conjuring trick, she proceeded, in *The Second Sex*, and the autobiographies, to invent the impossible, unillusioned ground on which to stand. Is this bad faith? It seems so heroical a version of it, if so, that it deserves another name. She dared to lay her own life on the line – treat herself (the author, not some other decorous character) as a representative figure. Authority may be a confidence trick, but we need it as a weapon against authority. As we approach the end of the twentieth century, and fundamentalisms, nationalisms and movements for Life revive, her demystificatory tactics seems less dated than they did.

Notes

1 *The Force of Circumstance* (1963), trans. Richard Howard (New York: Putnam, 1976), p. 237.

2 *When Things of the Spirit Come First* (1979), trans. Patrick O'Brian (London: Flamingo, 1982), p. 47.

3 *The Prime of Life* (1960), trans. Peter Green (Harmondsworth: Penguin Books, 1962), p. 223.

4 'Mon expérience d'écrivain' (1966), in Claude Francis et Fernande Gontier, *Les Écrits de Simone de Beauvoir* (Paris: Gallimard, 1979), pp. 439–57: 439: 'Écrire un roman, c'est en quelque sorte pulvériser le monde réel.'

5 Nathalie Sarraute, *Tropisms and The age of suspicion* (1939), trans. Maria Jolas (1950) (London: Calder and Boyars, 1959), pp. 32–3.

6 Roland Barthes, *Writing Degree Zero*, trans. Annette Lavers and Colin Smith (New York: Hill and Wang, 1968), p. 33.

7 Susan Rubin Suleiman, 'Simone de Beauvoir and the writing self', *L'Ésprit Créateur*, 29:4 (1989), 42–51: 46. I produced a fairly detailed analysis of Beauvoir's games with point of view in *She Came to Stay* in my book *Women in the House of Fiction* (London: Macmillan, 1992), where there is also a discussion of Beauvoir's refusal to celebrate a separate women's writing: see pp. 1–12.

8 He first made the point in the 1940s; see also, for example, Lévi-Strauss, *Structural Anthropology* (1958), trans. C. Jacobson and B. Grundfest Schoepf (New York: Basic Books, 1963): 'it may be disturbing to some to have women conceived as mere parts of a meaningful system' (p. 61).

9 Toril Moi, *Simone de Beauvoir: The Making of an Intellectual Woman*, (Oxford: Basil Blackwell, 1994), p. 66.

10 *Letters to Sartre* (1990), trans. Quintin Hoare (London: Radius, 1991), p. 451.

11 Elaine Marks, 'Transgressing the (in)cont(in)ent boundaries: the body in decline', *Yale French Studies*, 72 (1986), 181–200: 193–4.

12 Angela Carter, *The Sadeian Woman* (London: Virago, 1979), p. 11.

13 'Must we burn Sade?' (1953), in *Privilèges* (Paris: Gallimard, 1955), and in *Faut-il brûler Sade?*, Collection Idées (Paris: Gallimard, 1955).

14 Margaret Atwood, *Surfacing* (1973) (London: Virago, 1979), p. 181.

15 Margaret Atwood, *The Handmaid's Tale* (1985) (London: Virago, 1987), p. 83.

16 Nathalie Sarraute, *Portrait of a Man Unknown* (1948), trans. Maria Jolas (London: Calder and Boyars, 1963), p. 8.

17 Jean-Paul Sartre, *Being and Nothingness* (1943), trans. Hazel E. Barnes (London: Methuen, 1969), p. 609.

18 Moi, *Simone de Beauvoir*, p. 30.

19 Marks, 'The body in decline', pp. 189–90.

20 Judith Butler, 'Sex and gender in Simone de Beauvoir's *Second Sex*', *Yale French Studies*, 72 (1986), 35–50: 45.

21 Ibid., p. 40.

22 Ibid., p. 48.

23 These arguments burgeoned in Judith Butler's *Gender Trouble: Feminism and the Subversion of Identity* (New York and London: Routledge, 1990) and *Bodies That Matter*, where she writes: 'Performativity describes this relation of being implicated in that which one opposes, this turning power against itself to produce alternative modalities of power': *Bodies That Matter* (New York and London: Routledge, 1993), p. 241.

24 *Adieux: A Farewell to Sartre* (1981), trans. Patrick O'Brian (London: André Deutsch and Weidenfeld and Nicolson, 1984), p. 125.

25 Christine Brooke-Rose, *Stories, Theories and Things* (Cambridge: Cambridge University Press, 1991), pp. 250–64.

26 Deirdre Bair, 'Simone de Beauvoir: politics, language and sexual identity', *Yale French Studies*, 72 (1986), 149–64: 154, n.

27 Phyllis Rose, *The Penguin Book of Women's Lives* (London: Viking, 1994), p. 19; the Kennedy Fraser quotation comes from *The New Yorker*, 6 November, 1989.

28 Rose, ibid., p. 24.

5

A certain lack of symmetry: Beauvoir on autonomous agency and women's embodiment

CATRIONA MACKENZIE

> The terms *masculine* and *feminine* are used symmetrically only as a matter of form, as on legal papers. In actuality the relation of the two sexes is not quite like that of two electrical poles, for man represents both the positive and the neutral, as is indicated by the common use of *man* to designate human beings in general; whereas woman represents only the negative, defined by limiting criteria, without reciprocity ... just as for the ancients there was an absolute vertical with reference to which the oblique was defined, so there is an absolute human type, the masculine. (Simone de Beauvoir)[1]

In the Introduction to *The Second Sex* Beauvoir lays out for the reader the conceptual grid that will be employed in her analysis of woman's situation. A number of interconnected categories and oppositions feature significantly in this grid, categories and oppositions which Beauvoir claims she derives directly from Sartrean existentialism. Distinctions such as subject/object, transcendence/immanence, authenticity/bad faith and concepts such as 'freedom' and 'the project' are thus introduced from the outset. In the body of the text these are supplemented by others such as self-consciousness/Life. Chief among these interpretative categories is the opposition Essential One/Inessential Other. Beauvoir asserts that this opposition, and in particular the category of the Other, is 'as primordial as consciousness itself', figuring in all mythologies and cultures (SS16). Primordial or not, if we are to believe her it seems that an understanding of the philosophical implications of this category had to wait for the phenomenology of Hegel and the ontology of Sartre.[2] It is their understanding of the self/other opposition that Beauvoir claims she is using to throw light on the situation of women.

Given the extent of authorial guidance as to how the text should be read *The Second Sex* should by rights present the conscientious reader with no major interpretative obstacles. So what is to be made of the fact that the text is knotted with contradictions? In recent criticism one tendency has been to argue that these internal difficulties arise as a result of Beauvoir's application to woman's situation of the very categories, including that of the Other, which she regards as facilitating her analysis.[3] These arguments suggest that these categories in their original Hegelian and Sartrean contexts are inextricably connected with a fundamental hierarchical opposition between masculine and feminine in which the feminine is associated with whatever is devalued and to be transcended. Beauvoir's ability so strikingly to illuminate the situation of women is thus all the more remarkable. It is an achievement despite, rather than because of, her philosophical framework.

Another view, that of Moira Gatens, is that Beauvoir's assessment of her own philosophical approach in *The Second Sex* has the effect of making her contribution to philosophy invisible.[4] Michèle Le Doeuff has suggested that in their relationship to philosophy women historically have acted as vestals, preserving, commemorating and commenting upon the work of the great philosophers but adding no words of their own to the text of philosophy.[5] Gatens argues that it is not that women *add* no words of their own, it is rather that they *claim* no words as their own. Beauvoir's analysis of the situation of women is an instance of just this syndrome, since she herself tells the reader that her analysis is entirely consonant with Sartrean existentialism. However her text belies this claim. To take Beauvoir at her word and hence to regard the internal contradictions of *The Second Sex* as arising chiefly out of the philosophical constraints Beauvoir has imposed on herself is thus to underestimate the complexity of both Beauvoir's project and her text.[6]

The argument of this essay assumes that both of these approaches to *The Second Sex* are correct. I want to show how

Beauvoir's analysis of woman's situation simultaneously uses, is limited by, and reveals the limitations of, some of the philosophical presuppositions from which she begins. In particular, I shall show how her account of the way in which oppression structures the psyches and the bodies of women, is both constrained by and calls into question the account of autonomous agency, derived from themes in the work of Hegel and Sartre, which also provides the philosophical perspective from which she develops her analysis of oppression.[7] As a result, while Beauvoir's conception of autonomy opens up the theoretical space for an analysis of oppression, it also commits her to the problematic view that women's embodiment makes ethical authenticity, or autonomy, more difficult for women to achieve than it is for men.

This essay is divided into two parts. The first part situates Beauvoir's analysis of sexual oppression in the context of her broader ethical concerns, through a reading of the interconnections between *The Second Sex* and *The Ethics of Ambiguity*.[8] The second part develops the argument that there is a tension between Beauvoir's ethical concerns, in particular her account of autonomous agency, and her characterisation of women's embodiment.

The Ethics of Ambiguity, published in 1947, two years before *The Second Sex*, is concerned primarily with questions of freedom, choice and ethical responsibility. Beauvoir's concern with ethics has a double aspect. On the one hand she is interested in articulating the conditions of possibility for ethics in general; on the other hand she seeks to understand the difference between autonomous, authentic ethical agency and ethical failure or heteronomy. In particular she is interested in investigating the *reasons* for heteronomy. It is this investigation in *The Ethics of Ambiguity* which gives rise to her analysis of women's oppression in *The Second Sex*.

My discussion of Beauvoir's accounts of autonomy and oppression focuses in particular on her notion of woman as Other. I argue that if we situate the notion of woman as Other within the broader context of Beauvoir's ethical concerns three distinct though related notions of the other emerge: others; the Inessential Other or 'object'; the Absolute Other. In the first of these uses, that is as referring to others, the notion of the other is central to Beauvoir's account of autonomy. For she thinks that genuine autonomy requires an ethical commitment to the autonomy of others. This ethical requirement to recognise the freedom of others provides the moral framework within which Beauvoir can condemn oppression as an evil. Oppression arises when, instead of recognising that others are the condition of possibility of our own freedom, we regard them either as an intolerable limit to our freedom or else as expendable in the interests of our freedom. In contrast to the reciprocal recognition which characterises a genuinely ethical relation to others, oppression is thus defined as an asymmetrical and ossified relation in which the other is treated not as a self-determining subject but as a thing, or 'object', an Inessential Other. This is the second of Beauvoir's interpretations of the self/other distinction.[9] In her readings of myth and literature Beauvoir uses the third sense of the notion of the other, the other as Absolute Other, to identify an extreme expression of the process of objectification — the myth of 'femininity'. Here Beauvoir can be taken to show how 'Woman' as Absolute Other functions as a metaphor of whatever is repressed or excluded in the self-constitution of phallocentric systems of signification.[10]

The great strength of Beauvoir's account of oppression lies in the way it is able to explain the process of internalisation, and what is particularly striking about her explanation is that it locates the effects of internalisation not merely in the beliefs of the oppressed but in their bodies and body-images. This makes clear the connection between the truncated ethical possibilities of the oppressed and their bodily situations. But Beauvoir's presentation of women's bodily situations exhibits the same tensions that are in evidence elsewhere in her work. My argument in the second part of this essay is that these tensions arise from a distinction between the immanent and the transcendent body upon which Beauvoir's conception of embodiment implicitly draws. While this distinction provides the theoretical framework for Beauvoir's analysis of oppression as a process which latches on through the body, her ideal of the transcendent body presupposes a problematic view of autonomous agency as control over the body by a supposedly sexually neutral 'will' or consciousness. This view is problematic not only because this supposedly sexually neutral 'will' turns out implicitly to be associated with an idealised masculine body, which is the paradigm of the transcendent body, but also because it involves an inadequate conception of embodied subjectivity and hence of autonomous agency. This leads to a fundamental tension, within Beauvoir's philosophical project as a whole, between her call for a relation to the other founded on a genuine recognition of the radical otherness of the other, and the fact that her analysis of woman's situation leaves Beauvoir unable to provide an ideal of autonomous agency that is capable of incorporating a recognition of both the specificity and the variety of women's bodily perspectives.

Freedom and oppression

Ethics, ambiguity and others

Beauvoir's project in *The Ethics of Ambiguity* is not to formulate a normative system of ethics. As she rather dismissively explains in rejecting the very possibility of such an ethic, 'Ethics does not furnish recipes any more than do science or art' (EA134). Her ethic is rather an ethics of the 'situation', an ethics of action. It is an ethic which stresses the particularity of each moral agent and each moral situation and which argues that moral choice is a question of individual action in response to the specificity of each situation. No prior determination of value, in other words, can indicate how a person should act in any particular situation. Ethics is rather a question for each individual of deciding how he or she wants to live. But because human freedom is the condition of possibility of ethics, this question must be posed again and again, at each moment.

Beauvoir's ethics thus locates the source of moral value in the moral autonomy of each individual. But her conception of autonomy nevertheless sanctions neither ethical inconsistency nor ethical anarchy. According to Beauvoir, our choices are always made in the context of our previous and possible future moral choices and, more importantly, in the context of relations with others. These factors both structure our ethical possibilities in specific ways and mean that with the freedom to make choices comes also the responsibility for the choices we make. This responsibility is not merely responsibility for oneself but also involves responsibility to recognise the freedom of others, to the extent that our choices create or close off the ethical possibilities of others and vice versa. Thus, although Beauvoir rejects the idea of an absolute moral code, she nevertheless thinks that we can distinguish good actions from bad, or, in existentialist terms, authentic from inauthentic choices. *The Ethics of Ambiguity* is an account of the requirements for authentic, autonomous action – namely taking responsibility for our freedom, both individually and collectively – as well as an explanation of some of the reasons for ethical failure. *The Second Sex* is an extended analysis of one of these reasons – sexual oppression.

Beauvoir's central claim in *The Ethics of Ambiguity* is that it is the fundamental and inescapable ambiguity of the human situation that both makes possible and gives rise to the need for ethics. She characterises this ambiguity in terms of a series of interconnected oppositions: between nature and consciousness; subject and object; life and death; externality and internality; the present and the future; the individual and the collectivity; particularity and impartiality. Echoing Kant's idea that human beings belong to both the noumenal and the phenomenal worlds, her view is that human life is situated ambiguously between these oppositions. Beauvoir grounds her analyses of ambiguity, freedom, authenticity and choice in certain epistemological and ontological doctrines of Hegel and Sartre. From Sartre she derives the claim that ambiguity arises from the structure of human consciousness, specifically from its non-coincidence with, or lack of, Being and as a consequence from the fact that the meaning of human existence is never fixed. To Hegel she owes the insight that self-consciousness arises not in the interiority of the Cartesian *cogito* but in intersubjective recognition.[11]

Freedom For our purposes here it is not important to enquire into the details or assess the veracity of Sartre's account of consciousness. What is salient however is Beauvoir's claim in *The Ethics of Ambiguity* that, as it stands, this ontology opens up but does not itself provide an ethical perspective. Her intention is thus to extrapolate from the Sartrean analysis of consciousness a number of implications about the nature of value, freedom, choice and action that will provide the basis for an existential ethic. The first requirement of any such ethic is a recognition that the negativity or lack which, according to Sartre, constitutes consciousness must be positively affirmed as the foundation of all signification. Value arises only insofar as there is a consciousness which is able imaginatively to disengage itself from immersion in the world and, in defining its own relation to the world, posit the world as meaningful: 'By uprooting himself from the world, man makes himself present to the world and makes the world present to him' (EA12). In other words, although consciousness does not bring Being into existence, in constituting itself it structures the world as a synthetic and organised totality. In Beauvoir's terminology, consciousness is the 'disclosure of Being'. What this means is that value is not given *a priori*. Rather it arises from the relationship between consciousness and the world.

It is of course Hegel's insight that meaning and value are grounded in reflective awareness of the dialectical relationship between ourselves as subjects and the world which is the object of our consciousness. For Hegel, however, because the development of self-consciousness occurs within the process of the dialectical unfolding of Spirit, the dialectical oppositions between subject and object and between Spirit and self-consciousness are eventually reconciled or *aufgehoben* (sublated) in Absolute Knowledge. Thus the totality which self-consciousness seeks to articulate is universal and Absolute. By contrast for Beauvoir, who rejects the concept of Spirit, no such reconciliation between consciousness and its objects and between the for-itself and value are possible. Rather human life, and hence ethics, is the attempt to live the ambiguous tension between these oppositions. Neither can there be a universal totality. This is why for Beauvoir it is not 'impersonal, universal man who is the source of values, but the plurality of concrete, particular men projecting themselves towards ends on the basis of situations whose particularity is as radical and irreducible as subjectivity itself' (EA17).

Following Sartre, Beauvoir also claims that the negativity which characterises consciousness is the source of freedom. It is only because consciousness exists as a 'disclosure of Being' that I am free to determine my mode of relation to the world. For

Beauvoir, however, although it is the structure of human consciousness which makes freedom possible, freedom is not a given. Rather it must be willed and won. The authentic ethical agent is the individual who, rather than attempting to coincide with Being, actively seeks to disclose Being and thus wills their own freedom. Beauvoir's very Kantian notion of 'willing' freedom or 'transcendence' is best explicated through the notions of facticity – freedom's 'other' in opposition to which it defines itself – and the 'project'. The term 'facticity' refers to the cluster of contingent yet inescapable factors which structure both human existence in general and individual existences. Facticity is thus the resistance which the world opposes to our wills, but it is a resistance without which freedom could not function. Like Kant's dove,[12] I exert my will, I exercise choice in relation to a world structured by facticity. To will my freedom just is to achieve autonomy within the inescapable limits imposed by facticity, and thus to transcend or surpass facticity.

If facticity is the ground from which freedom takes off, the 'project' is the means by which freedom is concretely realised. For unless freedom can express itself in action, in the choice of particular ends and activities, it remains a purely abstract notion. The term 'project' has two connected senses. In its first sense a project is any willed activity by means of which an individual consciously acts upon the world, thereby both transforming the world and defining herself in terms of her future possibilities. Considered separately from one another however, as discrete choices, such projects cannot constitute authentic action. For a project could be chosen one moment and abandoned the next, in which case the notion of choice would be indistinguishable from impulse while the ambiguity of existence would become indistinguishable from absurdity. In order for action to be the realisation of freedom, therefore, it must exhibit a unity which unfolds in time. An action can only be authentic to the extent that it is founded upon past actions and projected towards future actions. The possibility of ethics thus arises only for a being conscious of its own historicity and temporality. This gives us the second sense of the term 'project': the project as original project or choice. A project is original not in the sense that it is temporally prior to or separate from particular projects but in the sense that it justifies them. The fact that our freedom can only become concrete through these freely chosen but fundamentally contingent projects entails an inescapable tension in our perspective on and attitudes towards our projects. Viewed from an external perspective they are arbitrary and without justification. Viewed from an internal perspective they confer meaning upon our existence.

Others   The existentialist notion of the project as the concrete realisation and unfolding of freedom echoes one of the founding themes of Hegelian metaphysics – the theme of externalisation.[13] But for both Sartre and Beauvoir, Hegel's greatest insight is his account of self-consciousness in the *Phenomenology of Spirit*, which charts the development of subjectivity as a process of intersubjective relations. In the master-slave dialectic Hegel shows how self-consciousness arises only in relation to another self-consciousness. It is only through their confrontation with one another, through a recognition of their identity in difference, that subjects constitute themselves as subjects and that self-consciousness becomes concrete. This insight is incorporated into Beauvoir's ethics in the view that freedom can be realised only in the context of relations with others. It is transformed into the basis of a theory of oppression by the claim that the actions of an individual can only be considered ethical, or authentic, to the extent that they embody a recognition of the freedom of others.

Beauvoir's characterisation of our relations with others manifests her typical preoccupation with ambiguity. She stresses the tension in our dealings with others between a concern for justice, which requires that we treat individuals impersonally and impartially, and the ethical importance of the particular attachments and affections between particular individuals, affections and attachments which often conflict with the demands of justice. She points to a similar tension between a Kantian demand that we treat persons as ends in themselves rather than as means, and a utilitarian concern to minimise total suffering. Further, while violence against persons is an inexcusable atrocity in which the other becomes for us a mere thing, violence against certain individuals is in some instances necessary to preserve the freedom of the collectivity. By now it should come as no surprise that Beauvoir's account of our relations with others does not offer a solution which will either dissipate these tensions or reconcile them. Once again, ethics is necessary because these tensions are endemic to human social life. It is inconceivable to imagine a future in which individuals will not make opposing and irreconcilable choices, in which our projects will not compete with the projects of others, in which the diversity of our particular interests can be finally harmonised.

Beauvoir locates the ambiguity inherent in our relations with others in the plurality of human consciousness, in the fact that though related to one another human beings are nevertheless separate from one another. Thus, although from an external perspective our situations are similarly conditioned by our finitude and mortality, those situations as lived are irreducibly different. From one perspective this irreducible difference and the conflict to which it often gives rise might make it appear that for each subject the existence of others appears as a threat to her own projects. Beauvoir argues, however, that this perspective misunderstands the nature of freedom. It is only insofar as there are others who, by exercising their freedom in projects, disclose and transform the world, that there can be a world at all in relation to which the individual defines herself or himself. Others therefore open out possibilities for us in relation to which or against which we define our possibilities.

But others can only open out our possibilities if they themselves can create their own possibilities, that is if their possibilities for transcendence are not frustrated by their situation. In *The Ethics of Ambiguity* Beauvoir distinguishes two ways in which our undertakings may be frustrated by our situation. On the one hand we often confront natural obstacles and disasters as well as the ever-present risk of death. But these factors, cruel and contingent though they may be, are not limitations on our freedom. Rather they define our human condition. To the extent that we resign ourselves in the face of them and give up hope, then we have failed to come to terms with that condition. On the other hand, because our freedom is exercised only in the context of relations with others, our undertakings can be frustrated by their refusal to recognise that freedom. 'Only man can be an enemy for man; only he can rob him of the meaning of his acts and his life because it also belongs to him alone to confirm it in its existence, to recognise it in actual fact as a freedom' (EA82). It is this situation which defines oppression, which is therefore never 'natural' but always arises in the context of relations between subjects.

Before turning to a detailed account of Beauvoir's analysis of oppression I want to make it clear exactly how she defines oppression in contradistinction to the ethical demand that we recognise the freedom of others. It should be apparent from what has been said so far that Beauvoir thinks that mutual recognition between subjects is not only possible but is also ethically required. But such recognition she argues, alluding to the outcome of Hegel's master-slave dialectic, cannot be achieved in relations of domination and subordination. What then is involved in genuine recognition? In brief remarks on love and friendship in both *The Ethics of Ambiguity* and *The Second Sex* Beauvoir suggests that genuine recognition of the other requires an equality and symmetry between subjects. This involves renunciation of any attempt either to merge our subjectivity with that of the other or to subsume the other under our own projects. We affirm ourselves as subjects only by accepting the freedom and independence of the other. Recognition therefore requires recognition of the otherness of the other, of their difference from ourselves: 'It is only as something strange, forbidden, as something free, that the other is revealed as an other. And to love him genuinely is to love him in his otherness and in that freedom by which he escapes. Love is renunciation of all possession, of all confusion. One renounces being in order that there may be that being which one is not' (EA67). Beauvoir makes it clear in *The Second Sex* that although our relations with others cannot always involve such reciprocal recognition, love and friendship 'are assuredly man's highest achievement, and through that achievement he is to be found in his true nature', that is, as a being which in renouncing *mere being* also renounces possession (SS172).

These remarks, in which Beauvoir clearly indicates that reciprocal recognition is possible and requires simultaneous recognition of the other, as both like ourselves, as a transcendent subject, and as irreducibly other, make a rather sharp break from the ontology of *Being and Nothingness*. For while Sartre also acknowledges that self-consciousness arises only in the context of our relations with others, he explicitly precludes the possibility of mutual recognition between transcendent subjects. As Genevieve Lloyd has argued, for Sartre the self as revealed by the other is not the transcendent self of the for-itself which is always escaping towards its own possibilities.[14] It is rather being-for-others, a self experienced through the emotions in which I experience myself not as transcendent but as objectified by the Other. Although for Sartre the very structure of human consciousness means that I cannot ever *become* this object which I experience myself as being, relations with others are nevertheless a perpetual struggle in which, in the Look, each subject either objectifies the other or tries to resist objectification by the other. In other words, for Sartre, Beauvoir's ideal of mutual recognition by each subject of the other as a free being is not possible. As I have argued however it is this ideal which, for Beauvoir, opens up the theoretical space for an analysis of oppression.[15]

Authenticity, bad faith and oppression   From the preceding analysis, the requirements for autonomous agency should be reasonably clear. But it should also be clear that authentic agency is not easy to sustain. If freedom must constantly be won we face every moment an existential choice between accepting freedom, ambiguity and their attendant anguish or, in 'bad faith', attempting to flee that anguish by refusing freedom. For both Sartre and Beauvoir the privileged zone of bad faith is our relations with others when we attempt to escape the struggle between subjects for recognition. The subject who is acting in bad faith fails to resist the other's attempt to objectify him. He allows himself to be objectified by the other and identifies himself with the object to which the other has reduced him, that is, he becomes the Inessential Other against which the subject defines himself as the Essential One. Bad faith in our relations with others is thus the supreme example of heteronomy or failure of ethical will. But whereas Sartre identifies every failure to achieve authentic subjectivity as bad faith, for Beauvoir not all cases of failure to achieve autonomy are instances of bad faith. For what the notion of bad faith fails to explain is the phenomenon of systematic oppression, which is the case when the other systematically

refuses my freedom and closes off my possibilities: when, instead
of understanding that my freedom is the guarantee of his own,
he sees my freedom only as a threat and limit to his own; when,
instead of recognising me as a subject he permanently reduces me
to the status of object or Inessential Other:

> my freedom, in order to fulfil itself, requires that it emerge into an
> open future: it is other men who open the future to me, it is they
> who, setting up the world of tomorrow, define my future; but if,
> instead of allowing me to participate in this constructive moment,
> they oblige me to consume my transcendence in vain, if they keep
> me below the level which they have conquered and on the basis of
> which new conquests will be achieved, then they are cutting me
> off from the future, they are changing me into a thing. (EA82–3)

For Sartre every time an individual loses her or his grip on transcendence it is because he or she has allowed it to happen. Thus
every instance of subordination, limitation, failure of will, in
relations with others is an instance of bad faith on the part of the
individual subject. Furthermore because the bad faith of one or
other of the parties in any encounter between subjects is un-
avoidable, there is no possibility of genuine reciprocity between
subjects.

By contrast, for Beauvoir failure to achieve transcendence
cannot always be explained in terms of *individual* bad faith but
is often a function of certain forms of *social* relations which she
characterises by means of the opposition Essential One/Inessential
Other. Her use of this opposition is thus significantly different
from Sartre's use of the same opposition.[16] While for Sartre it
designates the structure of all of our individual relations with
others, for Beauvoir it comes into play when human relations are
distorted by social relations of domination and subordination. I
have tried to establish that it is because she upholds the ideal of
genuine reciprocity that Beauvoir's account of our relations with
others is able to illuminate the phenomenon of structural oppression in a way that the Sartrean account of bad faith cannot.

Woman as Inessential and Absolute Other
Beauvoir's analysis of woman's situation works by playing off
against each other the two notions of the other which I have identified so far. Her claim is that social relations between the sexes

preclude mutual recognition between two free subjectivities. Rather these relations are structured as an ossified and asymmetrical opposition between Essential One and Inessential Other, an opposition in which one social group, men, are always the essential, transcendent subjects, while another, women, are permanently reduced to the status of the Inessential Other or object. The resultant curtailment of women's freedom in social relations is mirrored and reinforced by, and also helps set up, a series of constraints on women's abilities to exercise their freedom in projects. These constraints, which are variously legal, economic, historical, physical, psychological and so on, are such that they close off to women the social space required for transcendence. Given her conception of the human subject as freedom however, what Beauvoir needs to explain is how a free being can become unfree in this kind of way, how she can become the Other. In other words she needs to explain how and why women come to submit to their oppression. Beauvoir oscillates between two different answers to this question, answers which are often in tension with one another. The first answer explains how oppression becomes 'naturalised' by being 'internalised'.[17] The second answer is given in terms of the notion of 'bad faith'. In the following analysis I want to explain how Beauvoir arrives at these answers but also to show how her analysis of 'internalisation' is constrained by, but also reveals the limitations of, the Sartrean account of the subject as radical freedom from which it starts.

One of the insidious aspects of oppression, according to Beauvoir, is the way in which it becomes naturalised, the way in which certain characteristics of the oppressed group, characteristics which arise as a result of and in response to oppression – that is, in response to being treated by the other as an 'object', in response to severely restricted social opportunities – come to be seen as 'natural', inescapable facts which are then used to explain and justify the social relations from which they arise. But oppression cannot work if the oppressed refuse to identify with the oppressor's definition of themselves. Such refusal would signal the onset of hostilities between oppressor and oppressed. Oppression works best when the process of naturalising oppression actually structures both the oppressed's beliefs about themselves and their modes of relation to the world, that is, when the oppressed constrain their own possibilities while believing that these possibilities are constrained by some natural, inescapable facts about themselves. In other words the hallmark of oppression is its invisibility to the oppressed.

It is clear that Beauvoir's attempt to account for this phenomenon, the phenomenon of internalisation, puts a great deal of pressure on the Sartrean account of consciousness from which both her ethics and her feminism start. For this idea of internalisation cannot be explained by a Sartrean account of our relations with others, nor can it be expressed within the language of bad faith. In Sartre's account of my being-for-others, although the other can regard me as an object and although I can experience myself as an object for the other I can never actually *become* an object *for myself*. Even in 'bad faith' when I allow the other to limit my possibilities, this is ultimately just a pretence; my subjectivity is always transcending itself towards its own possibilities. However, Beauvoir's recognition of internalisation as a psychological phenomenon which structures the oppressed's relation to the world and to others requires that women do not just *play* at being the Inessential Other, they actually *become* inessential, that is, they become objects even for themselves. In fact, according to Beauvoir, the result of oppression is that women are both subjects and objects *for themselves* simultaneously. This analysis raises two questions. First, what exactly does Beauvoir mean by saying that the oppressed person is both subject and object for herself? Secondly, how does Beauvoir reconcile her conclusion with the Sartrean premise that consciousness is a being continually surpassing itself toward its own future possibilities?

In answer to the first question, Beauvoir seems to understand the process of internalisation as a kind of psychic alienation which alienates women from their subjectivity. Internalisation is a process of becoming for oneself less than an autonomous human subject, becoming for oneself an 'object'. As I will argue in more detail later, for Beauvoir this process of becoming for oneself an object is of necessity a process which takes hold in and through a person's body and body-image. A person becomes an object for herself when she experiences her body as alien to her subjectivity, rather than as the direct expression of her subjectivity.[18] But what is this subjectivity from which woman is alienated? The answer to this question shows how Beauvoir's account of oppression, though it clearly marks a break from the Sartrean account of consciousness, also remains within the orbit of Sartre's views – thus answering the second question just raised. For Beauvoir the subjectivity from which woman is alienated is the human subject as sexually undifferentiated freedom. This subject, the consciousness which is always surpassing itself toward its own future possibilities, exists prior to and in some sense outside of the social relations of domination and subordination. Thus as her dictum 'One is not born, but rather becomes, a woman' indicates, Beauvoir wants to say that women's subjectivity is constructed in and by relations of power; but she also wants to posit a residual, sexually indifferent subjectivity which somehow escapes the determinations of power.[19] On the one hand this enables her to give an account of resistance, which is understood as the revolt of a free subject against the forces which work to cut her off from her freedom. On the other hand it requires an analysis of complicity as a form of bad faith.

Beauvoir argues that women become objects even for themselves not just because their possibilities are foreclosed by social relations and structures of domination and subordination but also because they are actually complicit with their oppression. Not only do women just accept men's constructions of the world and of themselves, they actually go about turning themselves into the creatures that men expect them to be. Another way of putting this would be to say that women turn femininity into a project; they make the sorts of choices that, instead of aiming towards transcendence, actually close off their own possibilities. As Beauvoir details in 'Justifications', Part VI of *The Second Sex*, in their dreams of romantic love, in their own narcissistic pre-occupation with their appearances, in their various rejections of rationality, women turn themselves into 'objects' and so systematically give up their claim to be regarded as autonomous subjects.

While the phenomenon of complicity certainly presents a challenge to any theory of oppression, the problem with Beauvoir's analysis is that, because she retains the Sartrean notion of subjectivity as radical freedom, she has to explain complicity as a question of 'choice', that is as a question of women's collective bad faith: 'If woman seems to be the inessential which never becomes the essential, it is because she herself fails to bring about this change' (EA19). So although it is true that women are oppressed, they have furthered their own oppression because complicity is easier than the arduous task of resisting oppression and accepting responsibility for one's own freedom. In bad faith women have sought to escape this responsibility by simply accepting the world as men present it to them, rather than asserting their own subjectivities and so creating value. Even so-called 'feminine' values are masculine constructions which have served simply to further women's oppression: 'In truth women have never set up female values in opposition to male values; it is man who, desirous of maintaining masculine prerogatives, has invented that divergence' (SS96). The question that needs to be asked however is *why* women's bad faith takes this rather than the reverse form. Why is it men rather than women who have set themselves up as transcendent subject? In the second part of this essay I argue that, despite its productivity for an analysis of oppression, Beauvoir's ideal of autonomy actually commits her to the view that the only values worth having are those which men have established. That is to say, one reason why women have accepted the world as men present it to them is because the only thing that on her view really differentiates them from men, namely their bodies, cannot be sources of value at all. Thus it looks as though women's bad faith is an inevitable outcome of their facticity. Before turning to this argument, however, I want to examine Beauvoir's third use of the category of the other – as designating the Absolute Other. Here Beauvoir uses the notion of bad faith in a surprising and illuminating way to condemn man's role as oppressor.

The experience of alterity, Beauvoir suggests, is an inescapable feature of consciousness: in its relationship both with the world and with others consciousness is defined as a being which exists at a distance from itself, it is a being whose mode of existence is to be other than itself. This alienation manifests itself in the ambiguity of the human situation. Human beings are both part of nature, yet distanced from it; death represents an absolute limit to our possibilities, yet it is only our awareness of death that enables us to constitute life as meaningful; it is only in relation to others that our freedom is defined, yet our relations with others are necessarily conflictual, and so on. Beauvoir's suggestion seems to be that the category of the Absolute Other is a projection of our anguish in the face of this ineradicable alterity and the ambiguity which is its consequence. We attempt to escape ambiguity by projecting it onto the Absolute Other, we define ourselves as transcendence of the Absolute Other which we posit, but this Other can also be the repository of our hopes and ideals. In short, the Absolute Other is whatever the subject is not, whatever he or she hopes to escape or whatever he or she aspires towards. As such, the category of the Absolute Other is dialectically necessary to the subject who posits it.

Beauvoir's claim is that while many signifiers have been used to represent the Absolute Other, the signifier 'Woman' is privileged among them as 'the material representation of alterity' (SS211). 'Woman' is a signifier which represents whatever fear, desire, hope, ideal it is the projection of. This is why, as Beauvoir shows, the signifier 'Woman' can support so many contradictory predicates and why 'femininity' gets defined as essentially mysterious and contradictory. Understood in this third sense, Beauvoir's employment of the notion of the Other is thus closely aligned with the way in which the category of the Other has been understood in those feminisms strongly influenced by Derridean deconstruction, such as those of Le Doeuff and Kristeva.[20] But although the signifier 'Woman' is referentially ambiguous, the problem for *women* is that 'Woman' is a masculine construction by means of which men seek to define and limit women. Rather than recognising women as free subjectivities, men compel women to live out their own myths of 'femininity'. The motivation for this is bad faith. What men seek in condemning women to the status of Absolute Other is what the masterly consciousness seeks from the slave – non-reciprocal recognition from a being who will mediate for him his ambiguous relationship to the world and to others: 'caught between the silence of nature and the demanding presence of other free beings, a creature who is at once his like and a passive thing seems a great treasure' (SS739). By identifying women with the Absolute Other, men therefore simultaneously affirm and deny women's subjectivity; women become both subject and object, the other but the other who can be possessed. It is because women are free subjectivities who resist or subvert in various ways as well as comply with these myths, that coercive social structures limiting their possibilities are necessary.

Women, transcendence and the female body[21]

> Her body is not perceived as the radiation of a subjective person-ality, but as a thing sunk deeply in its own immanence; it is not for such a body to have reference to the rest of the world, it must not be the promise of things other than itself: it must end the desire it arouses. (SS189)

According to Beauvoir, the opposition which, in addition to that between Subject and Other, quintessentially characterises the ambiguity of the human situation, is the duality of body and consciousness. Characteristically, Beauvoir regards this duality as irreducible. She thus rejects both mentalist and materialist explanations of the mind–body relation. In fact her position, like that of Merleau-Ponty, reverses the order of priority of Cartesian interactionism.[22] Human beings are not essentially a *res cogitans* (thinking thing) somehow conjoined to a *res extensa* (extended/ material thing). Rather, existence is necessarily *embodied* existence. Our bodies define our situation in the world; con-sciousness is a relation to the world from a particular bodily perspective: 'To be present in the world implies strictly that there exists a body which is at once a material thing in the world and a point of view towards this world' (SS39). This duality of body and consciousness entails, according to Beauvoir, that the significance of the body itself is also fundamentally ambiguous. On the one hand, as a material 'thing' the body is continuous with the rest of the natural world. Hence it is subject to causal laws and represents merely one moment in the life of the species. Considered as such the body is pure immanence. On the other hand, as the perspective of an individual consciousness, the body is the concrete expression of that individuality, the instrumen-tality of the will. It is with this transcendent body that the subject undertakes projects and interacts with others. The ambi-guity of embodiment means, therefore, that while our bodily situations and capacities limit our possibilities they also open out possibilities for us.

But if the body defines our situation then it becomes sensible to ask whether sexually different bodies perceive the world from different perspectives, whether they limit or open out different possibilities for the embodied subject. This question is perhaps the motivating question of *The Second Sex*, and Beauvoir's answer to it is affirmative. Her claim is that the perspectives and possibilities made available by women's embodiment are not only different from those made available by men's embodiment but also drastically more limited. But the reasons for her answer are not clear. In fact she seems to give several complex and interesting, but ultimately incompatible, reasons for this answer. In this part of the essay I attempt to disentangle these reasons as well as to show how the tensions within her account of women's embodiment reveal difficulties with her understanding of autonomous agency. My argument is that at least two different reasons for Beauvoir's answer can be discerned in *The Second Sex*. The first explains women's different bodily perspectives and possibilities in terms of their oppression and suggests that if women were not socially subordinate then their embodiment would not be experienced as so much more limiting than men's. The second reason seems to ground the limitation of women's embodiment not just in their oppression but also in their reproductive capacities. I shall argue that although these two answers are incompatible they both arise from the distinction between the body as immanent and the body as transcendent which underlies Beauvoir's account of the ambiguity of embodiment. What makes a feminist appropriation of this distinction problematic is that the kinds of bodily activity which are characterised as quintessentially immanent, and against which the ideal of the transcendent body is defined, are activities typically associated with the female body, in particular with its reproductive capacities.

Oppression and the 'female' body as immanence

Beauvoir's analysis of women's bodily situation is crucial to the success of her argument against women's social subordination. She is explicit that one of the main ways in which this subordination has been naturalised is by recourse to the supposed 'facts' of female biology, which are said to explain women's passivity and dependence, and which bind women to the care of children. This is why woman's 'body is not perceived as the radiation of a subjective personality, but as a thing sunk deeply in its own immanence'. In order to counter this view, Beauvoir needs to show three things. First, she needs to show that women's bodies, like the bodies of men, are transcendent bodies. That is, she needs to disconnect women's subjectivities and their bodies from this image of the female body as inherently immanent. Second, she needs to show why this conception of the female body as immanent is instrumental in maintaining women's oppression. Third, she needs to explain why this connection is so readily made, why it is that women's bodies are 'not perceived as the radiation of a subjective personality'.

Beauvoir undertakes the first two tasks concurrently by means of a series of phenomenological descriptions of women's lived experience of their bodies. These descriptions, which occupy most of Parts IV and V of *The Second Sex*, begin with the young girl's experience of her body in childhood and then proceed to characterise the way in which that experience changes from puberty through sexual initiation, marriage, motherhood and old age. Beauvoir's central argument, which emerges during the course of these descriptions, is that the process of becoming a woman is a process of coming to experience one's body less and less as transcendent and more and more as signifying immanence. In early childhood, she claims, girls as well as boys experience their bodies as transcendent, as 'the instrument that makes possible the comprehension of the world' (SS295). This experience of the body is primarily neither sexual nor sexually differentiated; the body is rather experienced by both sexes primarily as a motility in which the child is not aware of her or his body as a physical thing. While this experience of the body continues in some ways for girls until puberty, it is simultaneous with an increasing awareness of their bodies as sexually marked bodies, that is as passive 'objects'. Beauvoir is explicit that this experience of the body as passive object arises as a result of women's situation, in particular as a result of their differential treatment which begins in early infancy and becomes more and more marked as childhood progresses. The result is that while the boy becomes 'aware of his body as a means for dominating nature and as a weapon for fighting' (SS307), the girl, by contrast, rather than seeing her body as instrument, is taught to make herself and her body into an object until, by the time the child reaches puberty, she 'feels that her body is getting away from her, it is no longer the straightforward expression of her individuality; it becomes foreign to her; and at the same time she becomes for others a thing: on the street men follow her with their eyes and comment on her anatomy. She would like to be invisible; it frightens her to become flesh and to show her flesh' (SS333).

However Beauvoir also seems to suggest that the differences between male and female anatomy conspire to reinforce these socially-produced differences. For instance, she seems to accept the weight given by psychoanalysis to the difference between the visibility of the male penis and the invisibility of the female vagina.[23] Thus she claims that the difference in the structure of their sexual organs encourages the boy's experience of his body as transcendent and the girl's experience of hers as immanent. This is because the very visibility of the penis means that it can become for the boy not only a plaything and compensation for the lost maternal object, but also an objective expression of his subjectivity, an *alter ego*. By this means even bodily acts like urinating, in which the body seems most thing-like, can become a means for transcendence – hence those competitions between little boys to see who can urinate the furthest. By contrast, the invisibility of the girl's vagina, the fact that it is inside her body, means both that she is 'from the start much more opaque to her own eyes, more profoundly immersed in the obscure mystery of life, than is the male' and that 'the little girl cannot incarnate herself in any part of herself' (SS306). Instead she identifies herself with a passive substitute like a doll which she sees as both her whole self but also as an external object. This simply reinforces the child's narcissism, unlike the penis which directs attention away from the self, so accounting for the precocious narcissism of little girls and its tendency to remain throughout women's adult life.

Now Beauvoir makes it clear that it is not this anatomical difference *per se* which gives rise to the difference between the girl's and the boy's experiences of their bodies, but rather the social significance of that difference, the fact that the penis is a symbol of a socially-valorised masculinity. Thus the girl experiences her body as immanent because it is a socially-devalued body. At the same time, however, Beauvoir's characterisations of the girl's body as 'more profoundly immersed in the obscure mystery of life' suggests that she also gives some credence to the idea that the female body is inherently more immanent than the male body. This ambivalence is particularly evident in some of Beauvoir's descriptions of women's lived experiences of menstruation, sexuality, pregnancy and maternity. There are passages for instance which characterise female sexuality as at once passive and voracious, passages which claim that the female body is an hysterical body, passages which describe menstruation as a heavy burden, humiliating and shameful, and passages which describe pregnancy and maternity as alienation – the obliteration of the individual by the demands of the species. What seems to emerge from these passages is a number of recurring motifs. These are that the female body is passive, that it is experienced by women as a burden that stands between them and their individuality and that it subjects women to the demands of nature. Thus, unlike man's body which he experiences primarily as transcendent, the female body is experienced by women mostly as immanence.[24]

The question that needs to be addressed then is this. How can these motifs be reconciled with Beauvoir's analysis of oppression? I want to argue that Beauvoir's text presents two answers to this question. The first answer also provides the first reason for her answer to the question posed earlier, namely the question of why women's embodiment opens up more limited perspectives and possibilities than men's embodiment. This answer is suggested by some fairly explicit instructions Beauvoir gives as to how should such passages should be interpreted. They are, she says, accounts of how women experience their own bodies as a result of oppression.[25] Thus those descriptions which represent the female body as immanent, far from proving problematic for Beauvoir's analysis of oppression, in fact provide powerful proof of women's oppression.[26] What they show is that oppression constructs women's subjectivity by marking the body as a passive, sexual object. The oppressed subject comes to see herself as object because she experiences her own body as an object, as a physical thing, rather than as transcendent. As a result of oppression her body is not just an object for others, but an object for herself. Although she is a subject she becomes an object for herself because she does not experience her body as the instrumentality of her will, but rather as the plaything of forces over which she has no control. This analysis explains my earlier claim that for Beauvoir the oppressed person is both subject and object *for herself* because she experiences her body as alien to her subjectivity.

In keeping with this analysis, it could also be argued that the phenomenological experiences which Beauvoir describes are symptoms of rebellion. The girl's disgust at the smell of menstrual blood, the fact that her vaginal emissions provoke in her an experience of abjection,[27] are her means of revolt against her oppression. In other words, since she has no other means of fighting her situation, her distress with the passivity to which she is condemned manifests itself in a self-destructive disgust at her own body. This analysis of Beauvoir would place her much closer to contemporary psychoanalytic feminist interpretations of such 'feminine' disorders as anorexia and hysteria than is often credited.[28]

This interpretation is certainly supported by a strong strand of thought in *The Second Sex*. It also conforms to the explicit logic of the text, namely the logic of existence preceding essence. Moreover, if this interpretation of Beauvoir's presentation of the female body is conjoined with her deconstruction of the myth of 'femininity', it could also be argued that Beauvoir's analysis shows that not only is gender a cultural construct, so too is sexual difference.[29] Just as there is no necessary connection between women and the myths of femininity, so too there is no necessary connection between women as transcendent or autonomous subjects and the immanent 'female' or 'feminine' body. Like 'femininity', the 'female' body is itself just a cultural artefact. Men's and women's bodies are equally subject to bodily processes and they are equally both the expression of a free individuality and mere moments in the perpetuation of the species. It is the cultural construction of femininity alone that signifies woman's body as immanent in its relation to reproduction and to its bodily functions. Thus, once women are given the space to exercise their autonomy, women's bodies will no longer be seen as 'feminine' bodies, that is, as bodies sunk in immanence. Rather they will be both perceived and experienced as the expression of a sexually undifferentiated and transcendent subjectivity.

While I think that Beauvoir is certainly making a claim such as this she also seems to suggest that the connection between women and the immanent 'female body' is not completely arbitrary. Rather it is insofar as women's bodies are reproductive bodies that they are connected with this immanent 'female body' and this is a further reason why women's bodies open out fewer possibilities than men's bodies. The problem is that on Beauvoir's analysis the 'female' or 'feminine' body has become a metaphor for immanence or heteronomy – explaining the rather disturbing similarity between some of Beauvoir's phenomenological descriptions and Sartre's notorious holes and slime metaphors of *Being and Nothingness*.[30] This is why some of the images Beauvoir uses to describe this body are images which associate it with nature at its most inert; the 'female' body is 'fleshly', 'stagnant', swamplike, 'mucous' and leaky like a dead body, smelling like 'wilted violets'; it is an 'involuntary' body. It is also why it is insofar as she experiences her body as a 'feminine' body that the young girl experiences it as shameful and humiliating. But if the 'female' body is a metaphor for immanence then on Beauvoir's analysis reproduction can only ever be culturally signified as passivity, as immanence, which explains why she regards technological interventions into the reproductive process as essential for the liberation of women.[31] Ironically, it also explains how Beauvoir is able so successfully to criticise the patriarchal equation of women with their reproductive capacities. If reproduction signifies immanence, this gives added strength to the claim that women have been oppressed insofar as their possibilities have been seen to be limited to reproduction.

But Beauvoir could argue that these two reasons explaining the limitations of women's embodiment are not as incompatible as I have suggested. In fact the idea that reproduction itself is limiting can be made compatible with the oppression thesis through the notion of 'facticity'. If it is a biological 'fact' that reproduction ties women more to the species than men, that their physiology renders their sexuality more passive and their bodies weaker than men's, then this is simply a question of 'facticity' and there is no point rebelling against it. What is important is the way we signify our facticity, and constitute ourselves as a transcendence of it. The rejection of oppression is a rejection of a particular way of signifying women's facticity. This is the second answer suggested by Beauvoir's text to the question of how some of her descriptions of female embodiment can be reconciled with her account of oppression. It is a neat answer. But it isn't satisfactory because the distinction between 'facticity' and 'value' is not quite as neutral as it appears. Neither is Beauvoir's presentation of the biological 'facts'.

Life, self-consciousness and the transcendent body

Although at a biological level the lives of both male and female individuals are to a certain extent subject to the dictates of the life of the species, according to Beauvoir there is a crucial difference between man's subjection to the species and woman's. Man's individuality is thoroughly integrated into the life of the species. He senses no contradiction between his own individual projects and the demands of the species. Woman's individuality, on the contrary, 'is opposed by the interest of the species; it is as if she were possessed by foreign forces – alienated' (SS57). At this same biological level, the genitalia and sexual experiences of male and female also differ. The penis is animated, a 'tool', the vagina an 'inert receptacle' (SS54). For the male, although intercourse represents the transcendence of the individual towards the species, it is simultaneously 'an outward relation to the world and to others', and a confirmation of his own individuality. For the female, intercourse can only be 'an interior event', a renunciation of her individuality for the benefit of the species. The asymmetry between the single moment in which the male transcends himself towards the species in the ejaculation of sperm, and the lifelong servitude of the female to her offspring accounts for this difference. The result is: 'From puberty to menopause woman is the theatre of a play that unfolds within her and in which she is not personally concerned. ... Woman, like man *is* her body; but her body is something other than herself' (SS60–1).

Now Beauvoir presents 'the enslavement of the female to the

species' as though it is a simple question of biological 'fact'.[32] Actually this presentation of female biology is structured by a distinction between life and self-consciousness which derives from Beauvoir's reading of Hegel's account of the origin of self-consciousness. In the terms of this distinction, human self-consciousness is defined in opposition to the desire for self-preservation, and the interests of the individual define themselves in opposition to those of the species. Consequently any bodily process which is associated with the maintenance and preservation of species-life seems to undermine the autonomous self-constitution of the individual subject. Such processes therefore cannot be represented as *activities* of an agent. Rather, they are merely passive *events* in nature, events in which the individual must submit unconsciously to the dictates of nature. It should now be clear why, for Beauvoir, the body *qua* reproductive body signifies immanence and why reproduction alienates women from their individuality – explaining why Beauvoir denies any activity associated with the reproductive process the status of a project:

> The woman who gave birth, therefore, did not know the pride of creation; she felt herself the plaything of obscure forces, and the painful ordeal of childbirth seemed a useless or even troublesome accident. But in any case giving birth and suckling are not *activities*, they are natural functions; no project is involved; and that is why woman found in them no reason for a lofty affirmation of her existence – she submitted passively to her biologic fate. (SS94)

What remains unexplained however is why human self-consciousness is defined in opposition to the maintenance and preservation of life. Again Beauvoir's reading of Hegel is relevant here, for she argues that human individuality defines itself only through conscious confrontation with death, through the real or metaphorical risk of life. Male supremacy emerged, she claims, out of man's involvement in activities like hunting and warfare in which, through the risk of life, he transformed mere self-preservation into an activity or a project. To the extent that woman, by virtue of her reproductive capacity, was excluded from such activities she remained 'closely bound to her body, like an animal', doomed merely to repeat life, rather than exercise mastery over it.[33]

What is to be made of this explanation? Michèle Le Doeuff, comparing this explanation with sociobiological explanations of women's 'inferiority', has argued that it should be read as a deliberate non-explanation on Beauvoir's part. Her claim is that by acting as a non-explanation the purpose of this explanation is to show that women's oppression arises without reason, that it is completely arbitrary — hence this story of the origin of women's oppression is quite consistent with the oppression thesis.[34] I disagree. Given my analysis of the way in which Beauvoir's interpretation of male and female biology is structured by the oppositions between life and self-consciousness, and species and individual, it is clear that this explanation is crucial for understanding Beauvoir's views on the significance of women's embodiment. For it makes it clear why, oppression aside, women's bodies are not and cannot be perceived as 'the radiation of a subjective personality': because woman's body *qua* reproductive body or *qua* 'female' body not only signifies but immerses woman in 'Life' as repetition, against which transcendence as value is defined. But this in turn makes it clear that the distinction between the body as immanent and the body as transcendent is itself sexually marked. In other words, the reproductive body as immanence implicitly defines the ideal of the transcendent body. In contrast to the reproductive body which, in its passive functioning, dooms the subject to repetition and immerses her in nature, the transcendent body, by means of which the autonomous subject is able to surpass the brute givens of facticity, is a pure instrumentality of the will, an active body which surpasses itself as material thing. Clearly Beauvoir is aware that no human body can always be transcendent; both male and female bodies are subject to processes which are beyond the voluntary control of the subject. Nevertheless the implicit contrast between the transcendent body and the reproductive body makes the reproductive 'female' body the paradigmatic metaphor of the body as passive and involuntary. By contrast, the transcendent body presupposes a certain idealised conception of the male body as a body which, in principle at least, is under the voluntary control of intellect and will.

This explains why Beauvoir's appropriation of the distinction between the body as immanence and the body as transcendence to illuminate women's situation gives rise in her text to two incompatible accounts of the significance of women's embodiment. On the one hand, this distinction enables her to account for oppression as an experience in which, because she feels her body as alien to her subjectivity, as immanent, the oppressed subject is both subject and object for herself simultaneously. On the other hand, because the ideal of the body as transcendent is defined in opposition to the reproductive body, woman's body *qua* reproductive body will always be alien to her *qua* autonomous subject.

The implication of this argument is that Beauvoir associates autonomous subjectivity with masculinity. I have already argued that Beauvoir's analysis of oppression posits a residual, sexually undifferentiated subjectivity which remains somehow untouched by the mechanisms of oppression and which is the locus of the subject's resistance to her oppression. It has also been shown that there is an intimate connection between the notion of the autonomous subject and the ideal of the body as transcendence. The subject asserts herself as freedom in and through her body which, as transcendent, is the instrumentality of her will. But if the ideal of the transcendent body presupposes a masculine body then the human subject as freedom is not sexually undifferentiated at all. Beauvoir's residual subjectivity is in fact a masculine subjectivity. What this means is that women can only exercise their autonomy, in projects and in relations with others, to the extent that they transcend their bodies *qua* reproductive bodies. In other words, women can only be authentic subjects by denying the ethical significance of their sexually specific bodily perspectives. Beauvoir makes this clear when she argues, in her discussion of the emergence of male supremacy, that the value created by men deprives the reproductive body – which merely repeats rather than transcends Life – of all value: 'woman also aspires to and recognizes the values that are concretely attained by the male. He it is who opens up the future to which she also reaches out' (SS96).

But how does all this square with Beauvoir's claim that a genuinely ethical relation with others requires that we recognise the other in 'his otherness and in that freedom by which he escapes'? How does it square with her claim that ethics must start from the recognition that human beings are irreducibly plural? For from the preceding analysis it seems that Beauvoir's conception of autonomous subjectivity requires a fundamental sameness of the human being which underlies and transcends sexual differentiation. Mutual recognition is a recognition of the otherness of the other only insofar as he or she is the *same* as me. I want to suggest that the problem with Beauvoir's account of autonomous agency, and the reason why she is unable to incorporate within it a recognition of the differences between bodily perspectives, is that the distinction between the immanent and the transcendent body commits her to the view that transcendence, or autonomous agency, is achieved through an exertion of will by means of which the subject gains self-mastery by exercising control over her or his immanent body. But given this conception of autonomy it is almost inevitable that women's bodily processes will be represented as passive, natural *events* and that women will appear as merely subject to these processes, rather than as active agents with respect to them.[35]

Notes

1 Simone de Beauvoir, *The Second Sex*, trans. H. M. Parshley (Harmondsworth: Penguin Books, 1972), p. 15. Subsequent page references in parentheses in text.

2 G. W. F. Hegel, *Phenomenology of Spirit*, trans. A. V. Miller, with an analysis of text and foreword by J. N. Findlay (Oxford: Clarendon Press, 1977); Jean-Paul Sartre, *Being and Nothingness*, trans. Hazel E. Barnes (New York: Philosophical Library, 1972).

3 See for example: Genevieve Lloyd, 'Masters, slaves and others', *Radical Philosophy*, 34 (1983), Special Issue on *Women, Gender and Philosophy*; Elizabeth Spelman, 'Woman as body: ancient and contemporary views', *Feminist Studies*, 8:1 (1982), 109–31; and my article 'Simone de Beauvoir: philosophy and/or the female body', in Elizabeth Gross and Carole Pateman (eds), *Feminist Challenges: Social and Political Theory* (Sydney: Allen & Unwin, 1986), pp. 144–56.

4 Moira Gatens, 'Feminism, philosophy and riddles without answers', in Gross and Pateman (eds), *Feminist Challenges*, pp. 13–29.

5 Michèle Le Doeuff, 'Women and philosophy', translated by Debbie Pope, *Radical Philosophy*, 17 (1977), 2–11. However, despite the fact that, in keeping with this argument, Le Doeuff calls *The Second Sex* 'a morganatic wedding-present' and a 'labour of love', in her own work on Beauvoir Le Doeuff's main aim is to show how Beauvoir actually transforms Sartrean

existentialism in applying it to the situation of women. See Michèle Le Doeuff, 'Operative philosophy: Simone de Beauvoir and existentialism', trans. Colin Gordon, *Ideology & Consciousness*, 6 (1979), 47–57, and the more extended discussion of the intellectual and erotic relationship between Sartre and Beauvoir in *Hipparchia's Choice*, trans. Trista Selous (Oxford: Basil Blackwell, 1991).

6 For another very interesting re-assessment of Beauvoir's intellectual relationship to Sartre along these lines, see Sonia Kruks, 'Gender and subjectivity: Simone de Beauvoir and contemporary feminism', *Signs*, 18:1 (1992), 89–110.

7 Beauvoir rarely uses the term 'autonomy'. My discussion uses the term 'autonomy' and Beauvoir's preferred terms 'transcendence', 'freedom' and 'authenticity' interchangeably.

8 Simone de Beauvoir, *The Ethics of Ambiguity*, trans. Bernard Frechtman (Secaucus, N.J.: Citadel Press, 1975). Subsequent page references are in parentheses in the text. For other discussions of the relationship between *The Ethics of Ambiguity* and *The Second Sex* see Sonia Kruks, 'Gender and subjectivity'; Linda Singer, 'Interpretation and retrieval: rereading Beauvoir', in *Hypatia Reborn: Essays in Feminist Philosophy*, eds Azizah Y. Al-Hibri and Margaret Simons (Bloomington: Indiana University Press, 1990), pp. 323–35; and Toril Moi, *Simone de Beauvoir: The Making of an Intellectual Woman* (Oxford: Basil Blackwell, 1994), pp. 148–9.

9 Kruks, 'Gender and Subjectivity', similarly identifies two distinct kinds of self/other relation in Beauvoir's work, which she characterises as the self/other relation between social equals (where otherness is mitigated by reciprocity) and the self/other relation between social unequals (where otherness entails subordination).

10 The term 'phallocentrism' is used to characterise discourses, texts and systems of signification which are structured around a hierarchical opposition between masculinity and femininity and in which femininity is defined solely in relation to an already defined masculinity, as either the same as, or a deviation from, it.

11 My presentations of the views of Sartre and Hegel in this essay focus only on those aspects of their work that are salient to an understanding of Beauvoir's appropriation of certain themes in their philosophies.

12 Kant uses the dove analogy in his *The Metaphysics of Morals*, trans. Mary Gregor (New York: Cambridge University Press, 1991).

13 In Hegel's system Spirit remains merely an abstract notion unless it becomes concrete by externalising itself in Nature and in human self-consciousness. Similarly in the master-slave dialectic, the slave's self-consciousness assumes concrete content when he externalises himself in labour.

14 Genevieve Lloyd, 'Masters, slaves and others'. For Sartre's discussion of the Look, see *Being and Nothingness*, pp. 252–82.

15 In effect, what I am arguing here is that Beauvoir's view of our relations

with others is closer to Hegel's more optimistic version of the self/other distinction in the master-slave dialectic than to Sartre's version of this distinction in *Being and Nothingness*. Marion Tapper has proposed a similar view, with respect to Beauvoir's analysis of love, in her article 'Sartre and de Beauvoir on love', *Critical Philosophy*, 2:1 (1985) 37–47.

16 This point is also made by Michèle Le Doeuff and Moira Gatens. Michèle Le Doeuff, 'Operative philosophy'; Moira Gatens, 'Feminism, philosophy and riddles without answers' in Gross and Pateman (eds), *Feminist Challenges*.

17 The term 'internalisation' is not actually used by Beauvoir herself. However, I would suggest it appropriately captures, without distorting, her view.

18 Sandra Lee Bartky's theory of psychological oppression is an elaboration of this conception of 'internalisation' as alienation. See Sandra Lee Bartky, *Femininity and Domination* (London: Routledge, 1990).

19 More recent analyses of the operations of power, such as that of Foucault, have questioned this notion of a residual subjectivity that somehow escapes the determinations of power. See especially Michel Foucault, *The History of Sexuality*, vol. 1, trans. Robert Hurley (New York: Random House, Vintage Books, 1980); *Power/Knowledge*, ed. Colin Gordon, (New York: Pantheon Books, 1980); *Discipline and Punish*, trans. Alan Sheridan, (Harmondsworth: Penguin Books, 1982). According to Foucault, the subject is not alienated from her or him self by oppression but is rather constituted as a subject within and by the network of practices through which power operates. Applying this analysis to the situation of women it might be argued that there is no residual sexually undifferentiated subjectivity which escapes the operations of power. Rather, within patriarchal social relations subjects are always already sexually differentiated subjects whose subjectivity is bound up with their sex in such a way that the one cannot be extricated from the other. In other words, as Marilyn Frye has argued, patriarchal social relations require a rigid sexual dimorphism in which subjectivity is only intelligible as sexually differentiated subjectivity; to be a subject is necessarily to be a sexed subject. See Marilyn Frye, 'Sexism', in *The Politics of Reality* (Trumansberg, New York: The Crossing Press, 1983). While I find Foucault's suggestion that subjects are constituted within and by relations of power illuminating, my concern is that the individual subject of experience as agent tends to disappear in his account of the operations of power, as well as in his notion of 'resistance'. Some interesting appraisals of the implications of Foucault's work for feminism can be found in some of the articles in Irene Diamond and Lee Quinby (eds), *Feminism and Foucault: Reflections on Resistance* (Boston: Northeastern University Press, 1988).

20 Here I am thinking particularly of Michèle Le Doeuff's reflections on women and the metaphor of femininity in the context of her analyses of the philosophical imaginary. Le Doeuff's readings of the way in which the metaphor of femininity functions in certain philosophical discourses are an elaboration of Beauvoir's point that 'femininity' as myth or metaphor is dialectically necessary to those systems of signification which define them-

selves in opposition to it. See Michèle Le Doeuff, *The Philosophical Imaginary*, trans. Colin Gordon (Stanford: Stanford University Press, 1989). Kristeva's view that the 'feminine' designates a position of critical marginality with respect to phallocentric discourses also echoes this view. See especially her articles reprinted in E. Marks and I. de Courtivron (eds), *New French Feminisms: An Anthology* (Brighton: Harvester, 1981): 'Woman can never be defined', pp. 137–41; 'Oscillation between power and denial', pp. 165–7. See also 'Women's time', pp. 187–213 in Toril Moi (ed.), *The Kristeva Reader* (Columbia University Press., N.Y., 1986) and 'Talking about polylogue' in Toril Moi (ed.), *French Feminist Thought: A Reader* (Oxford: Basil Blackwell, 1987). See also Jacques Derrida, 'Choreographies: an interview with Christie V. McDonald', *Diacritics*, 12 (1982), 66–76.

21 My argument in this part of the essay builds upon an earlier article on Beauvoir entitled 'Simone de Beauvoir: philosophy and/or the female body', *Feminist Challenges*. My later formulation of the argument here, however, is indebted to Iris Young's critique of the distinction, within existential phenomenology, between the body as transcendent and the body as immanent. See Iris Marion Young, 'Pregnant subjectivity and the limits of existential phenomenology', in Don Ihde and Hugh J. Silverman (eds), *Descriptions* (Albany, N.Y.: State University of New York Press, 1985).

22 See especially Maurice Merleau-Ponty's *Phenomenology of Perception*, trans. Colin Smith (London: Routledge and Kegan Paul, 1962).

23 Juliet Mitchell argues that Beauvoir's interpretation of psychoanalysis misreads Freud in a crudely determinist way, and that her account of the psychical significance of sex differences is derived mainly from the conservative woman psychoanalyst Helene Deutsch. See Juliet Mitchell, 'Simone de Beauvoir: Freud and the Second Sex' in Part Two, Section II of *Psychoanalysis and Feminism* (Harmondsworth: Penguin Books, 1975). I tend to agree with Mitchell on this point, but my interest here is mainly in the philosophical use to which Beauvoir puts her reading of psychoanalysis.

24 This point is illustrated quite graphically in the following four passages from different parts of *The Second Sex*. The first passage describes the young girl's experiences of menstruation, which Beauvoir calls 'the untidy event that is repeated each month':

> there are children who weep for hours when they realize that they are condemned to this fate. And what strengthens their revolt still further is the knowledge that this shameful blemish is known also to men; they would prefer at least that their humiliating feminine condition might remain shrouded in mystery for males. But no; father, brothers, cousins, all the men know, and even joke about it sometimes. Here disgust at her too fleshly body arises or is exacerbated in the girl. And though the first surprise is over, the monthly annoyance is not similarly effaced; at each recurrence the girl feels again the same disgust at this flat and stagnant odour emanating from her – an odour of the

swamp, of wilted violets – disgust at this blood, less red, more dubious, than that which flowed from her childish abrasions. (SS337–8)

The second passage is an account of the girl's experience of the body at puberty:

Apprehended through this complaining and passive flesh, the whole universe seems a burden too heavy to bear. Overburdened, submerged, she becomes a stranger to herself because she is a stranger to the rest of the world. Syntheses break down, moments of time are no longer connected, other people are recognized but absent-mindedly; and if reasoning and logic remain intact, as in melancholia, they are put to the service of emotional manifestations arising from a state of organic disorder. (SS353)

The third passage is an account of the difference between men's and women's experiences of their genitalia:

The sex organ of a man is simple and neat as a finger; it is readily visible and often exhibited to comrades with proud rivalry; but the feminine sex organ is mysterious even to the woman herself, concealed, mucous, and humid, as it is; it bleeds each month, it is often sullied with body fluids, it has a secret and perilous life of its own. Woman does not recognize herself in it, and this explains in large part why she does not recognize its desires as hers. These manifest themselves in an embarrassing manner. Man 'gets stiff', but woman 'gets wet'; in the very word there are childhood memories of bed-wetting, of guilty and involuntary yielding to the need to urinate. Man feels the same disgust at involuntary nocturnal emissions; to eject a fluid, urine or semen, does not humiliate: it is an active operation; but it is humiliating if the liquid flows out passively, for then the body is no longer an organism with muscles, nerves, sphincters, ... but is rather a vessel, a container, composed of inert matter and but the plaything of capricious mechanical forces. If the body leaks – as an ancient wall or a dead body may leak – it seems to liquefy rather than to eject fluid: a horrid decomposition.

Feminine sex desire is the soft throbbing of a mollusc. Whereas man is impetuous, woman is only impatient; her expectation can become ardent without ceasing to be passive; man dives upon his prey like the eagle and the hawk; woman lies in wait like the carnivorous plant, the bog, in which insects and children are swallowed up. She is absorption, suction, humus, pitch and glue, a passive influx, insinuating and viscous: thus, at least, she vaguely feels herself to be. (SS406–7)

The final passage is an account of how, according to de Beauvoir, women experience pregnancy and maternity:

The transcendence of the artisan, of the man of action, contains the element of subjectivity; but in the mother-to-be the antithesis of subject and object ceases to exist; she and the child with which she is swollen make up together an equivocal pair overwhelmed by life. Ensnared by nature, the pregnant woman is plant and animal, a storehouse of colloids, an incubator, an egg; she scares children who are proud of their young, straight bodies and makes young people titter contemptuously because she is a human being, a conscious and free individual, who has become life's passive instrument.

Ordinarily life is but a condition of existence; in gestation it appears as creative; but that is a strange kind of creation which is accomplished in a contingent and passive manner ... With her ego surrendered, alienated in her body and in her social dignity, the mother enjoys the comforting illusion of feeling that she is a human being *in herself, a value*.

But this is only an illusion. For she does not really make the baby, it makes itself within her; her flesh engenders flesh only ... Creative acts originating in liberty establish the object as value and give it the quality of the essential; whereas the child in the maternal body is not thus justified; it is still only a gratuitous cellular growth, a brute fact of nature as contingent on circumstances as death and corresponding philosophically with it. (SS512–14)

25 Thus in her discussion of menstruation she says:

In a sexually equalitarian society, woman would regard menstruation simply as her special way of reaching adult life; the human body in both men and women has other and more disagreeable needs to be taken care of, but they are easily adjusted to because, being common to all, they do not represent blemishes for anyone; the menses inspire horror in the adolescent girl because they throw her into an inferior and defective category. This sense of being declassed will weigh heavily upon her. She would retain her pride in her bleeding body if she did not lose her pride in being human. (SS340–1)

26 Linda Zerilli proposes a reading of Beauvoir's discussions of maternity that is consistent with this kind of interpretation. See Linda M. G. Zerilli, 'A process without a subject: Simone de Beauvoir and Julia Kristeva on maternity', *Signs*, 18:1(1992), 111–35. Zerilli suggests that readers ought not to take Beauvoir's remarks about the female body and maternity at face value. Rather they should be read as part of a rhetorical strategy that aims to expose and to subvert the dominant representations and experiences of women's bodies, in particular the maternal body, within patriarchal culture.

27 In *Powers of Horror* Kristeva characterises abjection as a feeling of disgust at the incorporated/expelled object (food, faeces, vomit, menstrual blood, etc.). According to Kristeva this disgust both signals the subject's recognition, and protects it from the recognition, that the expelled object is never fully expelled. Rather, it is 'something rejected from which one does not part' (p. 4), reminding the subject of its corporeality and threatening its stability and unity. Abjection is caused by whatever 'disturbs identity, system, order. What does not respect borders, systems, rules' (ibid.). See Julia Kristeva; *Powers of Horror*, trans. Leon Roudiez (New York: Columbia University Press, 1982). For a brief outline of Kristeva's account of abjection see Elizabeth Grosz, *Sexual Subversions* (Sydney: Allen & Unwin, 1989).

28 For an example see Grosz' analysis of the case of Dora, in Grosz, *Sexual Subversions*, pp. 134–9. For a rather different feminist analysis of anorexia, but one which relates interestingly to Beauvoir's analysis because it is also concerned with philosophical discussions of subjectivity, see Gillian Brown, 'Anorexia, humanism, and feminism', *Yale Journal of Criticism*, 5:1 (1991), 189–215.

29 Judith Butler argues this case in her article 'Variations on sex and gender: Beauvoir and Wittig', in Benhabib, S. and D. Cornell (eds), *Feminism as Critique* (Ithaca: Cornell University Press, 1987).

30 See *Being and Nothingness*, pp. 600–15. Some feminist interpreters of Sartre have argued that these metaphors do not render Sartre's whole philosophy irredeemably sexist because they function in his text merely as metaphors. See Christine Pierce and Margery Collins, 'Holes and slime: sexism in Sartre's psychoanalysis', in Carol C. Gould and Marx W. Wartofsky (eds), *Women and Philosophy* (New York: Capricorn, 1976). The idea that one can always distinguish the metaphorical aspects of philosophical texts from their conceptual content has been radically questioned by many recent writers, most notably by Jacques Derrida. Derrida's analysis aside, in what follows I intend to show that in *The Second Sex* the very notion of the body as transcendent is defined in opposition to the immanent reproductive body.

31 In pointing to the importance for Beauvoir of interventions into the reproductive process I am not implying that self-determination with respect to reproduction is unimportant for women, nor am I denying the significance of some technological developments – especially in the area of contraception – in increasing women's capacities for self-determination in this respect. However, technological intervention into the reproductive process has not only had the positive effect of increasing women's capacity for bodily self-determination in certain respects, in some ways it has also helped reinforce both the representation of women as passive with respect to their bodily processes and the idea that self-determination involves control over the body. Given this, an adequate appraisal of the benefits and disbenefits for women of various technologies of reproduction, as well as of the moral issues raised by these technologies, must also involve a challenge to conceptions of autonomous agency, such as that of Beauvoir, as control over the body.

32 Recent feminist critiques of science and the philosophy of science have uncovered the extent to which some biological accounts of sex differences are structured on sexist assumptions about female sexuality. See for example Ruth Hubbard's article 'Have only men evolved?' in Sandra Harding and Merrill Hintikka (eds), *Discovering Reality: Feminist Perspectives on Epistemology, Ontology, Metaphysics, and Philosophy of Science* (Dordrecht: Reidel, 1983).

33 The following excerpts from Part II, Ch. 1, entitled 'The Nomads', provide the textual support for this account of Beauvoir's explanation of the origin of women's subordination:

The warrior put his life in jeopardy to elevate the prestige of the horde, the clan to which he belonged. And in this he proved dramatically that life is not the supreme value for man, but on the contrary that it should be made to serve ends more important than itself. The worst curse that was laid upon woman was that she should be excluded from these warlike forays. For it is not in giving life but in risking life that man is raised above the animal; that is why superiority has been accorded in humanity not to the sex that brings forth but to that which kills.

Here we have the key to the whole mystery. On the biological level a species is maintained only by creating itself anew; but this creation results only in repeating the same Life in more individuals. But man assures the repetition of Life while transcending Life through Existence; by this transcendence he creates values that deprive pure repetition of all value ... [woman's] misfortune is to have been biologically destined for the repetition of Life, when even in her own view Life does not carry within itself its reasons for being, reasons that are more important than the life itself ...

The female, to a greater extent than the male, is the prey of the species; and the human race has always sought to escape its specific destiny. The support of life became for man an activity and a project through the invention of the tool; but in maternity woman remained closely bound to her body, like an animal. It is because humanity calls itself in question in the matter of living— that is to say, values the reasons for living above mere life – that, confronting woman, man assumes mastery. Man's design is not to repeat himself in time: it is to take control of the instant and mould the future. It is male activity that ... has prevailed over the confused forces of life; it has subdued Nature and Woman. (SS95–7)

34 Michèle Le Doeuff, 'Operative philosophy', 47–57.

35 This representation of women's bodily processes also informs much of the contemporary ethical debate over issues connected with reproduction, from the abortion debate to free market justifications of surrogacy, in which bodily autonomy is equated with control over a body which is conceived as extrinsic to, sometimes the property of, the autonomous agent.

6

Reading, resistance and
disempowerment

STEPHEN HORTON

In this essay I offer a partial explanation as to why Simone de Beauvoir's *The Second Sex* has had relatively little impact upon the sphere of analytic philosophy.[1] This lack of impact is somewhat surprising since Beauvoir's volume, given its style and wide-ranging content, has much in common with certain aspects of the analytic tradition in philosophy. In places *The Second Sex* has a depth of analysis and rigour reminiscent of the work of an analytic philosopher and yet, at the same time, it is wide ranging in that it does not restrict itself to any particular area of discourse. Indeed, during the course of her arguments Beauvoir considers, amongst other things, the social, political, ethical, moral and scientific aspects of the condition of the second sex.[2] The tendency to grant oneself licence to comment upon a diverse range of subject areas is one of the hallmarks of the analytic tradition. (Although to draw this parallel too strongly would be to underplay both the politics of Beauvoir's interventions and the pontifical nature of those of the analytic philosopher.) In addition, at least on initial examination, Beauvoir seems to be writing within the same Enlightenment tradition within which analytic philosophy locates itself.[3] The lack of interest shown by analytic philosophers in *The Second Sex* cannot have resulted from the fact that the text was originally written in French since it appeared in its only English translation within four years of initial publication in France.[4] Equally, it cannot be explained simply in terms of the existential bias of the text — particularly since the sole

English translation seems to understate somewhat this aspect of Beauvoir's theoretical position.[5] Therefore, other reasons must explain this lack of interest in Beauvoir's *The Second Sex* on the part of analytic philosophers. It is with a search for some of these reasons that this essay will concern itself.

I suggest that there are two interconnected aspects of Beauvoir's text that are responsible for this apparent lacuna. The first results from what is, even in the English translation, Beauvoir's most obvious central thesis: 'One is not born, but rather becomes, a woman. No biological, psychological, or economic fate determines the figure that the human female presents in society; it is civilisation as a whole that produces this creature, intermediate between male and eunuch, which is described as feminine' (SS295). Following Sonia Kruks,[6] I hold that one of the implications of the above thesis is the undermining of one of the Enlightenment's most precious myths, namely the existence of a stable, self-conscious, fully rational subject. To accept or even to consider seriously Beauvoir's thesis, as I shall show, would be to bring into question the most fundamental support of the analytic philosophical tradition: without the existence of such a subject the neutrality and therefore the power-base of analytic philosophy would be severely undermined. I shall discuss this aspect of Beauvoir's text in the first part of this essay.

However, it should be noted that Beauvoir can in no sense be said to be the originator of such criticisms. Indeed, criticism of the Enlightenment's notion of the subject has a long history dating back to at least the work of Ferdinand de Saussure,[7] whose influence runs through the work of such modern day (continental) philosophers as Jacques Derrida[8] and into the work of such postmodernists as Jean-François Lyotard,[9] and Ernesto Laclau and Chantal Mouffe.[10] For example, in their first major work together, Laclau and Mouffe describe their notion of the subject thus:

> Whenever we use the category of the 'subject' in this text, we will do so in the sense of 'subject positions' within a discursive structure. Subjects cannot, therefore, be the origin of social relations .... From the discursive character of all subject positions, nothing follows concerning the type of relation that could exist among them. As every subject position is a discursive position, it partakes

of the open character of every discourse; consequently, the various positions cannot be totally fixed in a closed system of differences.[11]

Granted that nothing can be said to follow, necessarily, from the nature of the subject, followers of the Enlightenment tradition (such as analytic philosophers) are, as I shall show, deprived of an easily available source of justification and power for their various projects. Indeed, in the words of Derrida, 'in the absence of a centre of origin, everything [becomes] discourse ... that is to say, a system in which the central signified, the original or transcendental signified [here the Cartesian subject], is never absolutely present outside a system of differences.'[12] Nevertheless, what makes Beauvoir so dangerous to the discourse of analytic philosophy is that she, unlike Derrida *et al.*, at one and the same time raises the possibility of challenging the Enlightenment's notion of the subject, yet clearly remains located within the Enlightenment tradition.[13] Indeed, it is this wish to remain within the Enlightenment tradition, whilst opening up the possibility of challenging its notion of the subject, that ultimately promises to damage the credibility of Beauvoir's project in *The Second Sex*. Thus, *The Second Sex* can be read as a warning to any who rely upon such a notion of the subject of the dangers of ever daring to question such a subject's viability.

This warning to the discourse of analytic philosophy manifests itself most clearly within *The Second Sex* with the emergence of an incongruity which results, in part, from Beauvoir's challenge to the Enlightenment's notion of the subject. This incongruity exposes a fundamental flaw in that faculty of the Enlightenment subject upon which both analytic philosophers and Beauvoir rely heavily, namely reason. Indeed, as this essay shows, invoking the power of reason as sponsor and protector brings with it some unexpected dangers. I shall discuss this incongruity in the second part of this essay.

The 'subject' of philosophy

In this section I investigate the implications of Beauvoir's position in *The Second Sex* for the notion of the 'subject' as used by analytic philosophers. My point of departure is Sonia Kruks's

1992 essay 'Gender and subjectivity: Simone de Beauvoir and contemporary feminism'.[14]

Kruks begins by noting certain problems with the postmodern notion of the subject.[15] Such a notion, it emerges, has a tendency to reduce the subject to a mere victim 'of the play of signifiers'.[16] This leaves little room for any genuine – that is, conscious – political activity.[17] Nevertheless, Kruks holds that, despite these shortcomings, the postmodern view of the subject does have unequivocal merit.

One of the implications of the postmodern view of the subject, as noted in my initial section, is that 'subjectivity is never "pure" or fully autonomous but inheres in selves that are shaped by cultural discourses and that are always embodied – selves that thus are also gendered.'[18] The positive effect of this view is that it undermines certain essentialist and universalist tendencies present within the Enlightenment ideal of the subject. Discourses which rely upon the Enlightenment notion of the subject tend to presuppose a self modelled on that of the Cartesian *cogito*. This self is unique, stable, coherent and fully rational.

In its extreme form, analytic philosophy reduces the self to only that which is rational. The following quotation is taken from a 1912 text by Bertrand Russell, one of the founders of the analytic tradition: 'the free intellect will value more the abstract and universal knowledge into which the accidents of private history do not enter, than the knowledge brought by the senses, and dependent, as such knowledge must be, upon an exclusive and personal point of view and a body whose sense-organs distort as much as they reveal.'[19] Although this view was expressed early in the second decade of the twentieth century, its universalist sentiments, derived from its faith in the unbiased nature of the power of reason, still permeate much of the work of those influenced by or working within the analytic tradition. One example is John Rawls's *A Theory of Justice*.[20] In the following quotation we find Rawls offering an explanation and justification for his theoretical starting point for the formulation of his theory of justice:

> The essential point is that we need an argument showing which principles, if any, free and equal *rational persons* would choose ...

> My suggestion is that we think of the original position as the point of view from which noumenal selves see the world ... The description of the original position interprets the point of view of the noumenal selves, of what it means to be a free and equal *rational being*.[21] (My emphasis.)

This text continues to be treated as seminal by many of those who teach and write about that variety of social and political philosophy still taught to the large number of students 'brought up' in the analytic tradition of philosophy.

This faith in the impartial power of reason spills over not only into logic, epistemology and political philosophy but also into moral philosophy and applied ethics. A currently popular introductory book to moral philosophy, Jonathan Glover's *Causing Death and Saving Lives*,[22] relies heavily upon the universalising and impartial aspects of reason in order to construct its particular blend of applied ethics.

Given that the analytic philosopher is trained *par excellence* in the use of this power of reason she, or more likely he, finds herself in a unique position. She is in a position to pursue knowledge for knowledge's sake, whether it be in the field of logic, ethics or politics, untainted and unrestricted by mundane concerns. Indeed, to adapt an idea of Elizabeth Spelman's:

> Once the concept of 'rational person' is divorced from the concept of 'historically and culturally located person', conceptual room is made for the idea of a person who is no particular historical and/or culturally located/gendered person – he or she has no colour, no accent, no sex, no particular characteristics that require having a body. He or she is somehow all and only 'rational person'; that is her/his only identifying feature. And so it will seem inappropriate or besides the point to think of persons in terms of sexual, cultural, racial or class characteristics.[23]

Without such a notion of the self and its associated ideal of reason, it is difficult to see how the romantic and popular view of the philosopher, which according to the OED is one who 'devotes himself [sic] to the search of fundamental truth', could be maintained. It is this supposedly dispassionate and therefore independent power of reason that enables the analytic philosopher to speak with authority upon matters as diverse as religion, politics, morality and science: 'The eternal rule of right reason,

virtue, and knowledge is the source of all progress, when humanity heeds it, rather than those desires that depart from it.'[24] It is
my aim here, with the help of Beauvoir's *The Second Sex*, to bring
into question the very autonomy of this miraculous power.

The value of Beauvoir's work in this respect is the challenge
she poses to the abstract notion of the 'subject' of analytic philosophy. This challenge is somewhat more tangible than that offered
by the poststructuralists and postmodernists since she does not
seek to dispose of the subject altogether, but gives a rather more
complex view of its situation and the influences upon it. Thus,
although throughout *The Second Sex* Beauvoir clings to an almost
Sartrean reverence for freedom – 'the individual defines himself
[*sic*] by making his own choices through the world about him'
(SS80–1) – this freedom is tempered by the constraints of an individual's social location: 'it must be repeated once more that in
human society nothing is natural and that woman, like much
else, is a product elaborated by civilization' (SS734).[25] In other
words, by situating the subject in the tension-ridden 'spaces'
between freedom and the social influences around her or him,
Beauvoir can, as Kruks so succinctly puts it:

> both acknowledge the weight of social construction, including
> gender, in the formation of the self and yet refuse to reduce the self
> to an 'effect'. She can grant a degree of autonomy to the self – as is
> necessary in order to retain such key notions as political action,
> responsibility, and the oppression of the self – while also acknowl-
> edging the real constraints on autonomous subjectivity produced
> by oppressive situations.[26]

Interestingly, in contrast, Keefe reads Beauvoir's opposition
between freedom and the effects of the social as a flat contradiction, rather than as a dynamic tension in the way Kruks
suggests.[27] This is very much how such a tension would be read
by an analytic philosopher. Indeed, without the 'law of noncontradiction', Enlightenment reason as employed by the analytic
philosopher would lose one of its most powerful allies.[28] (It seems
to have escaped the notice of such philosophers that it is this very
'law' which prevents the rational resolution of such debates as
those between supporters of freewill and their determinist oppo-
nents which continue to rage within the analytic tradition of
philosophy.)

The image of a socially-located self which Beauvoir constructs clearly takes us a long way from the unity and intactness of the subject of either Sartrean existentialism or the discourse of analytic philosophy. Yet it does not take us quite as far as the disseminated subject of postmodernity, typically described as 'a subjectivity which is precarious, contradictory and in process, constantly being reconstituted in discourse each time we think or speak'.[29] Beauvoir, therefore, seems to indicate the necessity of retaining enough substance for the subject to give the notion of 'political action' credence, whilst bringing into question the wisdom of the unswerving dedication given to the model of the abstracted, rational self by uncritical supporters of the Enlightenment project.[30] Indeed, in *The Second Sex*, although Beauvoir continually emphasises the profound effects upon the individual of its social environment, (e.g. SS31, 47, 69, 84, 307 and 734) she emphasises and re-emphasises the possibility of this individual making genuinely free choices. (e.g. SS80–1, 321, 391 and 539) For example: 'the idea of liberty is not incompatible with the existence of certain constants' (SS78). 'The truth is that [in determining a woman's sexuality] there is never a single determining [social/psychological] factor; it is always a matter of choice, arrived at in a complex total situation and based upon a free decision .... Environmental circumstances, however, have a considerable influence on the choice.' (SS437). Why is it so important that the 'subject' of analytic philosophy resists becoming affected by the mundane effects of the social? In short, if it cannot resist such 'contamination' then it would be forced to admit its own complex social situation. Once immersed in such social complications and their ensuing power relations, it would be difficult for analytic philosophers to continue to take for granted their logic-based universality and, therefore, the myth it supports of a society comprised of free and equal rational beings. It is the possibility of such a myth that endows analytic philosophy with the power-base it requires to pontificate upon matters moral, political and ethical. Indeed, to adapt a comment of Mark Poster's (written whilst discussing the work of Michel Foucault), without this possibility the writers of such philosophical texts would have to recognise their employment of a theoretical framework: 'which is always partial, always limited in the field in which it illuminates and therefore can never serve as an exclusive, all-encompassing foundation for [a moral, ethical or political] theory.'[31] However, to be fair to analytic philosophers, the potential for partiality of a theory such as Rawls's has not escaped all commentators working within this tradition. For example, Milton Fisk notes the following problems with the methodology Rawls employs in deriving his 'neutral' theory of justice:

> This defence of the neutrality of the reflective sense of justice depends on showing that the conception of humans as by nature free, equal, and rational itself has title to neutrality. This title, however, is defective in several ways ... [T]his conception of human nature is supported only by showing that certain values characteristic of the institutions of liberal democracy are associated with it ... There are alternative conceptions of human nature ... The existence of ... alternative conceptions of human nature undercuts the title to neutrality of the liberal conception. It [thus] appears that Rawls' working conception of human nature does not supply the principles of justice he derives from the original position with moral weight outside the context of liberal democracy.[32]

Thus, holds Fisk, the ultimate result of Rawls's theory is to lend stabilising support to the *status quo* of western liberal democratic societies. This occurs, comments Fisk, because of the model of reason employed by Rawls, namely 'analytic reason', which 'merely refines and abstracts from something it identifies as a consensus'.[33] Therefore: 'It is not accidental, then, that [Rawls's] theory mobilises analytic reason, with its reputation for thoroughness, objectivity, and hence the permanence of its product, to provide the conception that is the basis for [his theory].'[34] Despite Fisk's warning, and his associated recommendation that what he labels 'analytic reason' should be tempered with a sense of history, the myth of the fully rational self and the reputation of reason's inherent neutrality continue to grant each other sustenance which, in turn, grants power to those possessors of analytic reason. Indeed, even Fisk never fully challenges this analytic notion of reason; he restricts himself to a suggestion as to a certain temperance in its use. Further, it never occurs to Fisk to question directly the role of the philosopher as neutral 'outsider' in discussions of justice, morality and the morass of modern society. Rather, he concentrates on the philosopher's misuse of the tools available to him: in the case of Rawls, Fisk highlights his employment of contract theory, his associated misuse of the power of analytic reason and the abstracted social subject upon which both rely. Thus, despite his often weighty criticisms, Fisk essentially leaves intact the myth that provides the basis for what perhaps could be described as the 'contract' of Enlightenment thinking and the projects to which it lends credence – namely a self which is unique, stable, coherent and fully rational.

As to how analytic philosophy uses the myth of the unique, stable, coherent and fully rational self to avoid the taint of the mundane, here Beauvoir provides us with an important insight. Although writing specifically about the myth of 'woman', her comments seem to apply equally well to the 'deeper' myth of the Enlightenment subject and the myth of 'Man as rational animal' which it supports. Indeed, as I shall show, a mechanism similar to the one that Beauvoir describes in the following quotation grounds what I will call the process of 'liberation by assimilation':

> There are different kinds of myths. This one, the myth of woman, … is a static myth. It projects into the realm of Platonic ideas a reality that is directly experienced or is conceptualized on a basis of experience; in place of fact … it substitutes a transcendental Idea, timeless, unchangeable, necessary. This idea is indisputable because it is beyond the given: it is endowed with absolute truth. Thus, as against the dispersed, contingent, and multiple existences of actual women, mythical thought opposes the Eternal Feminine, unique and changeless. If the definition provided for this concept is contradicted by the behaviour of flesh-and-blood women, it is the latter who are wrong: we are told not that Femininity is a false entity, but that the women concerned are not feminine. (SS282–3)

Analogously, the chosen methodology of philosophers working within the analytic tradition is heavily dependent upon stable, pre-existent, almost concrete, concepts. Thus, the starting point of any project for such philosophers is to focus upon the definition of – or 'unpacking' of – the presupposed concepts connected with the subject area under investigation and the interrelations between such concepts. Granted this methodology, the analytic philosopher cannot concern himself too greatly with evidence of an empirical kind. Rather, he must restrict himself, with regard to the subject matter being examined, to the abstract realm of conceptual interrogation and definition. Inevitably such investigations, especially of the ethical, moral and political kind, must start with some conception/definition of the individual. Indeed, without some notion of what it means to be a 'person' the analytic philosopher would have nothing to predicate such concepts as 'equality', 'freedom' and 'justice' of in his discussions. I have already noted the favoured and ideal notion of the subject employed by the analytic philosopher, namely that of 'rational person'. It is at this juncture that we find the source of the analytic philosopher's power over the realms of the moral, ethical and political. This power seeks to ground itself in two ways. Firstly, the philosopher, having so defined the subject, can then immediately, as just such a 'rational person', recognise himself as a representative of such individuals; indeed, granted his special training *vis-à-vis* the power and use of reason, perhaps an ideal representative. Secondly, given that by definition (at least, by analytic philosophy's definition) to be 'human' requires that one be 'rational', the results of his inquiries will have relevance not only for himself but for *all* rational individuals in similar general circumstances. That such philosophers remain inspired in this respect by the ghost of Plato's 'philosopher ruler' is obvious:

> the true philosopher, ... whose mind is on higher realities, has no time to look at the [actual] affairs of men, or take part in their quarrels with all the jealousy and bitterness they involve. His eyes are turned to contemplate fixed and immutable realties, a realm where there is no injustice done or suffered, but all is reason and order, and which is the model he imitates ... as far as he can.[35]

This faith in the power of reason pervades one of the few texts written in the analytic style of philosophy to discuss Beauvoir's *The Second Sex* in any detail, namely Janet Radcliffe Richards's book *The Sceptical Feminist*.[36] She insists that: 'Feminists can get nowhere without logic and science.'[37] And again, a little later, that: 'It is essential that in addition to their concern for individuals and their experiences feminists must learn the logic and science which have been the traditional preserve of men.'[38] Why should learning such a skill present a problem? Surely, and this is Radcliffe Richards's point, the best way to tackle the patriarchal tendencies within modern western democratic societies is for women to take on men and beat them at their own game, thus demonstrating the equal worth of women? It is at this point, however, that the notion of 'liberation by assimilation' gains its purchase.

By reifying reason in such a way, its supporters grant to its purveyors enormous powers. As is implied in the above discussion, analytic philosophers have a tendency to view themselves as reason's quartermasters. Coincidentally, this latter group is comprised, in the main, of just those persons who wield the most power politically and economically within western liberal democratic societies: white, middle-class males. Indeed, although the following remark of Le Doeuff's (made during her discussion of the work of Beauvoir in her *Hipparchia's Choice: An Essay Concerning Women, Philosophy, etc.*) concerns Sartre, it could just as well have been made about the majority of analytic philosophers: 'At its imaginary level, Sartre's philosophy rests on his social experience as a man, a European and a philosophy teacher which, taken as a whole, is an unequivocal experience of domination.'[39] Thus, it seems, being a representative of reason frequently coincides with being a representative of the most powerful interest group within the most powerful societies in the world. Beauvoir seems to hint a warning against such suspicious coincidences: 'Art, literature, philosophy, are attempts to found the world anew on a human liberty: that of the individual creator; to entertain such a pretension, one must first unequivocally assume the status of a being who has liberty' (SS720).

How does one assume the status of such a being? Radcliffe Richards offers the following counsel:

> Feminism on the whole is still relatively little concerned with [analytic] philosophy. It tends to be preoccupied with debates about what might broadly be called factual matters: the history of women's oppression, differential treatment of girls and boys, the effect expectation has on performance, economics and power, women's role in children's books, male sexual fantasy, anthropological studies of women, political methods, and so on. Disagreements are of a kind to be decided by further empirical evidence.[40]
>
> [Thus,] feminism often suffers from staying too close to women, and not looking enough at the general principles which have to be worked out and then applied to women's problems.[41]

Therefore, it seems, at least if one acts upon Radcliffe Richards's advice, that the way to attain the required status of a 'being who has liberty' is to cast off the specificity of being a woman and to take on the universalist mantle of the analytic philosopher.

However, it is not difficult to see why so few contemporary feminist philosophers have heeded her words. Indeed, to follow Radcliffe Richards's advice would be for them to cast off exactly that which defines the problems with which feminist thought most productively engages, namely the discursively specific positions of women located within the power-infested matrix of the social. To do this would be to surrender to the most disempowering aspects of that image of the subject generated by the Enlightenment, namely (to borrow two phrases from Beauvoir) its inherently 'masculine authority' (SS611) granted to it by the 'magic male essence' (SS611) of logic and its counterpart reason. Beauvoir issues the following warning of the consequences to any woman who would contemplate such a surrender: 'she gives up criticizing, investigating, judging for herself, and leaves all this to the superior caste' (SS611). Therefore, perhaps, Radcliffe Richards should have paid more heed to Beauvoir's warnings: 'it is important to understand ... that even when he [here the analytic philosopher] was still perplexed before the mysteries of Life, of Nature, and of Woman, he was never without his power' (SS104). Thus:

> It is understandable ... that woman takes exception to masculine logic. Not only is it inapplicable to her experience, but in his hands, as she knows, masculine reasoning becomes an underhand form of force; men's undebatable pronouncements are intended to confuse her. The intention is to put her in a dilemma: either you agree or you do not. Out of respect for the whole system of accepted principles she should agree; if she refuses, she rejects the entire system ... [I]n yielding to him, he would have her yield to the convincingness of an argument, but she knows that he has himself chosen the premises on which his rigorous deductions depend. As long as she avoids questioning them, he will easily reduce her to silence; nevertheless he will not convince her, for she senses his arbitrariness. And so, annoyed, he will accuse her of being obstinate and illogical; but she refuses to play the game because she knows the dice are loaded. (SS623–4)

An incongruity in Beauvoir's *The Second Sex*

However, despite Beauvoir's warnings regarding masculine logic and the destabilising potential of her *The Second Sex* for the Enlightenment's notion of the subject (and its implications for analytic philosophy), it remains possible to read this work as an expression of Beauvoir's faith in the Enlightenment project as a source for the possibility of liberation. It is the presence of this incongruity within *The Second Sex* which provides the potential for an even greater, although more subtle, unsettling force upon the analytic philosophical tradition.

Despite the potential within Beauvoir's text to undermine the Enlightenment's notion of the subject, she herself does not hesitate to employ the tools of Enlightenment reason when constructing her critique of patriarchal society. It is unsurprising that Beauvoir should adopt this approach granted the subject position from which she wrote: that is, as a woman who had imbibed and, therefore, been constructed by (to borrow a phrase from Moi) 'the rules of reason as taught in French academic philosophy at the time'.[42] However, any unself-reflexive adherence to such rules brings with it certain dangers.

The employment of these rules dictated that Beauvoir's work should conform to an accepted set of values. These values supported, however, a model of reason which was the very epitome of male logic and rationality; the very model against which Beauvoir issued those warnings that were noted in the first part of this essay. Nevertheless, to be fair to Beauvoir, it is doubtful whether without the employment of such rules she, as a 'mere' woman, could have gained the credibility for *The Second Sex* that she needed for it to achieve maximum impact. That is, it was her position within French philosophical academia that allowed her access to a broad audience and, therefore, granted her the power and position to speak for the 'second sex'. It was perhaps this fact that led her to regard, to employ another of Moi's phrases, '[l]ucidity, intelligence, rationality [as] key values in her textual universe'.[43] However, as Mary Evans notes, it was, paradoxically, her apparent 'uncritical belief in what she describes as rationality'[44] that led her to universalise from her own subject position in such a way as to construct the subject positions of those for whom she sought to speak largely in her own image. Or, as succinctly put by Moi, 'Beauvoir in fact generalises her own condition, apparently without any recognition that it is *herself* who provides the paradigm case.'[45] Ultimately, continues Evans, this leads to her: 'negation and denial of various forms of female experience, and her tacit assumption that paid work and contraception are the two keys to the absolute freedom of womankind, [which] all suggest a set of values that place a major importance on living like a childless, rather singular, employed man.'[46]

Granted the value system that Beauvoir had to employ to make her voice heard, it is not at all surprising that on occasions this voice works against those whom she takes herself to represent. Indeed, in several places in *The Second Sex* Beauvoir seems to be expressing the sentiment that, given the opportunity, woman could rise above what she (Beauvoir) appears to suggest are the limitations of her sex. For example: 'if she is given opportunity, woman is as rational, as efficient, as a man; it is in abstract thought, in planned action, that she rises most easily above her sex. It is much more difficult, *as things are*, for her to escape from her woman's past, to attain an emotional balance that nothing in her situation favours' (SS539).[47] Having, then, achieved this feat, such a woman would then, presumably, be as good a man as any man. That is, granted the opportunity, she could be as rational, as efficient and even as emotionally balanced as a man. However, as suggested in the first part of this essay, to invoke such a strategy of analysis risks invoking, along with it, the logic of what I called there 'liberation by assimilation'. Indeed, implicit in the above quotation from *The Second Sex* is the reflection of a still not uncommon attitude amongst males that women are affected by a certain emotional instability that prevents them ever genuinely exhibiting the kind of rationality and efficiency which come 'naturally' to men. (On such an account, any woman who exhibited such a trait would be regarded as the very odd exception to the rule.) Thus, it seems that, having warned women against the dangers of employing male-dominated logic and reason, Beauvoir's initial reliance upon it in *The Second Sex* leads her, in places, full circle.

What, therefore, Beauvoir seems to have failed to realise is that by employing the power of reason as she does she is falling in with a doxa that, as Le Doeuff points out, allows male philosophers to portray women as 'dear creatures lacking in reason, who need looking after and must be locked away in their homes'.[48] That is, once one adopts the techniques of a discourse which is, by definition, superior and thus excludes all those discourses that it does not define in its own image, then one risks setting in motion the sort of ideological equipment which, as noted in the first section of this essay, Beauvoir seems to warn supports and promotes the value of one discourse over that of another. It is the discovery of this subterfuge that undermines the very impartiality upon which the discourse of analytic philosophy prides itself. It is also this subterfuge that allow those philosophers who rely upon Enlightenment reason their power to pontificate and be heard: 'A philosopher rarely accepts the existence of a politics which is not entirely that of the philosophers: "Either it is I who command, encompass and elucidate in the final instance, or it does not exist, other than as an object of contempt."'[49] All this suggests a limitation on the ability of reason to speak for those not cast in its own image. An image which is 'coincidentally' ridden through and through with those very traits most valued by what remain male-dominated discourses, for example, analytic philosophy. This doxa emerges clearly – unsurprisingly – in Janet Radcliffe Richards's *The Sceptical Feminist*. Here we have a woman discussing the issues of feminism from the subject position of an analytic philosopher. She suggests – again unsurprisingly, granted that she is working within the analytic tradition in philosophy – that feminists should adopt a strategy supported by the sort of sentiments expressed in the last quotation given above from Beauvoir's *The Second Sex* (SS539). Indeed, Radcliffe Richards expends a great deal of energy trying to convince feminists that they should adopt 'reason' and 'rationality' as the basis for the construction of their theoretical positions. Those who would challenge her suggested approach she labels the bearers of 'the fruits of unreason'.[50] These bearers, coincidentally, turn out to be anyone who seeks to challenge the form of rationality that Radcliffe Richards wants to defend; a 'rationality' defined in just those terms necessary to support the discourse of analytic philosophy, namely one based on a respect for the universalising power of logic and reason. So strong is Radcliffe Richards's conviction about these values that she informs us that any feminist thinker or philosopher who resists a rationality based on such ideals would be 'cling[ing] to the very deprivation of which women complain, and [thus] try[ing] to move into liberation loaded with the heaviest chains of their oppression'.[51]

The danger present, therefore, within Beauvoir's text, and by implication any feminist text which relies *uncritically* upon the power of reason, is that, ultimately, the text will serve to disempower that very group it wishes to empower, namely women. By uncritically invoking reason as the overseer of one's project one cannot avoid invoking those values upon which reason relies and which, by definition, anyone who opposes it cannot possibly possess, that is, lucidity, intelligence and rationality. Having undertaken such an invocation, one is then forced to discriminate between those cast in reason's own image and the bearers of the 'fruits of unreason'. Once in this position reason, rather than representing an empowering and universal force, becomes vehemently partial, disempowering those it deems not 'worthy' to be bearers of its own fruits: in this particular case, the majority of women. Having reached such a conclusion, it is difficult not to begin to suspect the supposedly unquestionable neutrality of reason. Once such doubts are raised, it becomes difficult for the members of any discourse that relies upon reason for its power of pontification to maintain the illusion that the subject positions of its representatives are more impartial than those of any other discourse. Although this aspect of Beauvoir's *The Second Sex* represents a somewhat subtle disturbance to the equilibrium of analytic philosophy, it may well explain, at least in part, analytic philosophy's almost structural resistance to the products of any discourse that question the supposedly innate capacity of reason to transcend the specificity of the subject positions of those who invoke its power.

In summary, what I have argued in this second section is that one of the more subtle threats Beauvoir's *The Second Sex* poses to analytic philosophy is that it has the potential to act as a destabilising 'mirror' to analytic philosophy's own lack of self-reflexivity. One result of careful study of this text is that it can serve to expose a fundamental incongruity within any feminist discourse that relies too heavily upon reason for its power-base.

In *The Second Sex* this incongruity manifests itself in the form of a tension between the project of the text, i.e. an exposé of patriarchal society, and the presuppositions employed and wholly visible in the text's very structure. These presuppositions involve a reliance upon notions of 'rationality' and 'reason', which themselves support a value system which actively discriminates against women (and, in fact, *anyone* not cast in its own image). Whilst it may not be easy for feminist discourses to re-evaluate their employment of the power of reason as a potential ally, it is *wholly* more difficult for a discourse such as analytic philosophy to do so. That is, granted that analytic philosophy relies heavily upon the values embodied in the Enlightenment notion of reason to give it its power-base and credibility, to admit any limitations upon the universalising power of such a faculty would be tantamount to admitting one's own partiality. Once in such a position, it would be very difficult for analytic philosophers to resist being pulled down from their mountain: 'In every Olympus there is a supreme god; the magic male essence must be concentrated in an archetype of which father, husband, lovers, are only faint reflections' (SS611).

Conclusion

In this essay I have suggested that analytic philosophy's apparent lack of interest in Simone de Beauvoir's *The Second Sex* results from its inability to treat Beauvoir's text with philosophical respect. This is because to do so would be for it to open a Pandora's box that it currently lacks the self-reflexivity to deal with. Indeed, to question the Enlightenment's notion of the subject would lead, in the first instance, to an exposé of analytic philosophy's in-built white, middle-class, male bias. Analytic philosophy is currently able to disguise this bias by using a notion of the subject that enables it to define all in its own image. Thus, analytic philosophy grants itself the power to universalise, thereby enabling itself to speak for all 'reasonable' people. This inevitably leads those who unquestionably follow the analytic tradition in philosophy down the path of what I have called 'liberation by assimilation'.

However, I have also suggested that Beauvoir's *The Second*

Sex has the potential to act as an even greater destabilising force against analytic philosophy. That is, by seeming to commit those very sins that she appears to warn us against, Beauvoir exposes a fundamental flaw in the power of Enlightenment reason: that is, despite Enlightenment reason's overt declaration of impartiality, it has a covert logic which serves to disempower any person or group not cast in its own image. Thus, if analytic philosophy were to recognise this flaw in the power of Enlightenment reason, to remain true to itself it must either surrender its law of noncontradiction or recognise itself as having to hold simultaneously both 'P' and 'not-P',[52] namely that at one and the same time the power of Enlightenment reason is both impartial and partial. Either way, it would find itself in a very uncomfortable position.

However, the purpose of this essay is not to sound the death knell for analytic philosophy. It is rather to issue a warning of the limitations of the discourse and to indicate the abuses that can and do arise from ignoring such limitations. It is here, more importantly perhaps, that analytic philosophers have something to learn from their counterparts in the continental tradition. Nevertheless, although there is much to be wary of in analytic philosophy, there is also much of value in its techniques and practices. For example, there is a certain, currently influential, tendency within continental philosophy, in particular within certain extreme aspects of its poststructuralist and postmodernist trends, to overemphasise the hermetic nature of language and discourse, thus seeming to rule out, on an *a priori* basis, the possibility of communication between discourses.[53] However, granted a certain conceptual awareness, it becomes clear that it is impossible to make any sense of specific notions of 'difference' without presupposing some pre-existent grounds for agreement. Indeed, without such grounds it would be impossible to mark the presence of any differences at all. It is via its power to note such inconsistencies and presuppositions that the steadying influence of the analytic tradition may most beneficially make its presence felt. Therefore, I am not advocating that we throw out the proverbial baby with the bath water. However, the question does arise of where to start such a fundamental re-evaluation of the discourse. As to the nature of this re-evaluation, perhaps we should look again to Beauvoir for a clue: 'Woman is the victim of no mysterious fatality; the peculiarities that identify her as specifically a woman get their importance from the significance placed upon them. They can be surmounted, in the future, when they are regarded in new perspectives' (SS736).

Notes

1   By 'analytic philosophy' I mean that tradition of philosophising which has been omnipresent in its influence until relatively recently in the English-speaking world, particularly in Britain. The central characteristic of this school of philosophy is a faith in the Enlightenment's project of replacing confusion with clarity, employing a model of transcendental reason and its accompanying model of Cartesian subjectivity.

2   All favoured areas for discussion for the analytic philosopher.

3   All this aside from the fact that, arguably, Beauvoir has been one of the most influential figures on twentieth-century feminist philosophy.

4   Simone de Beauvoir, *The Second Sex*, trans. and ed. H. M. Parshley [1952] (Harmondsworth: Penguin Books, 1972). All subsequent page references are in parentheses in the text.

5   For some critiques of the problematic translational aspects of Parshley's volume see: Judith Okely, *Simone de Beauvoir: A Re-Reading* (London: Virago, 1986), pp. 52 and 60; M. G. Dietz, 'Introduction: debating Simone de Beauvoir', *Signs*, 18:1 (1992), 74–88: 76; Toril Moi, *Simone de Beauvoir: The Making of an Intellectual Woman* (Oxford: Basil Blackwell, 1994), p. 281n.

6   Sonia Kruks, 'Gender and subjectivity: Simone de Beauvoir and contemporary feminism', *Signs*, 18:1 (1992), 89–110.

7   Particularly his seminal work: *Cours de linguisitique générale* [1915], translated into English as the *Course in General Linguistics*. There are at least two English translations of this text: Ferdinand de Saussure, *Course in General Linguistics*, trans. W. Baskin (London: Fontana/Collins, 1974); Ferdinand de Saussure, *Course in General Linguistics*, trans. R. Harris (London: Duckworth, 1983).

8   For, perhaps, Derrida's most influential text see *Of Grammatology* [1967], trans. G. C. Spivak (Baltimore and London: Johns Hopkins University Press, 1976).

9   See, for example, *The Postmodern Condition: A Report on Knowledge* [1979], trans. G. Bennington and B. Massumi (Manchester: Manchester University Press, 1984), p. 40. Here Lyotard, somewhat surprisingly using the work of Ludwig Wittgenstein (a founding figure of analytic philosophy), speaks of the dissemination of the Enlightenment subject between and within the language games (discourses) of postmodern society.

10 Ernesto Laclau and Chantal Mouffe, *Hegemony and Socialist Strategy: Towards a Radical Democratic Politics* (London: Verso, 1985).

178 Simone de Beauvoir's *The Second Sex*

Ibid., p. 115.

12 Jacques Derrida, *Writing and Difference* [1967], trans. Alan Bass (London: Routledge and Kegan Paul, 1978), p. 280.

13 Although, as will become apparent, the challenge to the Enlightenment subject made possible by Beauvoir's *The Second Sex* does not result in the total dissemination of the subject, unlike the challenges made by such post-Enlightenment philosophers as Derrida, Lyotard, etc.

14 Kruks, 'Gender and subjectivity', 89–110.

15 Ibid., 89ff.

16 Ibid., 90.

17 For a valuable discussion of this and other shortcomings related to the postmodern notion of the 'subject' see S. Best and D. Kellner, *Postmodern Theory: Critical Interrogations* (London: Macmillan, 1991).

18 Kruks, 'Gender and subjectivity', 91.

19 Bertrand Russell, *The Problems of Philosophy* [1912] (Oxford: Oxford University Press, 1967), p. 93.

20 J. Rawls, *A Theory of Justice* (Oxford: Oxford University Press, 1973).

21 Ibid., pp. 255–6.

22 J. Glover, *Causing Death and Saving Lives* (Harmondsworth: Penguin Books, 1977).

23 See: E.V. Spelman, *Inessential Women: Problems of Exclusion in Feminist Thought* (London: The Women's Press, 1988), p. 128.

24 T. J. Reiss, 'Revolution in bounds: Wollstonecraft, women, and reason', in: L. Kauffman (ed.), *Gender and Theory: Dialogues on Feminist Criticism* (Oxford: Basil Blackwell, 1989), pp. 11–50: 46.

25 Margaret Simons also notes the presence of this tension in *The Second Sex*. See M.A. Simons, 'Lesbian connections: Simone de Beauvoir and feminism', *Signs*, 18:1 (1992), 136–61: 159.

26 Kruks, 'Gender and subjectivity', 92.

27 Terry Keefe, *Simone de Beauvoir: A Study of Her Writings* (London: Harrap, 1983), p. 112.

28 The 'law of noncontradiction' states that a proposition 'P' and its negation 'not-P' cannot both be true at the same moment in time and in the same respect.

29 Chris Weedon, *Feminist Practice and Poststructuralist Theory* (Oxford: Basil Blackwell, 1987), p. 33.

30 Linda Zerilli arrives at a similar conclusion via an examination of what she calls Beauvoir's 'discursive uses of the maternal'. See Linda M.G. Zerilli, 'A process without a subject: Simone de Beauvoir and Julia Kristeva on maternity', *Signs*, 18:1 (1992), 111–35.

31 M. Poster, *Foucault, Marxism and History: Mode of Production – vs – Mode of Information* (Cambridge: Polity Press, 1984), p. 91.

32 Milton Fisk, 'History and reason in Rawls' moral theory', in: N. Daniels, ed., *Reading Rawls: Critical Studies of 'A Theory of Justice'* (Oxford: Basil Blackwell, 1975), pp. 53–80: 57.

33 Ibid., p. 79.

34 Ibid., pp. 79–80.

35 Plato, *The Republic*, 2nd revised edn, trans. D. Lee (Harmondsworth: Penguin Books, 1987), 500b.

36 Janet Radcliffe Richards, *The Sceptical Feminist: A Philosophical Enquiry* (Harmondsworth: Penguin Books, 1982).

37 Ibid., p. 47.

38 Ibid., p. 49.

39 Michèle Le Doeuff, *Hipparchia's Choice: An Essay Concerning Women, Philosophy, etc.*, trans. Trista Selous (Oxford: Basil Blackwell, 1991), p. 75.

40 Radcliffe Richards, *The Sceptical Feminist*, p. 18.

41 Ibid., p. 19.

42 Moi, *Simone de Beauvoir*, p. 67.

43 Toril Moi, *Feminist Theory and Simone de Beauvoir* (Oxford: Basil Blackwell, 1990), p. 73.

44 Mary Evans, *Simone de Beauvoir: A Feminist Mandarin* (London: Tavistock, 1985), pp. 56–7.

45 Moi, *Simone de Beauvoir*, p. 67. However, as Moi indicates, this is not to say that this universalist strategy always works against Beauvoir's case in *The Second Sex* (p. 176). Whilst I, at least in part, agree with Moi's point here, it is, I hold, those places where Beauvoir's text fails to do this that provide the sort of disruption for analytic philosophy that I am indicating here. However, I am still far from convinced that any text that relies uncritically upon the universalising aspect of reason, as Beauvoir's text still does even on Moi's own admission, can escape as effectively as Moi thinks from reason's disempowering potential.

46 Evans, *Simone de Beauvoir*, p. 57.

47 Similar sentiments seem little more than just below the surface on, for example, SS269, 308, 353 and 718.

48 Le Doeuff, *Hipparchia's Choice*, p. 35.

49 Ibid., p. 110.

50 Radcliffe Richards, *The Sceptical Feminist*, Chapter 1.

51 Ibid., p. 49.

52 For a definition of the 'law of noncontradiction' see footnote 28.

53 For a valuable discussion of the implications of the more extreme tendencies within postmodernist and poststructuralist thought see: Christopher Norris, *Uncritical Theory: Postmodernism, Intellectuals and the Gulf War* (London: Lawrence and Wishart, 1992).

7

To become or not to become; or, Must two be second? Simone de Beauvoir and *The Second Sex* in conversation

NICOLE WARD JOUVE

Heloise and Paula are friends. Not close, but friends. They have known each other a long time. Feminism in its heyday has brought them together. They have met in the sea, swimming among black rocks, in the cove near a common friend's home in the Mediterranean. Paddling in the water, its blue darkened by the rocks, they had been cagey with each other. Since then, they have spent enjoyable time together. There has been warmth, and caring, and the exchange of affectionate and heartfelt and supportive letters. Both are French.

Heloise is famous. Since that first meeting in the sea, she has written much, and gained quite a reputation. Paula has written a little, which has been well-received. Well-received enough for her to be asked to chair a discussion of Heloise's work at a symposium. Paula, who has enthusiastically kept up with her friend's work, has re-read Heloise's books, preparing questions she hoped would be astute. Heloise has prepared herself, got mentally attuned.

Paula asks a question about fairness. Inequalities between women. Heloise turns on her. 'If you're worried about equality', Heloise says, 'that's your problem.'

Paula feels affronted. She thought the question was abstract, not personal. Heloise has put her publicly on the spot. As Paula reflects on the incident, it occurs to her that what Heloise has said tallies with what she writes. Asking for equality for women is simply wanting to reproduce a faulty state of things, rather than changing it: more women having a share of power in a world that is in a bad way is simply going to perpetuate the bad. Much better work to change things, make room for alternative values, seek to escape from hierarchies and binaries that always privilege some at the expense of others, explore sexual difference as mobility and interplay, not as a competition between rival monoliths. Heloise holds by her own version of what is known as New French Feminisms. 'I've been silly', Paula thinks. 'I shouldn't have asked that question.' But isn't Paula cross with herself for having, by an uncensored question, publicly revealed something about her deep-down feelings about Heloise? Something very simple: Paula is not worried about women's equality with men, but about women's equality among themselves. More specifically, and it hurts Paula to have to admit it: she is envious of what she feels to be Heloise's success. Her superiority. Heloise was the star being questioned. Paula was the interviewer. Crowds had flocked in on Heloise's account, not Paula's. Heloise's mind is swifter, grander, more powerful: Paula's getting worsted in the debate has made that obvious. Heloise is famous: Paula is not. Heloise is first: Paula is second.

She was right, Paula thinks: it is my problem. We can truly be friends only once I like and accept myself enough to feel I am fine as I am. Then I can like and accept her as she is. As long as I want her place, her success – and I can't have them – we might as well forget it. I will remain second. In my mind. And I will resent her for it.

Paula dreams that she is in a dark hall, like a cinema before the screening starts. There are students sat in loose rows. Paula has invited her friend Dot to attend. Dot is a novelist, all curly blonde hair, like an angel. Students ask questions and Dot takes it upon herself to answer. She answers brilliantly, funnily. Her blonde hair shines. She's got the audience captivated. She moves around amid the rows. It was to be Paula's show, her lecture. Paula tells herself, 'let her get on with it, you know she's the one who's got the charisma'. This is a dream but Paula's mind is curiously alert, it thinks, 'in her chart Dot has her sun conjunct with Venus, it shows she's attractive, she's seductive, she's got magnetism.'

Paula makes herself remember that her own sun isn't conjunct with her Venus. She tells herself, 'you're a Cancerian, a watery one, a deep one, one not for show. You're a mirror. Dot is a Leo, full of light. Follow her, be her servant, let her take the lead. She's the one who's got the capacity for power.'

Paula wakes up. The dream is making a lot of things clear. She reflects upon how, after years and years of putting a man – her man – upon a pedestal, now that she is separated from him she has without noticing it put a number of women – friends, associates, writers – Dot, Heloise – upon a pedestal too. As if Paula needed someone else to be in charge, needed a comfortable hiding-place in someone's shadow, as their attendant, their admirer, their disciple. Whenever she gets praised, offered positions of power, how self-denigrating she becomes! She avoids responsibilities – she might chair a debate with Heloise, but only as Heloise's follower. Recently, on a Spanish trip, Paula hired a car with two friends: she let them do the driving. Paula sat in the back and navigated. It is other people, always, who seem to Paula to have a centre, authority. She plays the part of the guest, the nomadic visitor, unsure of where she belongs. Always she chooses the part of the *Seconde*. The others are Ones. To herself, Paula is an Other.

Paula now wonders: does she instinctively fall into the role she was born for – to serve? Or is she being a coward, taking refuge under the shadow of others, shrinking from responsibilities, intellectual or otherwise, afraid to lead, to assert, to become visible? Did marriage and motherhood do that to her, or did she construct herself into that kind of wife, that kind of mother? Is she being a hypocrite, not daring to *be* what she is? For it isn't as if Paula were a sweet comfortable unambitious accommodating little thing – oh no – she has to admit to that. 'Would I be envious of the "stars", would I have the dreams I have', Paula asks herself, 'if I didn't *want* stardom? And my feminism', Paula thinks, 'what about it? Didn't I become a feminist to rebel against gods of my own making – father, uncle, teachers, husband – all those I put on a pedestal, those I expected to lead, drive, act out, conquer, in *my* place? But I didn't dare be who I was. I let others do it for me. Then I got angry – envious. I found Feminism, its warmth and largesse, the idea of a community of women all

working with and *for* me, and asked Feminism to do my
rebelling, my claiming the first place, for me. I hid under its
skirts, I sallied forth from under the ample skirts of the likes of
Heloise to dare bark at the legs of the passing patriarchs. But now
that Feminism has come of age, that it is full of infighting, of
diversities and resentments all of its own, I don't like it half so
much, do I? No room for seconds in there any more, is there?
Well – yes – plenty of room for seconds like me. Only, this time
I am second to women, not men. I can't blame my sex for my
secondness. I have to blame myself.' Paula is uncomfortable with
what she seems to be seeing.

So uncomfortable that at a conference she corners two old
friends. Josephine is a theorist. Anne – well, Anne is Anne. She
is now into spirituality and femininity and all sorts. But they've
travelled the same roads – they've all been feminists – still are in
some ways. Jo certainly is. Tall, slim, Amazon-like Jo with her
sharply-tailored trousers and waistcoats, her dark close-cropped
hair moulding her handsome face. 'I want to have a discussion
about *The Second Sex*,' Paula tells Jo and Anne. Can we make
time?' They meet in a town café, after supper. The conference is
over, they've said their goodbyes, they have this luxurious spare
time in this strange provincial town: tomorrow they can go home.
But not tonight. They've cornered a pleasant table, brightly lit.
Through the ample glass front they watch the passers-by. It is
late spring, dying twilight. A deep pink glow lingers on the
houses across the street. The pavement is strewn with lime blos-
soms from the neighbouring park. The café is quiet. 'So you want
to talk about old Simone?' Jo asks Paula. 'Appropriate we should
meet in one of those cafés where she enjoyed writing.' 'And
debating', Paula rejoins. 'Well', Jo says. 'Shoot.' Jo stoops a bit
as if to listen to the smaller people around her, especially Anne
who is fair and petite and green-eyed and gently watchful. And
younger: a former pupil, turned friend.

'I've thought about this quite a bit', Paula says. 'So I'll start
with a little lecture. As I understand it, or remember it, *The
Second Sex* is about women being second by virtue (or vice) of
their sex. It opens with the idea of alterity. Throughout culture,
being human, though supposedly referring to a universal, has in

effect meant being male. Everything human — everything that makes for "transcendence" — has been attributed to the male sex. The male is the One, whilst the female is the Other.'

'It's quite a dazzling demonstration that opens *The Second Sex*', Jo rejoins. 'Beauvoir has such a clear, concise, efficient mind. Every debate that was going to surface in the late 1960s and 1970s in the Women's Movement, here in France especially, is examined in this opening: the structuralist, the psychoanalytic, the anthropological angle … I've heard Marcelle Marini say that it's always been supposed, and with Beauvoir's own agreement, that of the two Sartre was the better philosopher, and Beauvoir the better novelist. But posterity will reverse that judgement: Beauvoir will be seen as the better philosopher of the two. So much philosophical speculation is there in a nutshell.'

'It's precisely what I wish to contest', Paula replies. 'I don't mean that Beauvoir was not as good a philosopher as Sartre — very likely Marini is right. But how truly philosophical is all this?'

'Philosophical? What do you mean?', Anne asks.

'Bear with me. In the 1975 issue of *L'Arc*, *Simone de Beauvoir et la lutte des femmes*, which also contained Cixous's now famous essay 'Le rire de la Méduse', Beauvoir is reported as saying that the model she had used for her description of the alterity of the second sex was Hegel's dialectic of the master and slave, also used by Sartre for *L'Être et le néant,* written only a few years before. The one was published in the early 1940s, wasn't it, the other in 1949? In *L'Arc,* in the mid seventies, Beauvoir says she would use another model, the category of "la rareté", scarcity, developed by Sartre in his *Critique de la raison dialectique*, a work of the sixties. Very Malthusian for a left-wing couple if you ask me. But let that pass. But if she was the better philosopher, Jo, why did she have to kowtow yet again to that bloody man?'

'No need to be rude', Jo laughs. 'You can use somebody else's concepts, and do better things with them than they do. Paula, you're angry.'

Paula leans forward, her elbows on the table. She twists her long brown hair into a knot, as she always does when she is absorbed.

'I suppose I am. But whichever model you use, you end up with similar results. The master and slave model: two men fight for domination. The defeated one exchanges his life for slavery to the other. But though he be the slave, he is one better than the master in that he recognises the humanity of the master, whilst the master does not recognise the slave's humanity. Or take the scarcity model: there is not enough humanity to do the rounds, so men corner it whilst women go without. Now Beauvoir makes sexuality, indeed biology as interpreted by culture, replace group or tribe or class as the cornerstone of the master-slave divide: humanity, she says (and she means transcendence), has gone to the sex that kills rather than the sex which gives life. The same conclusion applies if you think in terms of scarcity. It's again women's biology, their reproductive system, that becomes the occasion or the pretext for their having to lump it in the race to the humanity feast-table: they can't get there fast enough. Jo, you're frowning.'

Jo stretches her long legs towards the next, empty, table.

'I feel very suspicious of your introjecting Malthus in all this. But I'll let it pass for now. Get to your point.'

'My point is that instead of remaining a dialectic, of there being a series of turn-abouts in the master and slave roles, the power positions as they are described in *The Second Sex* have become set once and forever. In Hegel the master will only become fully human once he's also been led to recognise the slave's humanity. It's part of a movement. But throughout culture as Beauvoir describes it, man has remained the One. Woman the Other. She is and has been the Second Sex, if not for eternity, at least since the cave-age.'

'Hang on a minute', Jo interrupts. 'That she might not remain so for eternity may be precisely due to the dialectic potential of the Hegelian model. There can be a turning around. Change remains permanently possible. The slave can, by her uprising, by recognising her own capacity for transcendence, by taking on the parts the master had sought to keep for himself, persuade or force the master to recognise that she is a master too.'

'But', Anne interjects in her gentle, little girl's voice, 'can there be a world of masters?'

'What?'

'Can you have the One without the Other? Will the rising of women to transcendence end mastery? And if it's a case of scarcity, who then will go without? Will there be re-divisions, new kinds of hierarchies, with new Others appearing? Will it simply be the case that the more powerful, more gifted, richer, better-armed, thicker-skinned will simply rise to the top, as usual, and the less so, the less gifted, more timid, poorer, less advantaged, etc., sink to second place — it will just be that there will be women as well as men in both categories?'

'You've got it', Paula says. 'Well — not quite. I wasn't getting at it from that sort of angle.'

'If that's what you're getting at', Jo says impatiently, 'then what have you beaten the drums and summoned up a Council of the sages for? It's been argued over, one way or another, inside the women's movement both sides of the Atlantic, both North and South, for over a quarter of a century. Equality versus Difference. *Féminisme* versus *Psych et Po*. Anglo-American Feminisms versus so-called French Feminisms. Some, as Anne was doing, critique the concept of equality — they claim that if you simply redistribute rights or power and wealth you will change nothing, that change can only come from an acceptance of sexual difference. The opposite camp say that if you establish a woman-centred specificity, try to have *écriture féminine* or an alternative libidinal economy as it is called, or dig out for repressed womanly depths, then you're re-establishing the same old trope — going back to the female body — sexuality and the emotions and motherhood and all that. You're simply perpetuating something that's always been used to put women down, keep them out of things. Passivity, depth, maternal thinking … You make physiology, and its psychoanalytic build-up at the hands of culture into *Fate*: for what does the subconscious produce if not what culture's put there? Sexual difference, they say — the masculine-feminine polarities — permit old oppressions to continue. I endorse that. So did Simone. She goes for the jugular. "One is not born, one becomes a woman." In that "become" is our freedom. The logic that impels *The Second Sex* is beautifully clear.'

Jo drains her *ballon de rouge*. Combs her short hair with both sets of fingers, from the nape upwards.

'The book — as you must remember — goes on to analyse all the details of that "become". Formation, from the baby girl to the young girl and into age, sexuality from a to z, Situations … And then Beauvoir demonstrates all the consequences that flow from the production of the being that's called feminine. She does prove her point, over and over again, in a text brimming with quotations from wide cultural sources. She marries a beautifully anchored, practical and literary form of existentialism (no smoky baroque nonsense unlike her mate Sartre) with the ability never to lose sight of her central, and crucial, idea. Femininity *is* a construct. Like any form of sexuality. Exposing constructs frees you. Recent or not so recent theorists, based in the US mostly, de Lauretis, Butler, Haraway, Wittig, Riley, Garber, have explored and expanded that. It's the right direction to go. Beauvoir may not be referred to as often as she ought to be, but she is the seed – the pathfinder.'

'Well, there's my point.' Paula has waited for the full flow of Jo's enthusiasm to subside. 'I think it's not philosophical. I think Beauvoir is full of assumptions, of unargued assertions. No worse than Sartre, mind you, and I do agree she's more to the point – she doesn't try to cover her tracks, she doesn't go into rhetorical or romantic excess, she's better grounded. But she's still guilty of what she accuses men thinkers and writers of. Whilst demystifying she doesn't see how she herself mythologises.'

'I just don't get you. You're repeating yourself.'

Jo is getting annoyed, Anne observes. Paula breathes deeply, as if about to dive.

'For a start, Beauvoir – rightly mind you – exposes Benda, Leiris, and countless others, philosophers from Aristotle onwards, or poets, as having solemnly or angrily pontificated about women's inferiority. Unlike Woolf, who in *A Room of One's Own* analyses the emotional reasons behind the statements, sees how men turned their own *feelings*, of anger, of fear, their will to power, into arguments about women's supposed incapacities, Beauvoir is not interested in the reasons for the "otherization" as it is called, but in what is being said. In this she is miles more systematic and detailed than Woolf. She – rightly – denounces through what slippages "man" has come to be equated with "human", has monopolised Oneness, transcendence. But she never sees that she herself privileges those positions of power – Oneness, transcendence. And according to her it is transcendence that makes us human. She never questions what transcendence is – nor to what extent it may be connected to the phallus. She just takes it it's hierarchically superior to immanence, and she does not stop to think how absurd it may be to think of human beings as immanent. She wants transcendence. She wants It. She does think that women are inferior *on account of their bodies*. She despises women's bodies – her own body, her mother's in *Une Mort très douce* ... She wants what she perceives men as having. *The Second Sex* ends up telling women, "you can have one too darlings if you dare, and then you'll be alright". It proposes unexamined values which have their history, their moment in the history of often destructive and always fallible human beings, as absolutes. She never realises that it's her fantasy that's made those values into universals.'

'Which values?' Jo snaps.

'I've already mentioned transcendence. France hadn't been long out of Occupation. It was the post-war years. Freedom had its own particular charged meaning at that point: collaboration, passivity under the occupant and all that ... It's no accident, not only that Sartre in the period makes freedom into the absolute value – the attraction is that he makes it anarchic, not patriotic – so the French – we, I mean – can have their cake and eat it, be Romantic about freedom but not think too badly of ourselves for so few of us having been in the Resistance. Transcendence. It also has a lot to do with virility as it was constructing itself – since, dear Jo, we are talking about construction – in the Fascist period preceding the war and in the recreation of maleness that followed from the humiliations of the war. Existentialism is a very male movement. There aren't many females floating about in it any more than in the Surrealist movement, if you've noticed. A lot of it is about masculine angst. Sartre (or Camus for that matter) are reclaiming transcendence for the men of the left. Though to be fair to Sartre, Camus is by far the more macho of the two. But why is Beauvoir so sold on transcendence? Why does she so admire the boys?'

'I think', Jo says slowly, crossing and uncrossing her feet, apparently intent on her high-tech new trainers, 'that you're making a great deal rest upon one word. And you're producing a lot of specious political analysis. I'd need to have what you say backed up by a lot of hard evidence.'

'Hard?' Paula queries.

Anne laughs. Soothingly.

'Hang on a minute. You've got a point, Jo, but we can return to it later. What are you really driving at, Paula? I can sense – hear? – that you've got a bee in your bonnet.'

Paula finishes her beer. She licks the froth from the rim. Sits back in her chair.

'Want another round, ladies? I'm talking about envy. Penis-envy.'

'I don't believe this', Jo moans. 'Get me another *rouge*'.

Anne is into fruit-cocktails. They are elaborate affairs in this café – '*on a trouvé le lieu chic du coin*', Jo has pointed out. Anne's tall glasses come with kiwi slices and pineapple chunks which she spears with a stick crowned with a little paper parasol. They keep sinking, spurting juice, and she laughs. Paula has got herself a huge beer. A 'Formidable'. Anne's eyes widen: 'I didn't know you liked beer so much'. 'I don't', Paula replies. She drags at her long black pullover. 'Too bitter. This is sheer penis-envy disguised as café Existentialism. I'm telling myself, I'm telling the world, "I can drink a Formidable as well as any man. My bladder can hold a Formidable as well as any man's. My never having drunk beer in the past and my not being likely to do so in the future and my not even liking the taste of ruddy beer cannot trammel my freedom to drink a Formidable tonight." Plus, I want to get pissed.' 'Fair enough', Anne mildly concedes. 'As long as you don't start driving penknives into your hand, *ma chérie*, like that horrible Ivich in *The Roads to Freedom*. I hate the sight of blood.'

'What about penis-envy then?' Jo asks.

'My contention', Paula replies, 'is that *The Second Sex* offers its analysis as Existential Philosophy. But it is existential in a limited way. To me existence means the whole of what I am as a human being, the unconscious as well as the conscious. But that entire book comes from Ego. With a lot of Superego in *its* bonnet. Only mind is at work, what the brain can produce in the way of analyses and conscious perceptions. What fuels this book – why it is being written, and how this colours what is being said, is never looked at.'

'So?'

'So envy may well be at the bottom. Which makes it, not objective but subjective. Not Philosophy, but projection – of a person's psyche, of her moment in time, private and public. Of her *sex*.'

'It remains to be seen whether this could not be said of *all* Philosophies', Jo grumbles. 'Re-read Le Doeuff and Lloyd and Irigaray and Kofman and others.'

'But why envy?' Anne pipes up. 'Can you explain?'

'I'll try. It's not easy. It's come to me like a bolt out of the blue, apropos of a recent experience – why it was a bolt out of the blue is difficult to communicate. I chaired a debate with Heloise H* – a friend, as you know. Not a close friend, but a friend. We met in the sea. Years ago. That's always been a bond. For me. I asked a question about equality and she sent me packing – said it was my problem ...'

'She would', Jo growls.

'When I reflected about it afterwards, I realised I was deeply envious of her – her brilliance, her success. I realised that I felt *second* to her. She was right to have told me it was my problem. Because I needn't feel second. It was my feeling, my construction. She's always been lovely to me. I was the one who'd set up a competition in my head ...'

'With' (Jo breathlessly intervenes) 'the help of State institutions, Survival of the Fittest present-day ideologies, the French meritocracy system with its highly-competitive "concours", especially its *Grandes Écoles* (in which system let me remind you, dear Paula, you did quite well). With the encouragement of the market economy, best-sellers, the media craze for 'stars', the recession ... There *are* plenty of competitions out there. You didn't invent competitiveness, dear. It's the law of our economic survival. Heloise steps on your foot and you say sorry: learn to fight, stupid ...'

'That may be so', Paula laughs. 'But I'm after something deeper ...'

'Beware the search for depth that comes from frustration ... There's nothing deeper than the economy. It's underneath everything. It's the tortoise under the elephant. Scarcity. Sartre and Beauvoir had it right at the time of the *Critique de la raison dialectique*, when they tried to take some of Marxism's more

evident points on board. Today's world is becoming more insid-
iously savage as everything and everyone is being more visibly
drawn together, and it makes scarcity more obvious. With the
economic straits, the greater level of competition, the end of the
cold war that suddenly makes each and everyone into a potential
rival because there no longer are mysterious enemy camps, Iron
Curtains or Berlin Walls that force you to stick together: and
hasn't sisterhood got it in the wing! Competitiveness has got into
the Women's Movement: and the Movement itself is in a state of
recession and self-division along with all left-wing ideologies.
Stardom's become more desirable, and scarcer. It's a commodity
like everything else. It goes by more anarchic rules than it used
to. You're just a case in point, Paula. A pawn in the economic game,
that's discovered it's a pawn, not a queen. Once upon a time you
would have felt sisterly. Once upon a time you would have been
playing draughts, not chess. That was idealistic. The Women's
Movement protected women from the realities of power. Now
those realities have broken in. The world has changed.'

'You unregenerate Marxist', Anne laughs, 'let her finish.'

'You may be arguing for me without realising it', Paula says,
looking Jo straight in the eyes. She is going through her
Formidable in dutiful, quizzical sips, taking her mouth to her
outsize glass, frowning above it. Anne watches the two: the one
clumsy with her beer, long glossy hair sliding over her shoul-
ders, pushed back, swift hands twisting it back or into a bun; the
other sharp with her large liquid eyes, her helmet of black hair,
confident and self-forgetful with her *rouge*. Both excited.
Confrontational. 'Funny', Anne reflects. 'They're much closer in
their views and interests than they are to me – but they seem to
rile each other.' Jo, who deeply disagrees with Anne's views,
fondly patronises her, patiently hears her out – calls her '*Bout de
chou*' or '*Petite*'. 'Is it because she doesn't believe a word I say?'
Anne wonders.

'How am I helping you?' Jo asks of Paula. 'I thought I was
reminding you that what you want to psychologise as usual is
economic – it comes from the outside, not from the inside. As
Sartre and Beauvoir in my opinion rightly believed, psychology,
innerness, are never more than the interiorisation of a situation.'

Paula speaks slowly.

'I don't agree with that. There are particular reactions to situations, that come from inside, and there are projections, that make a person or situation appear such and such. Of two people going to work together in the morning, same sex, class, job, upbringing, the one may be expatiating on the grey horror of commuting to the treadmill, the other praising the loveliness of the spring day. But I was, as you've guessed, about to say that feeling envy about Heloise, feeling second to Heloise, made me realise that the state of feeling second was an inner state. That it concerned *me*, not Heloise or others. But what you've said tallies with my perception: a woman can be your rival, make you second just as much as a man. You say it's for economic reasons, I say it's for psychological ones. But the result is the same. What has our sex got to do with being second, with being other? Saying as – Angela Carter, was it? – did, that you have discovered you are a second-class citizen, is one thing. Attaching ideas of secondness to sex is another. It's a projection. To me that means that the main thesis of the book – that being second is bound up with femininity – doesn't hold.'

'You're mixing things up, Paula. If a woman like Heloise today can make you feel second just as much as a man, it's because we women have got on. Because progress has been made towards equality and the emancipation of women. When there were only a very few women writers, artists, politicians, there was no competition, they were the exception. 'Alone of all her sex', as English Marina Warner has called the Virgin Mary, or as Sartre regarded Beauvoir. She was his equal, he felt – he confessed to her – and that enabled him to feel macho to other women. Now that things are more democratic and women have achieved so much, now that – at least in the so-called West – any woman can get an education and aspire to become Prime Minister – whatever the subtle exclusions and discriminations still at work, and god knows how cunningly – whatever assumptions and mythologies remain embedded in culture – then perhaps women no longer are the second sex. Perhaps there no longer is any need for Feminism, groan groan. Perhaps the sap of feminism now goes into enlarging and reinforcing opportunities. It's become practical. Simone has not laboured in vain. Your feeling second to Heloise is a triumph.'

Paula sits back. Grimaces.

'I feel floored. But frustrated. Deeply, deeply frustrated. And I can't think clearly. My head is buzzing.'

'You don't have to finish that beer, *ma chérie*', Anne says. 'You don't have anything to prove. If what you really wanted is to get pissed and you're pissed – hallelujah!'

'Have I ever told you', Paula says, 'how I love the way you call your friends – you call me – *ma chérie*?'

'Now she's turning sentimental!' Jo looks exasperated.

'My turn to buy', Anne says. 'Another wine, Jo? Why don't you have something you actually like, Paula? Be a devil. What about a Glenfiddich?'

'They might not have it here', Jo says. 'And if she has a whisky now, we'll lose her for good. Get her a coffee. And a Vittel.'

'First I want a pee', Paula says. 'Then I want – a coffee, OK. *Bien tassé*. And a Perrier.'

'*Bien tassé* it will be, *ma chérie*.' Anne goes off to the counter. Paula crosses to the toilets.

'Make sure to use the men's', Jo shouts.

'There's only one, and it's Turkish', Paula shouts from the back. Some clients start and stare at her, at Jo. 'Make sure you do it standing then', Jo shouts. Two men glare. Two women look indignant.

For a while they make small talk. Then Anne takes things in hand. 'Hear her out', she says to Jo. 'Why do you jump on her every time she tries to explain?'

'She's trying to knock one of my idols. That's why. And her politics gets up my nose. You can dismiss any justified claim by accusing those who make the claim of envy. It's a well-known conservative ploy. Self-serving millionaires who accuse the have-nots of the base sin of envy so that their greed can go unrestrained. Wanting to demote *The Second Sex* on the grounds that it's about Simone being envious of men is right-wing rubbish. Part of the backlash.'

Anne simpers in a mock way. She puckers her face.

'Do you think we could be just a tiny weeny bit less confrontational? Just for a bit?'

Jo laughs. 'OK, you monkey. Paula, I'm all ears.'

Paula has sobered up somewhat. 'I've got to get back to envy', she says.

Jo sighs, 'Envy be it'.

'When I realised how envious I felt of Heloise', Paula says, 'how envious also I was of my friend Dot B*** — the novelist — I had a dream about her — it became clear to me that feeling or maybe even *being* second was a sort of choice. An inner choice. In this I am more Existentialist than you, Jo. And closer to the position that Beauvoir herself arrives at in her final section, which is that because we are human, i.e. free, we can always change our choices, work to become free: we don't have to remain the second sex. I don't think that Economics are as absolute as you do — that because a competitive ethos is prevalent on account of socio-economic pressures we will inescapably become rivals of one another. Maybe that's the way it tends to work. But I can't accept it as *doom*. You know, Heidegger and his "Intuition of Being" that makes it possible for us to stand back and seek the truth, that makes truth possible? I buy that. I *can* stand back. I don't *have to* be second. Rather, I make myself second through a multitude of often unconscious decisions. Envy arises because there is a certain temper inside me, the result of what life, and myself through thousands of conscious or unconscious decisions, have made me.'

'You mean, you could be as much of a star as Heloise if you wanted to?'

'No. I can't make myself cleverer or that much more pugnacious than I am. Mind you, for one Heloise who deserves her fame, is a fine writer and has outstanding intelligence, there are ten mediocrities who don't, but are clever and combative enough to get fame. Making it to the contemporary Pantheon does not depend on your being a god.'

'Or goddess?' Anne asks.

'Or goddess. But I don't *have to* be *comparative*. Second is ordinal. It implies a hierarchy — which Beauvoir equates with the One and the Other — which I'm not sure is right.'

'What you're saying', Anne intervenes again, 'is that you're not forced to compare yourself with Heloise — to be in competition with her — and that if you cease to be, then you can be who you are and she can be what she is?'

'That's right. If I were happy with myself – loved myself enough – if I were what I truly desire to be – then Heloise's success wouldn't bother me.'

'You're turning mighty moralistic the two of you', Jo growls. 'And – I've had my say – you're again ignoring economics. But what's that got to do with Beauvoir?'

Paula finishes her coffee. Puts her cup to her mouth, licks the sugar at the bottom.

'Plenty. For a start, does there have to be a *binary* hierarchy? Is sexual difference *the* basis of all hierarchies – I'm thinking here of the Aristotelian binaries, man/woman, mind/nature, etc. you know, the notion that man's supposed superiority to woman has been used to structure western thought, "man"'s domination over the world – the notion so eloquently attacked by Derrida and by Cixous …

'And by your friend Heloise – don't forget her', Anne adds.

'And by Heloise. You're right. She's very eloquent in her deconstruction of binaries. But if the first/second category re-emerges in an all-women, same-class, same-colour situation, like the ones I've been describing, and is produced by any competitive situation, how relevant is it to sexual difference? Perhaps there will always be some who are more than others, but that maybe a universal human problem rather than a system that would be made better if one of the categories – women – were removed from the system. It isn't specific to sexuality then, is it? The One/Other model comes to distort the relationship, it isn't ingrained in it. The evolution of the women's movement, its division along lines of homo/hetero, black/white, western/non-western, Muslim/liberal, (class, to be fair, was always there) has proved this, each newly-defined underclass accusing the others of making them second. As long as there were monoliths around, simple things everyone could safely resent, like men, or even better, 'the system', 'the patriarchy', and women could unite *en bloc* against them, fine. Once the movement was strong enough for women of colour, of the South, for lesbians or women of unrecognised ethnic groups to express their anger at having been passed over, bracketed, spoken for, then that recourse went.

'What (Paula continues) if Beauvoir had made what was a (powerful, universal) emotion (envy, resentment, wanting to blame somebody for having what you want) into a philosophical, almost metaphysical concept? The One – the Other. First, Second.'

'You're wandering again, Paula.' Jo is helping the waiter put their glasses and cups on his tray. She smiles at him, looking him straight in the eyes. He is annoyed, because they've kept going to the counter to order, instead of waiting until he spotted their call. 'I always come, but I do it at my own pace', he's said loftily to Paula who complained: 'But you never see our signals!' 'I've been in this café for twenty years, Madame, and no client has ever gone thirsty.' Paula has got her Glenfiddich after all, with some more Perrier. Jo is on her fourth glass of red wine. 'Come on, Paula, what about envy?'

'It's this essay that I read, which got me thinking' Paula says. 'In a book about Female Sexuality. An essay by an analyst called Maria Torok. She claims that both men and women patients feel jealousy, despair, depression, anguish, etc. but that only women connect these feelings – the lack of happiness – to the nature of their sex – their lack of a penis. It was the recurrence of this complaint in his women patients, she says, which led Freud to postulate a universal penis-envy in women – thus allowing anatomy to intervene. But, Torok argues, penis-envy can only be a subterfuge, a mask for something else, in *that it is an envy*. A desire can be satisfied – an envy, never. An envy can only lead to destructiveness – or more envy. Objects – even *the* Object – can only be the signs of unconscious desires or fears, mediators towards the goal of the impulse, which is the satisfaction of desire. You would be doing a disservice to the woman who complains of her lack of a penis if you were either to tell her (as Freud did), "yes, you *are* castrated" or (as Beauvoir is doing) "you only feel this lack because of the socio-cultural situation". In both cases you bar the door to satisfaction: for beneath the supposed penis-envy there hides an authentic desire, which has been forbidden, denied, suppressed. Under the idealised or phantasised penis there hides the womb, i.e. the little girl's own genital organisation, whose existence has been repressed, *refoulée*, denied, often by the mother. Torok agrees with Klein, Jones, Horney, Müller, that "an undiscovered womb is a denied womb". The girl's supposed anger with the mother for not having given her a penis (in Freud's scenario) is, for Torok, a compromise whereby the little girl buckles under her mother's denial of her own specific genitality and – to retain the love of the mother, not to face up to her own hatred for her mother – accepts the sacrifice that is being demanded of her. Accepting the suppression of her own legitimate desire, she protects the mother against her hatred – makes the suppressed desire illegitimate, substituting an inaccessible object (the penis) for the true one. Thus the inside of her body falls under the mother's control. Penis-envy is a disguised *revendication* – a disguised complaint, a reaching out. Maturing is finding the way to one's own desire – one's own satisfaction.

'Gosh, how very hetero', Jo moans. 'Dead straight – and hopelessly contorted. Tell me, Paula – how do these people arrive at all these veerings and twistings?'

'They listen. For years. And years.'

'Irrefutable experience, eh? How tedious if you haven't got it. How come these analysts argue so much among themselves, then – for they're like a basket of crabs, aren't they? Worse than the Balkans?'

'Do you think we might ask Paula to get to the point rather than discuss the merits or demerits of psychoanalysis?' Anne sounds gently chiding.

'Point taken, *bout de chou*. Yes, Paula – what are you getting at?'

'That the way Beauvoir writes about the female sex is a case in point. She phantasises about the penis – about transcendence. *L'homme* has had it far cushier in her book than I think is the case. She idealises. She imagines all men as gleefully sallying forth from their caves brandishing their clubs or going out to battle like Achilles in glorious armour, or as her own irrepressible Jean-Paul – rather than having as hard a time being men (whatever that means) as a lot of women have being women. As I have said, she wants It. But she wants it because she's got such a low opinion of her own sex – of her sex's sexuality, if you follow me. She's repressed her own true desire. A denied womb is a repressed womb.'

Jo shakes her head like a puppy out of water.

'Oi *la petite*,' she says 'do you hear what I hear? Simone – who had it so good with that squirt Jean-Paul, bless her generous heart or some other generous part of her anatomy – and with

Nelson Algren – and Claude – and a few others – not to mention
all the women who've surfaced in the recently-published letters
and biographies – whom she had affairs with – Simone –
repressed?'

Anne smiles.

'I hear. I'm not shocked. I'm intrigued. Where do you see this
idealisation, Paula? Where the repression?'

'In her selection of psychoanalysts to discuss, for a start.
Why has she read some and not others? I've got the book, I've
brought it!' Paula triumphantly picks up her bag from underneath her chair, pulls out from it two worn paperback volumes,
Gallimard. On both covers is the statue of a crouching Venus
bathed in golden light, about to rise. 'According to *all* analysts,
Beauvoir says, the same determining elements assign the same
fate to woman: "Her drama resides in the conflict between her
'viriloid' and her 'feminine' tendencies; the first are realised in
the clitoridian system, the second in vaginal eroticism." (DS1,59)
I take issue with "determining", which is a misunderstanding.
But if the division of female genitalia into clitoris and vagina, if
talk of a "phallic phase" is true of Freud, it isn't true, for instance,
of Ernest Jones: who warns against mistaken parallelisms
between the clitoris and the penis, since the clitoris is *part*, not
one of, the female sexual organs, plural. Nor is it true of Karen
Horney or Müller or of Klein, who claim that the little girl does
have an instinctive knowledge of her vagina. Klein argues that it
is the repression of the vagina (that becomes invested with the
little girl's fears concerning the inside of her body) that leads the
little girl to privilege the clitoris (Chasseguet-Smirgel: 49, 57). In
fact, this latter point clinches the Torok for me. Wasn't it fear of
the inside of her own body that made Beauvoir select the analysts
she did select, Freud, Deutsch, Stekel, who fed her prejudices?
The others were around to be read just as well. Why wasn't she
interested in what they had to say? Wasn't it out of the same fear
that made her so hostile to motherhood?'

'How so?' Anne is leaning forward.

Paula goes to a marker in her volume two. Her finger travels
down the page.

'She sees motherhood as alienation *per se*. Motherhood, she
argues, grants woman the fusion she has vainly sought in the

arms of the male, and that would make up for the pain of separation, of weaning. Through pregnancy and through giving birth, woman feels she ceases to be – I'm quoting – "*un objet soumis*" , a submissive object, "inferior to a subject". But she is not what she ought to be, "a subject anguished by its freedom". She is "this equivocal reality: life". Society congratulates her, consecrates her through the figure of the Virgin Mother. But – I quote again – "alienated in her body and her social dignity, the mother is under the pacifying illusion of feeling a being *in-itself,* a ready-made *value.*" Read the description of pregnancy and parturition that follows. The mother is subjected to a destiny that *transcends* her; she is "the prey of the species". A "polyp" is growing inside her. It is going to "fatten" – "*s'engraisser*" out of her substance – neither Sartre nor Beauvoir liked fat people, did they? – . Etc., etc. (DS2,157ff).'

'There may be a lot of truth in what she says', Jo observes. 'She is challenging false pieties.'

'For some, yes. But not for all. All the joy has gone out of childbearing. You're going to swear at my talking from experience again, Jo, but I've had three – they can be a bloody pain but also – what delight! Beauvoir writes as if what she says were purely objective – philosophical truths rather than aspects or dimensions of a reality – or some people's experience.'

'But she had to be provocative. She was taking on one of the greatest sacred cows of all times and places. She had to shock, to jolt sense into people. A lot of this is rhetoric. And funny.'

'But is it sense? Listen to her, comparing the advantages of the male adolescent with the disadvantages of the female. Because violence is allowed the male, he can use his fists to affirm his will, himself. He is not transcended by another. What she rather forgets, at this point, is that the fist-fight or gang-battle delivers a victor and a vanquished – a master and a slave – what does that do to the vanquished's wish for transcendence? Doesn't a lot of violence stem from impotence and frustration? Anyway – let that pass. The comparison is with the girl who, not being able to externalise her revolt or anger, becomes imprisoned in an abstract subjectivity. Beauvoir compares her to a Black man from the Deep South of the USA, *and* to a French*man* during the Occupation. The passage leads to thoughts about menstruation and hysteria (DS1,375-8). Beauvoir concludes that "woman's biological situation constitutes a handicap" (DS1,378). This handicap also affects her intellectual life (DS1,379ff). No wonder, if you accept this description and its premises – that the need to be "transcendent", to down your opponent, is what makes you human – that biological essentialism should turn out to be the devil incarnate.'

'Come on, Paula', Jo protests. 'You know perfectly well this is not the end point. Simone demonstrates how woman *has been made*, which makes it appear that she can unmake herself. There, I've got it', Jo adds, having got hold of the second volume and swiftly turning the pages at the end. '"Woman's destiny is not eternally fixed" (DS2,495). Here it is, black on white. Beauvoir explains how much easier puberty would be if it was turned towards a free adult future, how happier woman's eroticism if she was not put off by the destiny it entails (DS2,495–7). The half century or so that has followed *The Second Sex*, at least in the western world, has proved her right.'

'I'd be more convinced if her biological descriptions were not offered as so normative – if her relish for male transcendence did not go hand in hand with such a depreciation of the female sex. Listen to this.' (Paula is still turning the pages of volume one.) '"Man's sex is clean and simple as a finger; it exhibits itself innocently, as boys have often shown it to their pals, with pride and defiance; the female sex is mysterious for the woman herself, hidden, tormented, mucous, wet; it bleeds every month, sometimes it is soiled by humours, it has a secret and dangerous life" (DS1,456). Etc., etc.: man has a hard-on, woman "wets" , with urinary associations; her desires are felt in shame. Re-read Simone on her dying mother in *Une Mort très douce,* or on Sartre in old age in *La Cérémonie des adieux,* and see resurface the disgust about incontinence, the inability to control. The association with urine and faeces are hers. Rather like – Spinoza, is it, who found that the two holes between which the sexual organs lie make sex disgusting. All this stuff is loaded with Simone's own problems with her own body, her own passion for control, which she confuses with transcendence. Listen to this again: "to project a liquid, urine or sperm, does not humiliate: it is an active operation; but there is humiliation if the liquid escapes from the body passively, for then the body is no longer an organism, muscles, sphincters, nerves," and here I stress, "*under the brain's command*, expressing a conscious subject but a vase, a receptacle ... If flesh oozes – as an old wall or a corpse may ooze – it does not seem to emit a liquid, but to become liquefied. [...] Man pounces on his prey like the eagle and the kite; [woman] watches like the carnivorous plant, the marsh in which insects and children become mired'" (DS1,456–7).

'Wow!' Anne exclaims. 'I'd forgotten those bits.'

'Don't tell me this isn't about her own phobia. Don't tell me that whilst ego, brain, wants to be in charge, Id is not talking. I think it's talking about horror of the mother's body. Melanie Klein does say that envy – I return to envy, you see – goes back to "the earliest exclusive relation with the mother" (Klein, 212). Man's sex is here idealised because anger against the mother is so great, because the womb is so violently being suppressed.'

'It's the idea of everything being a fight – to establish one's power over the other – which I find hard to stomach', Anne intervenes. 'I just don't believe that the freedom and the ability to use your fists makes for transcendence. Being fully human – call it transcendent if you like – is a hell of a complicated business. Look at Mike Tyson – I was reading about him. The guy who'd written the article called him "a great fighter but not much of a man".'

'Granted', Jo says. 'But being your own master when it comes to acting is a major start. Without it there isn't even sanity. I don't agree with the two of you that analogies with the war or politics are wrong. Look at the history of hysteria. The one period in which there have been more men in the psychiatric hospitals than women was during and after World War I. The trauma of being shelled in trenches, of being subjected to idiotic orders – the experience of powerlessness – developed in the men the mental breakdown that women had been experiencing in the course of their ordinary lives. Madness is eloquent about such matters.'

'It still bothers me' – Anne is shaking her head – 'the relation between the sexes being conceived as a competition, a war. Was it Booker T. Washington who said that the only way to keep another person down was to stay down with them? If the sexual relation is based on domination, if it is a fight, how is that ever going to stop?'

'Some of us simply won't engage with blokes', Jo snorts.

'But at bottom that solves nothing', Anne replies.

'That's it', Paula says. 'How are things going to get better? As Beauvoir herself reminded Sartre in the seventies – the two of them had thought that the Communist revolution would bring about the desired change, different attitudes, the end of *all* struggles. There was this dream in the post-World War II years – throughout the de-colonisation period – that the uprising of the oppressed, the overthrow of the conquerors, would bring about access to transcendence for the downtrodden in their turn. With it would come political independence, new nationhood, access to a true self. Sartre did write the preface to Fanon's *The Wretched of the Earth*, which held out that hope – and a version of the same hope animates the ending of *The Second Sex*. Alas! We see things rather differently today, don't we? Look at Algeria – Rwanda ...'

'Hang on a minute!' Jo bursts out. 'Let's not go for simplistic analyses! What about the sequels left by colonialism – ancient structures destroyed, irksome privileges left standing, inappropriate structures in place, under-development – not to mention economic colonialism, the new imperialism of world capital creating new divisions, new forms of powerlessness ...'

'OK', Anne says. 'Let's leave the post-colonial world out of this. It still is true that the solution Beauvoir envisages – which is not far from the one that Wittig's *Les Guérillères* adumbrates – the end of the sex struggle after an uprising of the women, after they've seized power, asserted their imaginative and political transcendence – has not come to pass. If one remains with that model of a struggle – and if there is scarcity – the backlash at present, the attacks on affirmative action and the new Geneticism in the USA seem to testify that there is – where does one go?'

Jo moans. Comically makes as if to pull her short hair. Bangs her glass on the table: it is empty.

'But the two of you talk as if Beauvoir was *advocating* a struggle. She does encourage activity, independence on the part of women – but for Pete's sake, she is describing *things as they are*. She writes about the world as it is – not as we would like it to be. It is one in which women own – what? 1 per cent, 2 per cent of the world's wealth? Think of war-rapes – of peacetime rapes for that matter – of wife-battering – enslaving the women of one's defeated enemy – think of clitoridectomy – infibulation – foot-binding – harems – honour-killings – the lapidation of adulterous women – not to mention lower wages, denied access to education or the arts or the professions or wealth or the ballot-box or the army and church – all the catalogue of women's hell on earth that Wittig's female Virgil exhibits to her female Dante in her *Across Acheron*. You've got it cushy, you two – *we*'ve got it cushy. Look at where we are – what we're doing. Being free to go to a café in any town in France, spend the evening talking – free to talk about whatever we please, to say whatever we want, swear to our heart's content, drink ourselves silly – your turn to buy, Paula. Our having had access to an education that enables us to be as wise or stupid as the next man about any of the big wheels of culture – Aristotle, Spinoza, Sartre – we owe it all to women like Simone or the suffragettes – women who were brave enough to chain themselves to railings, go on hunger-strikes, write punchy books. Could we be sitting here talking, harmless as you might think it is, in the nineteenth century? Could we do it in Kigali? in Algiers? in Tibet? You've lost sight of the wood for the trees. You've become complacent. Yet there is need for vigilance. Watch out for the moral right. For Fundamentalisms of all sorts. Women may not have it so good in twenty or even ten years' time.'

There is silence while Paula orders. The three of them are now on joking terms with the waiter: they're the best customers in the place. Paula resumes. She's back on Perrier water. She looks thoughtful.

'You're using a big mallet to knock me on the head.'

'Oh no' – Jo moans comically. 'It's the other way round. The two of you are trying to make me into a giant – to make *The Second Sex* into a giant. You're just getting bashed by the wing of a windmill. You're full of high-falutin' stuff. I speak the voice of reality.'

'Are you, Jo?' Paula shakes her head. 'Or is the hell version mind-created? Remember – Simone herself, in one of her epigraphs, applies to women one of Sartre's sayings: "Victims some-what, somewhat accomplices, *like everybody else*". Clinging to a vision of women as down-trodden – victims – is becoming an accomplice in one's own victimisation. And wanting it to be universal. Like you – like many other French women of my class and generation, twenty, thirty years ago, I recognised myself in the account Beauvoir provides of female childhood, adolescence, and marriage. Backed up as it was by quotations from George Sand and Countess Tolstoy to Colette and Margaret Kennedy and Rosamund Lehmann, it seemed so accurate. But making all these forms of middle-class ... repression in the last century into a universal account of women's sexuality was *so* inaccurate in terms of the larger pattern. Yasmina tells me that in the Koran Muhammad spoke fervently *against* the sexual repression of women. That Ali, his son-in-law, explained that of the ten parts of sexual desire that Almighty God had created, He had given nine parts to women and one to men. Rather like Tiresias' answer to Zeus and Hera about women having seven times as much pleasure as men. Beauvoir is so scathing about the "*amoureuse*" and the "*mystique*". She only values what she calls activity, projection: aren't these particular, western values, made into absolutes? The whole thing is tautological. Projection is good, control is good: when they seem to be doing something that makes them happy like finding God or being in love, women aren't in control, *ergo* that's bad and women allow themselves to be passive, i.e. inferior. They're *the second sex*. It's Beauvoir's *a priori* that creates *secondness*.'

'That leads to an important question.' Anne suddenly looks animated. She is leaning forward. 'Must two be second?'

'What on earth do you mean?' Jo sounds impatient.

'Don't be angry, dear Jo. I can't think when people are angry with me.'

'I'm not angry, you darling little mouse. The two of you may be lined up against me, but I'm rather enjoying myself. Have your say. God knows we've had ours. I thought you were being surprisingly quiet. I was wondering what was up your sleeve. But your question is double Dutch to me.'

Anne beams one of her quizzical smiles at Jo.

'Two only becomes second once you start a competition – a line-up. 'Deuxième' – Beauvoir did say, *Le Deuxième Sexe*, not *The Second Sex*, which would have had no pejorative connotations – 'deuxième' suggests second-class, inferiority. And that's what the book says there is. But the number two is everywhere.

Numbers were born out of, thanks to, our bodies. Two eyes, two arms, two hands. One head, one nose. Our bodies speak one, speak two, speak three: even the male sex – one cock and two balls ... Not One, as is always said. Five fingers, which is four fingers and one thumb.'

'I like that', Paula smiles. 'What about the female sex, then? One clitoris, one vagina, but what about neck and hymen and labia ... does it make seven? Many, certainly. Right up Irigaray's street. *This sex which is not one* ...'

'What on earth are you getting at?' Jo snaps.

'There are so many forms of dualisms, not just the binary hierarchies that are attacked as phallogocentric. And forms of Trinitarian thinking. According to some, woman *in so far as she can become a mother*, is linked with the number two ...'

'Mother and child?' Paula asks.

'Among a host of other things, yes ... Is there something to be discovered, something archetypal in all this? Do numbers – not just two, but also three, and four – express forms of synchronicity? If we allow them to signify, can they not lead us to all sorts of insights? And isn't it terribly reductive to want two *only* to register as inferior?'

All three look up. The waiter is standing over them.

'What are you ...?' Jo begins, pointing to her friends' glasses. They're still half full. 'This time you've come too soon', she smiles at the waiter. 'We're not ready to order yet.'

'It's the end of my shift, Madame. Would you mind settling your bill?'

'Wallets out, everybody,' Jo orders. 'Is it this late? Christ – it is – must go to bed – rather sleepy actually.'

'So am I', Paula says.

The waiter half tears the bundle of chits. They wish him a very good night. He goes away, strapped in his big white apron, looking smug as well as melancholy.

'Cowards', Anne says. 'You want to run away just when I was about to start.'

'You can see why Sartre was forever writing about waiters.' Paula watches their waiter deposit his round tray at the counter, whisper conspiratorially with the cashier. 'It *was* a handsome tip. He could have smiled.'

'Might have done if we'd been blokes. All about economics, darlings.' Jo yawns. 'I keep telling you. Gender and class.' 'All about relations between people', Paula yawns back.

Works cited

Jo, Paula and Anne all discuss ...

Beauvoir, Simone de, *Le Deuxième Sexe*, 2 vols (Paris: Gallimard, 1949). Paula quotes from the two-volume Gallimard edition, Collection Idées, 1977. Translations by Nicole Ward Jouve, who also translated the whole of the above conversations. Paula had taped them, and got Jo's and Anne's agreement to have them transcribed and translated.

Beauvoir, Simone de, *L'Invitée*, (Paris: Gallimard, 1943)

—, *La Force des choses* (Paris: Gallimard, 1963)

—, *Une Mort très douce* (Paris: Gallimard, 1964)

—, *La Cérémonie des adieux* (Paris: Gallimard, 1981)

Sartre, Jean-Paul, *L'Être et le néant* (Paris: Gallimard, 1943).

—, *Critique de la raison dialectique* (Paris: Gallimard, 1960).

—, *La Nausée* (Paris: Gallimard, 1938).

—, *Les Chemins de la liberté*, 3 vols (Paris: Gallimard, 1945–49).

When talking, in passing, Jo, who reads English and is fairly well-versed in Anglo-American theory, has in mind ...

Bowlby, Rachel, *Still Crazy After All These Years: Women, Writing and Psychoanalysis* (London and New York: Routledge, 1992)

Braidotti, Rosi, *Nomadic Subjects: Embodiment and Sexual Difference in Contemporary Feminist Theory* (New York: Columbia University Press, 1994)

Butler, Judith, *Gender Trouble, Feminism and the Subversion of Identity* (London and New York: Routledge, 1990)

—, *Bodies that Matter* (London and New York: Routledge, 1994)

—, and Joan Scott (eds), *Feminists Theorize the Political* (London and New York: Routledge, 1992)

Cixous, Hélène, *Entre l'écriture* (Paris: des femmes, 1986)

de Lauretis, Teresa, *Technologies of Gender: Essays on Theory, Film and Fiction* (Bloomington: Indiana University Press, 1987)

Garber, Marjorie, *Vested Interests: Cross-Dressing and Cultural Anxiety* (New York and London: Routledge, 1992)

Haraway, Donna, *Simians, Cyborgs and Women: The Reinvention of Nature* (London: Free Association Books, 1990)

Huston, Nancy, *Journal de la création* (Paris: Seuil, 1989)

Irigaray, Luce, *Ce sexe qui n'en est pas un* (Paris: Minuit, 1977). Trans. by Catherine Porter with Carolyn Burke as *This Sex which Is not One*

(Ithaca: Cornell University Press, 1985)

—, *Speculum de l'autre femme* (Paris: Minuit, 1974). Trans. by Gillian Gill as *Speculum of the Other Woman* (Ithaca: Cornell University Press, 1985)

Kofman, Sarah, *L'Énigme de la femme, la femme dans les textes de Freud* (Paris: Editions Galilée, 1980) Trans. by Catherine Porter as *The Enigma of Woman, Woman in Freud's Writings* (London: Cornell University Press, 1985)

Kristeva, Julia, 'L'Héréthique de l'amour', *Tel Quel*, 74 (1977), 30–49; repr. in *Histoires d'amour* (Paris: Denoël, 1983). Trans. as 'Stabat mater' in *The Kristeva Reader*, ed. Toril Moi (Oxford: Basil Blackwell, 1986), pp. 160–86

Le Doeuff, Michèle, *L'Imaginaire philosophique* (Paris: Payot, 1984), trans. Colin Gordon as *The Philosophical Imaginary* (Stanford: Stanford University Press, 1989)

Lloyd, Genevieve, *The Man of Reason: 'Male' and 'Female' in Western Philosophy* (London: Methuen, 1984)

Nicholson, Linda J. (ed.), *Feminism/Postmodernism*, (London and New York: Routledge, 1990)

Riley, Denise, *Am I That Name? Feminism and the Category of Women in History* (Basingstoke and London: Macmillan, 1988)

Wittig, Monique, 'La Pensée straight', *Questions Féministes*, 7 (1980). Trans. in *Feminist Issues*, 1:1 (1980), and in *The Straight Mind and Other Essays* (Boston: Beacon and London: Harvester Wheatsheaf, 1992)

Paula has read/is thinking of ...

L'Arc, Special Issue: *Simone de Beauvoir et la lutte des femmes*, 61 (1975), especially. 'Simone de Beauvoir interroge Jean-Paul Sartre', 3–12, and the essay by Sylvie le Bon de Beauvoir, '*Le Deuxième Sexe*: l'esprit et la lettre', 55–61.

Chasseguet-Smirgel, Janine (ed.), *Recherches sur la sexualité féminine: recherches psychanalytiques nouvelles* (Paris: Payot, 1964). Maria Torok's essay, 'La Signification de l'"envie du pénis" chez la femme' is on pp. 181–220. Chasseguet-Smirgel discusses Klein on pp. 49 and 57.

Cixous, Hélène, 'Sorties', in Cixous H. and C. Clément, *La Jeune Née* (Paris: Union Générale d'Edition, coll. 10/18, 1975). Trans. by Betsy Wing, as *The Newly Born Woman* (Minneapolis: University of Minnesota Press, 1986); extracts repr. in Susan Sellers (ed.), *The Hélène Cixous Reader* (London and New York: Routledge, 1994) and Catherine Belsey and Jane Moore (eds), *The Feminist Reader* (Basingstoke and London: Macmillan, 1989).

Fanon, Frantz, *The Wretched of the Earth*, trans. Constance Farrington (Harmondsworth: Penguin Books, 1967).

Klein, Melanie, *Envy and Gratitude, and other works 1946–1963* (London: Virago, 1988).

Anne has read a lot ... But she doesn't get much of a chance to talk about any of it, does she?

Notes on contributors

MARGARET ATACK is Professor of French at the University of Leeds. Her publications include *Literature and the French Resistance: Cultural Politics and Narrative Forms 1940-1950* (1989) and *Contemporary French Fiction by Women: Feminist Perspectives* (co-edited with Phil Powrie, 1990). She is preparing a book on the cultural legacy of May 1968 in France.

RUTH EVANS is a Lecturer in English Literature at the University of Wales, Cardiff and a member of the Centre for Critical and Cultural Theory at Cardiff. Her publications include *Feminist Readings in Middle English Literature* (co-edited with Lesley Johnson, 1994) and contributions to the *Reader's Guide to Women's Studies* and the *Cambridge Guide to Women's Writing in English*. She is currently working on a book on difference and gender in premodern drama.

STEPHEN HORTON is a Lecturer in Philosophy at the University of Wales, Cardiff. He has recently completed his Ph.D., entitled *With Reference to Reference: A Study of the Complications of the Relationship Between Language Users and the World via a Defence of a Description Theory of Reference* (1996). His research interests include the philosophy of language, philosophical logic, the philosophy of science and the construction of possible points of contact between analytic philosophy and contemporary continental philosophy.

NICOLE WARD JOUVE is Professor of English Literature in the Department of English and Related Literature at the University of York. She is the author of *White Woman Speaks With Forked Tongue: Criticism as Autobiography* (1991), *Colette* (1987) and *Female Genesis: Creativity, Gender and Self* (forthcoming).

CATRIONA MACKENZIE is a Senior Lecturer in Philosophy at Macquarie University, Sydney. She has published papers on ethics and feminist theory in *The Austrialian Journal of Philosophy*, *Hypatia*, and in numerous edited collections. With Natalie Stoljar, she is co-editing a collection of essays entitled *Relational Autonomy: Feminist Perspectives on Autonomy, Agency and the Social Self* (forthcoming). She is also writing a book on autonomy, imagination and emotion.

CATHERINE RODGERS is a Lecturer in the Department of French at the University of Wales, Swansea, where she teaches French feminist theories, the *Nouveau Roman* and modern critical theories. She has published several articles on Marguerite Duras, and an interview with Elisabeth Badinter in *Signs*. She is currently working on a book of interviews with French feminists, concerning their reactions to *Le Deuxième Sexe*, and she is co-editing the proceedings of a conference on Marguerite Duras that she co-organised in London in January 1996.

LORNA SAGE is Professor of English Literature at the University of East Anglia, Norwich. She writes for the *Times Literary Supplement*, *The London*

Review of Books, and *The New York Times Book Review.* Her recent publications include *Women in the House of Fiction: Post-War Women Novelists* (1992) and *Angela Carter* (1994). She has also edited *Flesh and the Mirror: Essays on the Art of Angela Carter* (1994) and Katherine Mansfield's *The Garden Party and Other Stories* (1997), and is currently editing *The Cambridge Guide to Women's Writing in English.*

Bibliography

Editions of The Second Sex

Beauvoir, Simone de, *Le Deuxième Sexe*, 2 vols, Collection Blanche (Paris: Gallimard, 1949; repr. 1976)

——, *Le Deuxième Sexe*, 2 vols, Collection Idées (Paris: Gallimard, 1968)

——, *Le Deuxième Sexe*, 2 vols, Collection Folio (Paris: Gallimard, 1986)

——, *The Second Sex*, trans. and ed. H. M. Parshley (New York: Alfred A. Knopf, 1953)

——, *The Second Sex*, trans. and ed. H. M. Parshley (London: Jonathan Cape, 1953)

——, *The Second Sex*, trans. and ed. H. M. Parshley (Harmondsworth: Penguin Books, 1972; repr. 1974, 1975, 1976, 1977, 1984)

Other works by Beauvoir cited in this volume

Beauvoir, Simone de, *L'Invitée* (Paris: Gallimard, 1943). Trans. Yvonne Moyse and Roger Senhouse as *She Came to Stay* (London: Fontana, 1984)

——, *Pour une morale de l'ambiguïté* (Paris: Gallimard, 1947). Trans. Bernard Frechtman as *The Ethics of Ambiguity* (Secaucus, N.J.: Citadel Press, 1975)

——, 'Must we burn Sade?' (1953), in *Privilèges* (Paris: Gallimard, 1955), and in *Faul il brûler Sade?*, Collection Idées (Paris: Gallimard, 1955)

——, *Les Mandarins* (Paris: Gallimard, 1954). Trans. Leonard M. Friedman as *The Mandarins* (London: Fontana, 1986)

——, *La Force de l'Âge* (Paris: Gallimard, 1960). Trans. Peter Green as *The Prime of Life* (Harmondsworth: Penguin Books, 1962)

——, *La Force des choses* (Paris: Gallimard, Coll. Folio, 1963). Trans. R. Howard as *Force of Circumstance* (New York: Putnam, 1976); (Harmondsworth: Penguin Books, 1978)

——, *Une Mort très douce* (Paris: Gallimard, 1964). Trans. Patrick O'Brian as *A Very Easy Death* (Harmondsworth: Penguin Books, 1983)

——, *Quand prime le spirituel* (Paris: Gallimard, 1979). Trans. Patrick O'Brian as *When Things of the Spirit Come First* (London: Flamingo, 1982)

——, *La Cérémonie des adieux* (Paris: Gallimard, 1981). Trans. Patrick O'Brian as *Adieux: A Farewell to Sartre* (London: André Deutsch and Weidenfeld and Nicolson, 1984) (Harmondsworth: Penguin Books, 1986)

——, *Lettres à Sartre* (Paris: Gallimard, 1990). Trans. Quintin Hoare as *Letters to Sartre* (London: Radius, 1991)

Biographical studies

Appignanesi, Lisa, *Simone de Beauvoir* (Harmondsworth: Penguin Books, 1988)

Bair, Deirdre, *Simone de Beauvoir: A Biography* (London: Jonathan Cape and New York: Summit Books, 1990; repr. London: Vintage, 1991)

Crosland, Margaret, *Simone de Beauvoir: The Woman and her Work* (London: Heinemann, 1992)

Francis, Claude and Fernande Gontier, *Simone de Beauvoir* (Paris: Perrin, 1985)

Fullbrook, Kate and Edward Fullbrook, *Simone de Beauvoir and Jean-Paul Sartre: The Remaking of a Twentieth-Century Legend* (Hemel Hempstead: Harvester Wheatsheaf, 1993)

Jeanson, Francis, *Simone de Beauvoir ou l'entreprise de vivre* (Paris: Seuil, 1966)

General studies

Albistur, Maïté and Daniel Armogathe, *Histoire du féminisme français du moyen âge à nos jours* (Paris: des femmes, 1977)

Atack, Margaret, '*Le Deuxième Sexe*: subjects, subjectivities and gender', in D. Berry and A. Hargreaves (eds), *Women in Twentieth-Century Culture and Society: Papers in Memory of Andrea Cady* (European Research Centre, 1993), pp. 1–16

—, and Phil Powrie (eds), *Contemporary French Fiction by Women: Feminist Perspectives* (Manchester and New York: Manchester University Press, 1990)

Atwood, Margaret, *Surfacing* [1973] (London: Virago, 1979)

—, *The Handmaid's Tale* [1985] (London: Virago, 1987)

Badinter, Elisabeth., *L'Amour en plus: histoire de l'amour maternel, 17e–20e siècle* (Paris: Flammarion, 1980). Trans. by R. De Garis as *The Myth of Motherhood: An Historical View of the Maternal Instinct* (London: Souvenir Press, 1982)

—, 'Femmes, vous lui devez tout', *Le Nouvel Observateur*, 18–24 avril 1986, 39

—, *L'Un est l'autre, des relations entre hommes et femmes* (Paris: Odile Jacob, 1986). Trans. by Barbara Wright as *Man/Woman, The One is the Other* (London: Collins Harvill, 1989)

—, *XY, de l'identité masculine* (Paris: Odile Jacob, 1992)

Bair, Deirdre, 'Simone de Beauvoir: politics, language and sexual identity', *Yale French Studies*, 72 (1986), 149–64

Barthes, Roland, *Writing Degree Zero*, trans. Annette Lavers and Colin Smith (New York: Hill and Wang, 1968)

Bartky, Sandra Lee, *Femininity and Domination* (London: Routledge, 1990)

Baruch, E. Hoffman, *Women Analyse Women: In France, England, and the United States* (London: Harvester Wheatsheaf, 1988)

Beauvoir, Simone de, 'Simone de Beauvoir interroge Jean-Paul Sartre', *L'Arc*, 61 (1975), 3–12

Belsey, Catherine and Jane Moore (eds), *The Feminist Reader* (Basingstoke and London: Macmillan, 1989)

Best, S. and D. Kellner, *Postmodern Theory: Critical Interrogations* (London: Macmillan, 1991)

Bowlby, Rachel, *Still Crazy After All These Years: Women, Writing and Psychoanalysis* (London and New York: Routledge, 1992)

—, 'Flight reservations', *The Oxford Literary Review*, 10 (1988), 61–72

Braidotti, Rosi, *Nomadic Subjects: Embodiment and Sexual Difference in Contemporary Feminist Theory* (New York: Columbia University Press, 1994)

Brooke-Rose, Christine, *Stories, Theories and Things* (Cambridge: Cambridge University Press, 1991), pp. 250–64

Brown, Gillian, 'Anorexia, humanism, and feminism', *Yale Journal of Criticism*, 5:1 (1991), 189–215

Butler, Judith, 'Sex and gender in Simone de Beauvoir's *Second Sex*', *Yale French Studies*, 72 (1986), 35–50

—, 'Variations on sex and gender: Beauvoir and Wittig', in Benhabib, S. and D. Cornell (eds), *Feminism as Critique* (Ithaca: Cornell University Press, 1987)

—, *Gender Trouble, Feminism and the Subversion of Identity* (London and New York: Routledge, 1990)

—, *Bodies That Matter* (New York and London: Routledge, 1993)

—, and Joan Scott (eds), *Feminists Theorize the Political* (London and New York: Routledge, 1992)

Carter, Angela, *The Sadeian Woman* (London: Virago, 1979)

Certeau, Michel de, '"Making do": uses and tactics', in *The Practice of Everyday Life*, trans. Steven Rendall (Berkeley, Los Angeles and London: University of California Press, 1984)

Chapsal, M., 'Simone de Beauvoir, une femme qui parle parmi les femmes', *Elle*, 12 février 1979

Chasseguet-Smirgel, Janine (ed.), *Recherches sur la sexualité féminine: recherches psychanalytiques nouvelles* (Paris: Payot, 1964)

Chawaf, Chantal, 'La Chair linguistique', in Hélène Cixous (1976), p. 18. Trans. as 'Linguistic Flesh' in Marks and de Courtivron (eds), (1981), pp. 177–8

—, *Le Corps et le verbe, la langue en sens inverse* (Paris: Presses de la Renaissance, 1992)

Cixous, Hélène, 'Le Rire de la Méduse', *L'Arc*, 61 (1975), 39–54. Trans. by Keith Cohen and Paula Cohen as 'The laugh of the Medusa', in Marks and de Courtivron (eds) (1981), pp. 245–64

—, 'Sorties', in Cixous H. and C. Clément, *La Jeune née* (Paris: Union Générale d'Edition, coll. 10/18, 1975). Trans. by Betsy Wing as *The Newly Born*

Woman (Minneapolis: University of Minnesota Press, 1986); extracts repr. in Susan Sellers (1994) and Belsey and Moore (1989)

——, 'Des femmes en écriture (dossier réalisé par)', *Les Nouvelles Littéraires* (mai, 1976), 15–20

——, A. Leclerc and M. Cagnon, *La Venue à l'écriture* (Paris: U.G.E., 1977). Trans. by S. Cornell as *Coming to Writing and Other Essays* (Cambridge, Mass.: Harvard University Press, 1991)

——, *Entre l'écriture* (Paris: des femmes, 1986)

Compagnon, Antoine, *La Seconde Main, ou le travail de la citation* (Paris: Seuil, 1979)

Coole, Diana H., *Women in Political Theory* (Brighton: Harvester Wheatsheaf, 1988; 2nd edn 1993)

Davies, Howard, *Sartre and 'Les Temps modernes'* (Cambridge: Cambridge University Press, 1987)

De Lauretis, Teresa, *Technologies of Gender: Essays on Theory, Film and Fiction* (Bloomington: Indiana University Press, 1987)

Delphy, Christine, *Close to Home: A Materialist Analysis of Women's Oppression*, trans. and ed. by Diana Leonard (London: Hutchinson, 1984)

——, 'Rethinking sex and gender', *Women's Studies International Forum*, 16:1 (1993), 1–9

——, 'The invention of French feminism: an essential move,' *Yale French Studies*, 87 (1995), 190–221

——, and D. Leonard, *Familiar Exploitation, A New Analysis of Marriage in Contemporary Western Societies* (Cambridge: Polity Press, 1992)

Derrida, Jacques, *Of Grammatology* [1967], trans. G. C. Spivak (Baltimore and London: John Hopkins University Press, 1976)

——, *Writing and Difference* [1967], trans. Alan Bass (London: Routledge and Kegan Paul, 1978)

——, 'Choreographies: an interview with Christie V. McDonald', *Diacritics*, 12 (1982), 66–76

Dhavernas, M.-J., *Le Monde*, 15 avril 1986

Diamond, Irene and Lee Quinby (eds), *Feminism and Foucault: Reflections on Resistance* (Boston: Northeastern University Press, 1988)

Dietz, M. G., 'Introduction: debating Simone de Beauvoir', *Signs: Journal of Women in Culture and Society*, 18:1 (1992), 74–88

Dossier de presse Gallimard pour le décès de Simone de Beauvoir [Gallimard's press pack]

Duby, G., and M. Perrot (eds), *Histoire des femmes en Occident*, vol. 5 (Paris: Plon, 1992)

Duchen, Claire, *Women's Rights and Women's Lives in France, 1944–1968* (London: Routledge, 1994)

Elam, Diane, *Romancing the Postmodern* (London and New York: Routledge, 1992)

— and Robyn Wiegman (eds), *Feminism Beside Itself* (London and New York: Routledge, 1995)

Elle, Enquête «Que représente pour vous Simone de Beauvoir?», 28 avril 1986, 77–9

'Elles sont pour, Simone de Beauvoir, de la mémoire aux projets: rencontre du 16 décembre 1989'

Evans, Mary, *Simone de Beauvoir: A Feminist Mandarin* (London: Tavistock, 1985)

Fallaize, Elizabeth, 'Reception problems for women writers: the case of Simone de Beauvoir', in Diane Knight and Judith Still (eds), *Women and Representation* (Nottingham: Women Teaching French Occasional Papers 3, 1995), pp. 43–56

'Femmes, une autre écriture?', *Le Magazine Littéraire*, 180 (1982), 17–41

Fisk, M., 'History and reason in Rawls' moral theory', in N. Daniels (ed.), *Reading Rawls: Critical Studies of 'A Theory of Justice'* (Oxford: Basil Blackwell, 1975), pp. 53–80

Foucault, Michel, *The History of Sexuality*, vol. 1, trans. Robert Hurley (New York: Random House, Vintage Books, 1980)

—, *Power/Knowledge*, ed. Colin Gordon (New York: Pantheon Books, 1980)

—, *Discipline and Punish*, trans. Alan Sheridan, (Harmondsworth: Penguin Books, 1982)

Fouque, Antoinette, 'Moi et elle', *Libération*, 15 avril 1986

—, 'Femmes en mouvements, hier, aujourd'hui, demain (entretien)', *Le Débat*, 59, Gallimard (mars-avril, 1990), 126–43. Trans. with other essays in *Women in Movements, Yesterday, Today, Tomorrow and Other Writings* (des femmes (USA), 1992)

—, 'Il y a deux sexes', in M. Negrón, ed., *Lectures de la différence sexuelle* (Paris: des femmes, 1994), pp. 283–317

—, 'Paroles avec Antoinette Fouque [entretien avec Isabelle Huppert]', *Cahiers du Cinéma*, 477 (1994), pp. 36–49

—, *Il y a deux sexes, essais de féminologie, 1989–1995* (Paris: Gallimard, 1995)

Fraisse, Geneviève, *Révolution*, 18 avril 1986

Francis, Claude and Fernande Gontier, *Les Écrits de Simone de Beauvoir* (Paris: Gallimard, 1979)

Friedman, Susan Stanford, 'Making history: reflections on feminism, narrative, and desire', in Elam and Wiegman (eds), (1995), pp. 11–53

Frye, Marilyn, 'Sexism', in *The Politics of Reality* (Trumansberg, New York: The Crossing Press, 1983)

Gallop, Jane, 'Reading the mother tongue: psychoanalytic feminist criticism', *Critical Inquiry*, 14 (1987), 314–29

Garber, Marjorie, *Vested Interests: Cross-Dressing and Cultural Anxiety* (New York and London: Routledge, 1992)

Gatens, Moira, 'Feminism, philosophy and riddles without answers', in Elizabeth Gross and Carole Pateman (eds), *Feminist Challenges: Social and Political Theory* (Sydney: Allen & Unwin, 1986), pp. 13–29

Gauthier, Xavière, 'Lutte de femmes', *Tel Quel*, 58 (1974), 93–7

—, *Rose saignée* (Paris: des femmes, 1974)

—, 'Femmes, une autre écriture?', *Le Magazine Littéraire*, 180 (1982), 17

— and M. Duras, *Les Parleuses* (Paris: Minuit, 1974). Trans. by K. A. Jensen as *Woman to Woman* (Lincoln: University of Nebraska Press, 1987)

Genette, G., *Figures 1* (Paris: Seuil, 1966)

Gennari, Geneviève, *Simone de Beauvoir* (Paris: Éditions Universitaires, 1958)

Glover, J., *Causing Death and Saving Lives* (Harmondsworth: Penguin Books, 1977)

Grosz, Elizabeth, *Sexual Subversions* (Sydney: Allen & Unwin, 1989)

Guillaumin, C., *Sexe, race et pratique du pouvoir, l'idée de nature* (Paris: côté-femmes, 1992)

Halimi, Gisèle, *Le Lait de l'oranger* (Paris: Gallimard, 1988)

—, *La Cause des femmes* (Paris: Gallimard, 1992)

—, 'Plaidoyer pour une démocratie paritaire', in Gisèle Halimi (ed.), *Femmes, moitié de la terre, moitié du pouvoir* (Paris: Gallimard, 1994), pp. 11–22

Haraway, Donna, *Simians, Cyborgs and Women: The Reinvention of Nature* (London: Free Association Books, 1990)

Heath, Jane, *Simone de Beauvoir*, Key Women Writers (Hemel Hempstead: Harvester Wheatsheaf, 1989)

Hegel, G. W. F., *Phenomenology of Spirit*, trans. A. V. Miller, with an analysis of text and foreword by J. N. Findlay (Oxford: Clarendon Press, 1977)

Hubbard, Ruth, 'Have only men evolved?', in Sandra Harding and Merrill Hintikka (eds), *Discovering Reality: Feminist Perspectives on Epistemology, Ontology, Metaphysics, and Philosophy of Science* (Dordrecht: Reidel, 1983)

Huston, Nancy, 'Les Enfants de Simone de Beauvoir', *La Vie en Rose* (mars, 1984), 41–4

—, *Journal de la création* (Paris: Seuil, 1989)

Irigaray, Luce, *Speculum de l'autre femme* (Paris: Minuit, 1974). Trans. by Gillian Gill as *Speculum of the Other Woman* (Ithaca: Cornell University Press, 1985)

—, *Ce Sexe qui n'en est pas un* (Paris: Minuit, 1977). Trans. by Catherine Porter with Carolyn Burke as *This Sex which Is not One* (Ithaca: Cornell University Press, 1985)

—, F. Clédat, X. Gauthier and A.-M. Vilaine, 'L'Autre de la nature', *Sorcières*, 20 (1980), 14–25

—, *Et l'Une ne bouge pas sans l'autre* (Paris: Minuit, 1979). Trans. by H. V. Wenzel as 'And the one doesn't stir without the other', *Signs: Journal of Women in Culture and Society*, 7:1 (1981), 60–7

——, 'Interview', in E. Hoffman Baruch (1988), pp. 149–64

——, *Je, tu, nous, Pour une culture de la différence* (Paris: Grasset et Fasquelle, 1990). Trans. by A. Martin as *Je, Tu, Nous, Towards a Culture of Difference* (London: Routledge, 1993)

——, *J'aime à toi* (Paris: Grasset, 1992)

——, 'L'Identité féminine, biologie ou conditionnement social?' in Gisèle Halimi (ed.), (1994), pp. 101–8

——, 'The question of the other', *Yale French Studies*, 87 (1995), 7–19

Jardine, Alice, 'Interview with Simone de Beauvoir', *Signs: Journal of Women in Culture and Society*, 5:2 (1979), 224–36

——, *Gynesis: Configurations of Women and Modernity* (Ithaca and London: Cornell University Press, 1985)

Kauffman, L. (ed.), *Gender and Theory: Dialogues on Feminist Criticism* (Oxford: Basil Blackwell, 1989)

Kaufmann-McCall, Dorothy, 'Politics of difference: the women's movement in France from May 1968 to Mitterand', *Signs: Journal of Women in Culture and Society*, 9 (1983), 282–93

——, 'Simone de Beauvoir: questions of difference and generation', *Yale French Studies*, 72 (1886)

Keefe, Terry, *Simone de Beauvoir: A Study of her Writings* (London: Harrap, 1983)

Klein, Melanie, *Envy and Gratitude, and Other Works 1946–1963* (London: Virago, 1988)

Kofman, Sarah, *L'Énigme de la femme, la femme dans les textes de Freud* (Paris: Editions Galilée, 1980) Trans. by Catherine Porter as *The Enigma of Woman, Woman in Freud's Writings* (London: Cornell University Press, 1985)

Kristeva, Julia, 'L'Héréthique de l'amour', *Tel Quel* 74 (1977), 30–49; repr. in *Histoires d'amour* (Paris: Denoël, 1983). Trans. as 'Stabat mater' in Toril Moi (ed.), (1986), pp. 160–86

——, 'Le Temps des femmes', *33/44: Cahiers de Recherche de Sciences des Textes et Documents*, 5 (Winter, 1979), 5–19; repr. in Julia Kristeva, *Les Nouvelles Maladies de l'âme* (Paris: Fayard, 1993), pp. 297–331. Trans. by Alice Jardine and Harry Blake as 'Women's time' in *Signs: Journal of Women in Culture and Society*, 7 (1981), 13–35, and repr. in Toril Moi (ed.), (1986), pp. 187–213, and extracts in Belsey and Moore (eds) (1989), pp. 197–217

——, *Powers of Horror*, trans. Leon Roudiez (New York: Columbia University Press, 1982)

——, 'À propos des *Samouraïs* (entretien)', *L'Infini*, 30 (été, 1990), trans. Leon Roudiez as 'Concerning *The Samurai*', in Julia Kristeva, *Nations without Nationalism* (New York: Columbia University Press, 1993), p. 77–95

Kruks, Sonia, 'Gender and subjectivity: Simone de Beauvoir and contemporary feminism', *Signs: Journal of Women in Culture and Society*, 18:1 (1992), 89–110

Laclau, Ernesto and Chantal Mouffe, *Hegemony & Socialist Strategy: Towards a Radical Democratic Politics* (London: Verso, 1985)

L'Arc, Special Issue: *Simone de Beauvoir et la lutte des femmes*, 61 (1975)

La Vie en rose, 'Simone de Beauvoir, témoignages' (mars, 1984), 37–44

le Bon de Beauvoir, Sylvie, '*Le Deuxième Sexe*: l'esprit et la lettre', *L'Arc*, 61 (1975), 55–61

Leclerc, Annie, 'Patronne des femmes?', *La Croix*, 16 avril (1986)

——, *Parole de femme* (Paris: Grasset & Fasquelle, 1994)

Le Doeuff, Michèle, 'Women and philosophy', trans. Debbie Pope, *Radical Philosophy*, 17 (1977), 2–11

——, 'Operative philosophy: Simone de Beauvoir and existentialism', trans. Colin Gordon, *Ideology & Consciousness*, 6 (1979), 47–57

——, 'Simone de Beauvoir and existentialism', *Feminist Studies*, 6 (1980), 277–89

——, *L'Imaginaire philosophique* (Paris: Payot, 1984), trans. Colin Gordon as *The Philosophical Imaginary* (Stanford: Stanford University Press, 1989)

——, *L'Étude et le rouet, des femmes, de la philosophie, etc.* (Paris: Seuil, 1989). Trans. by Trista Selous as *Hipparchia's Choice: An Essay Concerning Women, Philosophy, etc.* (Oxford: Basil Blackwell, 1991)

——, 'On some philosophical pacts', *Journal of the Institute of Romance Studies*, 2 (1993), 395–407

——, 'Simone de Beauvoir: les ambiguïtés d'un ralliement', *Le Magazine Littéraire*, 320 (1994), 58–61; trans. as 'Simone de Beauvoir: falling into (ambiguous) line', in Margaret A. Simons (ed.), (1995), pp. 59–65

Leighton, Jean, *Simone de Beauvoir on Woman* (Cranbury, N.J. and London: Associated University Presses, 1975)

Lévi-Strauss, Claude, *Structural Anthropology* [1958], trans. C. Jacobson and B. Grundfast Schoepf (New York: Basic Books, 1963)

Lilar, Suzanne, *Le Malentendu du Deuxième sexe* (Paris: PUF, 1969)

——, *À propos de Sartre et de l'amour* (Paris: Grasset, 1969)

Lloyd, Genevieve, *The Man of Reason: 'Male' and 'Female' in Western Philosophy* (London: Methuen, 1984)

——, 'Masters, slaves and others', *Radical Philosophy*, 34 (1983), Special Issue on *Women, Gender and Philosophy*

Lyotard, Jean-François, *The Postmodern Condition: A Report on Knowledge* [1979], Theory and History of Literature, vol. 10, trans. G. Bennington and B. Massumi (Manchester: Manchester University Press, 1984)

——, *Le Postmoderne expliqué aux enfants* (Paris: Editions Galilée, 1988)

——, *The Differend: Phrases in Dispute*, trans. Georges van den Abbeele (Manchester: Manchester University Press, 1988)

——, *The Inhuman: Reflections on Time* [1988], trans. Geoff Bennington and Rachel Bowlby (Stanford: Stanford University Press, 1991)

Mackenzie, Catriona, 'Simone de Beauvoir: philosophy and/or the female body', in Elizabeth Gross and Carole Pateman (eds), *Feminist Challenges: Social and Political Theory* (Sydney: Allen and Unwin, 1986), pp. 144–56

Manifeste des 343, *Le Nouvel Observateur*, 5 avril (1971)

Marks, Elaine, *Simone de Beauvoir: Encounters with Death* (New Brunswick, N.J.: Rutgers University Press, 1973)

— 'Transgressing the (in)cont(in)ent boundaries: the body in decline', *Yale French Studies*, 72 (1986), 181-200

— (ed.), *Critical Essays on Simone de Beauvoir* (Boston: Hall, 1987)

—, and Isabelle de Courtivron (eds), *New French Feminisms: An Anthology* (Brighton: Harvester/Wheatsheaf, 1981)

Mathieu, N.-C., *L'Anatomie politique, catégorisations et idéologies du sexe* (Paris: côté-femmes, 1991)

Merleau-Ponty, Maurice, *Phenomenology of Perception*, trans. Colin Smith (London: Routledge and Kegan Paul, 1962)

Millett, Kate, *Sexual Politics* (New York: Doubleday, 1970; repr. London: Virago, 1977)

Mitchell, Juliet, 'Simone de Beauvoir: Freud and the second sex', in Part Two, Section II of Juliet Mitchell, *Psychoanalysis and Feminism* (Harmondsworth: Penguin Books, 1975)

Moi, Toril, *Sexual/Textual Politics: Feminist Literary Theory* (London and New York: Methuen, 1985)

—, *Feminist Theory and Simone de Beauvoir*, The Bucknell Lectures (Oxford: Basil Blackwell, 1990)

—, 'Appropriating Bourdieu: feminist theory and Pierre Bourdieu's sociology of culture', *New Literary History*, 22 (1991), 1017–49

—, *Simone de Beauvoir: The Making of an Intellectual Woman* (Oxford: Basil Blackwell, 1994)

— (ed.), *The Kristeva Reader* (Oxford: Basil Blackwell, 1986)

— (ed.), *French Feminist Thought: A Reader* (Oxford: Basil Blackwell, 1987)

Nicholson, Linda J. (ed.), *Feminism/Postmodernism* (London and New York: Routledge, 1990)

Norris, Christopher, *Uncritical Theory: Postmodernism, Intellectuals and the Gulf War* (London: Lawrence and Wishart, 1992)

Okely, Judith, *Simone de Beauvoir: A Re-Reading* (London: Virago, 1986)

Picq, Françoise, *Libération des femmes, les années-mouvement* (Paris: Seuil, 1993)

Pierce, Christine and Margery Collins, 'Holes and slime: sexism in Sartre's psychoanalysis', in Carol C. Gould and Marx W. Wartofsky (eds), *Women and Philosophy* (New York: Capricorn, 1976)

Plato, *The Republic*, 2nd revised edn, trans. D. Lee (Harmondsworth: Penguin Books, 1987)

Poster, M., *Foucault, Marxism and History: Mode of Production − vs − Mode of Information*, (Cambridge: Polity Press, 1984)

Prasteau, J., 'Suzanne contre Simone, Lilar contre Beauvoir', *Le Figaro Littéraire*, 29 sept.−5 oct. (1969), 25

Prost, G., 'Merci Simone', *Paris Féministes*, 26 mai (1986), 13−4

Rabaut, J., *Histoires des féminismes français* (Paris: Stock, 1978)

Rawls, J., *A Theory of Justice* (Oxford: Oxford University Press, 1973)

Readings, Bill and Bennet Schaber (eds), *Postmodernism Across the Ages* (Syracuse: Syracuse University Press, 1993)

Reiss, T. J., 'Revolution in Bounds: Wollstonecraft, Women, and Reason', in L. Kauffman (ed.), *Gender and Theory: Dialogues on Feminist Criticism* (Oxford: Basil Blackwell, 1989), pp. 11−50

Remy, Monique, *De l'utopie à l'intégration, histoire des mouvements de femmes* (Paris: L'Harmattan, 1990)

Richards, Janet Radcliffe, *The Sceptical Feminist: A Philosophical Enquiry* (Harmondsworth: Penguin Books, 1982)

Riley, Denise, *Am I That Name? Feminism and the Category of Women in History* (Basingstoke and London: Macmillan, 1988)

Rose, Phyllis (ed.), *The Penguin Book of Women's Lives* (London: Viking, 1994)

Russell, Bertrand, *The Problems of Philosophy* [1912] (Oxford: Oxford University Press, 1967)

Sage, Lorna, *Women in the House of Fiction: Post-War Women Novelists* (London: Macmillan, 1992)

Sarraute, Claude, 'Féminisme=humanisme', *Le Monde*, 6−7 avril 1975

Sarraute, Nathalie, *Tropisms and the Age of Suspicion* (1939), trans. Maria Jolas (1950) (London: Calder and Boyars, 1959)

—, *Portrait of a Man Unknown* (1948), trans. Maria Jolas (London: Calder and Boyars, 1963)

Sartre, Jean-Paul, *La Nausée* (Paris: Gallimard, 1938)

—, *Les Chemins de la liberté*, 3 vols (Paris: Gallimard, 1945)

—, *Critique de la raison dialectique* (Paris: Gallimard, 1960)

—, *L'Être et le néant* (Paris: Gallimard, 1943), trans. Hazel E. Barnes as *Being and Nothingness* (London: Methuen, 1969) (New York: Philosophical Library, 1972)

Saussure, Ferdinand de, *Course in General Linguistics*, trans. W. Baskin (London: Fontana/Collins, 1974); trans. R. Harris (London: Duckworth, 1983)

Savigneau, Josyane, 'La Mort de Simone de Beauvoir, une mère symbolique', *Le Monde*, 16 avril (1986), 19

Schor, Naomi, 'This essentialism which is not one: coming to grips with Irigaray', *Differences*, 1:2 (1989), 38−58

Schwartzer, A., *Simone de Beauvoir aujourd'hui, six entretiens* (Paris: Mercure de France, 1984)

Self, Will, 'Cult books 1966/1996: my generation', Observer *Life* Magazine, 21 January (1996), 32–3: 32

Sellers, Susan (ed.), *The Hélène Cixous Reader* (London and New York: Routledge, 1994)

Showalter, Elaine, *A Literature of Their Own: British Women Novelists from Brontë to Lessing* (Princeton: Princeton University Press, 1977)

Simone de Beauvoir Studies 3 (1985–86)

Simons, Margaret A., 'Lesbian connections, Simone de Beauvoir and feminism', *Signs: Journal of Women in Culture and Society*, 18:1, (1992), 136–61

— (ed.), *Feminist Interpretations of Simone de Beauvoir* (University Park: Penn State Press, 1995)

Singer, Linda, 'Interpretation and retrieval: rereading Beauvoir', in Azizah Y. Al-Hibri and Margaret Simons (eds), *Hypatia Reborn: Essays in Feminist Philosophy* (Bloomington: Indiana University Press, 1990), pp. 323–35

Spelman, E. V., 'Woman as body: ancient and contemporary views', *Feminist Studies*, 8:1 (1982), 109–31

—, *Inessential Women: Problems of Exclusion in Feminist Thought* (London: The Women's Press, 1988)

Stoekl, Allan, *Agonies of the Intellectual: Commitment, Subjectivity and the Performative in the Twentieth Century French Tradition* (Lincoln and London: University of Nebraska Press, 1992)

Suhamy, Henri, *Les Figures de style* (Paris: PUF Que sais-je, 1981)

Suleiman, Susan Rubin, 'Simone de Beauvoir and the writing self', *L'Esprit Créateur*, 29:4 (1989), 42–51

Tapper, Marion, 'Sartre and de Beauvoir on love', *Critical Philosophy*, 2:1 (1985), 37–47

Tidd, Ursula, 'Telling the truth in Simone de Beauvoir's autobiography', *New Readings*, 2 (1996), 7–19

Torok, Maria, 'La Signification de l'"envie du pénis" chez la femme', in Chasseguet-Smirgel (ed.), (1964), pp. 181–220

'Variations sur des thèmes communs', *Questions Féministes*, 1 (Nov., 1977), 3–19. Trans. in Marks and de Courtivron (1981), pp. 212–30

Vilaine, A.–M. de, 'Le Corps de la théorie', in 'Femmes, une autre écriture?' (1982), 25–8

Ward Jouve, Nicole, *White Woman Speaks With Forked Tongue: Criticism as Autobiography* (London: Routledge, 1991)

Weedon, Chris, *Feminist Practice and Poststructuralist Theory* (Oxford: Basil Blackwell, 1987)

Weir, Allison, *Sacrificial Logics: Feminist Theory and the Critique of Identity* (New York and London: Routledge, 1996)

Wenzel, H. V., 'Interview with Simone de Beauvoir', *Yale French Studies*, 72 (1986), 5–32

White, Hayden, 'The question of narrative in contemporary historical theory', in *The Content of the Form: Narrative Discourse and Historical Representation* (Baltimore and London: Johns Hopkins University Press, 1987)

Whitford, Margaret, *Luce Irigaray, Philosophy in the Feminine* (London: Routledge, 1991)

Whitmarsh, Anne, *Simone de Beauvoir and the Limits of Commitment* (Cambridge: Cambridge University Press, 1981)

Williams, Linda, 'Happy families? Feminist reproduction and matrilineal thought', in Isobel Armstrong (ed.), *New Feminist Discourses* (London and New York: Routledge, 1992)

Wittig, Monique, *Les Guérillères* (Paris: Minuit, 1969). Trans. by D. Le Vay as *Les Guérillères* (London: The Women's Press, 1980)

—, 'La Pensée straight', *Questions Féministes*, 7 (1980). Trans. in *Feminist Issues*, 1:1 (1980), and in *The Straight Mind and Other Essays* (Boston: Beacon and London: Harvester Wheatsheaf, 1992)

—, *The Straight Mind and Other Essays* (Boston: Beacon and London: Harvester Wheatsheaf, 1992)

Young, Iris Marion, 'Pregnant subjectivity and the limits of existential phenomenology', in Don Ihde and Hugh J. Silverman (eds), *Descriptions* (Albany, N.Y.: State University of New York Press, 1985)

Zéphir, Jacques, *Le Néo-féminisme de Simone de Beauvoir, trente ans après Le Deuxième Sexe, un postscriptum* (Paris: Denoël-Gonthier, 1982)

Zerilli, Linda M. G., '"I am a woman": female voice and ambiguity in *The Second Sex*', *Women in Politics*, 11:1 (1991), 93–108

—, 'A process without a subject: Simone de Beauvoir and Julia Kristeva on maternity', *Signs: Journal of Women in Culture and Society*, 18:1 (1992), 111–35

Index

Literary works are found under authors' names. If an idea is associated with a particular thinker or writer, then it is usually listed under that person's name. Existentialist categories are listed, as far as possible, under the headword 'existentialism'.